Understanding the Small Family Business

It is estimated that family businesses comprise between 60 and 90 per cent of all firms in Europe and the United States. This book makes an important contribution to the understanding of small family firms, bringing together a number of key themes in management/organisation studies.

The contributions in this book explore the relationship between work and the family in the context of the small business. The contributors demonstrate the complexities of this relationship, arguing that it is ambiguous and shaped by contradictory yet complementary discourses of control and nurturing. These ambiguities and contradictions are examined through three dominant discourses – rational, resource-based and critical – which are identified as shaping the development of family business research over the past thirty years.

Using a variety of theoretical and methodological approaches, including quantitative and in-depth case analyses, each chapter considers a different feature of small business organisation. These include:

- strategic change
- entrepreneurship
- corporate governance
- leadership
- finance
- training and succession.

Drawing on an international range of studies, this book also points to the future of research in this area, and indicates how support and policy initiatives may be directed in the future.

Denise E. Fletcher is Principal Lecturer at Nottingham Business School, teaching Business Development, Entrepreneurship and Research Methodology in the MBA and Master's programmes. She has also taught on small business and entrepreneurship courses delivered in Greece, France, Poland, the Czech Republic and Kenya. In the past ten years she has been working with small companies through a variety of research projects addressing business development issues in small firms. Her research interests also extend to family firms and her doctoral thesis was on the topic of strategic change issues in the small family business. She has participated extensively in European workshops, conferences and research projects, and has published widely in the small business literature.

Routledge Studies in Small Business
Edited by David J. Storey

Understanding the Small Family Business

Edited by Denise E. Fletcher

London and New York

First published 2002
by Routledge
11 New Fetter Lane, London EC4P 4EE

Simultaneously published in the USA and Canada
by Routledge
29 West 35th Street, New York, NY 10001

Routledge is an imprint of the Taylor & Francis Group

Typeset in Baskerville by Taylor & Francis Books Ltd
Printed and bound in Great Britain by The Cromwell Press,
Trowbridge, Wiltshire

British Library Cataloguing in Publication Data
A catalogue record for this book is available from the British Library

Library of Congress Cataloging in Publication Data
A catalog record for this book has been requested

ISBN 0–415–25053–6

Contents

Illustrations

Tables

Figures

Contributors

Susan Baines, Department of Sociology and Social Policy, Claremont Bridge Building, University of Newcastle, Newcastle.

Marc Cowling, Research Centre for Industrial Strategy, The Birmingham Business School, University of Birmingham, Birmingham.

Denise E. Fletcher, Nottingham Business School, The Nottingham Trent University, Burton Street, Nottingham.

Annika Hall, Jönköping International Business School, PO Box 1026, Jönköping, Sweden.

Carole Howorth, Institute for Enterprise and Innovation, Nottingham University Business School, Jubilee Campus, Wollaton Road, Nottingham.

Bengt Johannisson, Scandinavian Institute for Research in Entrepreneurship (SIRE), Vaxjo University, Vaxjo, Sweden.

Trevor Jones, Department of Strategy and Management, Leicester Business School, De Montfort University, Leicester.

Paul Karofsky, Center for Family Business and Management Science Group, College of Business Administration, Northeastern University, Boston, MA 02115.

Saija Katila, Department of Management of the Helsinki School of Economics and Business Administration, Helsinki, Finland.

Harry Matlay, The Business School, University of Central England, Franchise Street, Perry Bar, Birmingham.

Leif Melin, Jönköping International Business School, PO Box 1026, Jönköping, Sweden.

Robert Millen, Center for Family Business and Management Science Group, College of Business Administration, Northeastern University, Boston, MA 02115.

Barbara Murray, The Family Business Network, Lausanne, Switzerland.

Mattias Nordqvist, Jönköping International Business School, PO Box 1026, Jönköping, Sweden.

Elizabeth Oughton, Department of Sociology and Social Policy, Claremont Bridge Building, University of Newcastle, Newcastle.

Panikkos Zata Poutziouris, Manchester Science Enterprise Centre, UMIST, Fairburn Building, Manchester.

Monder Ram, Department of Strategy and Management, Leicester Business School, De Montfort University, Leicester.

Claudio A. Romano, AXA Family Business Research Unit, Dept. Accounting and Finance, Faculty of Business and Economics, Monash University, PO Box 197, Caulfield East, Victoria 3145, Australia.

Kosmas X. Smyrnios, AXA Family Business Research Unit, Dept. Accounting and Finance, Faculty of Business and Economics, Monash University, PO Box 197, Caulfield East, Victoria 3145, Australia.

David J. Storey, Centre for Small and Medium-Sized Enterprises, Warwick Business School, The University of Warwick, Coventry.

George A. Tanewski, AXA Family Business Research Unit, Dept. Accounting and Finance, Faculty of Business and Economics, Monash University, PO Box 197, Caulfield East, Victoria 3145, Australia.

Jill Thomas, Graduate School of Management, Adelaide University, Security House, North Terrace, Adelaide, SA 5005, Australia.

Paul Westhead, Institute for Enterprise and Innovation, Nottingham University Business School, Jubilee Campus, Wollaton Road, Nottingham.

Jane Wheelock, Department of Sociology and Social Policy, Claremont Bridge Building, University of Newcastle, Newcastle.

Mustafa R. Yilmaz, Center for Family Business and Management Science Group, College of Business Administration, Northeastern University, Boston, MA 02115.

Foreword

In the early 1990s Paul Westhead and I obtained a substantial grant from the Leverhulme Foundation to examine economic aspects of family businesses. At that time a Conservative administration was in power with, at least in public, a commitment to tax cutting. While no taxes are ever popular, the payment of inheritance tax on the assets of family businesses caused particularly strong feelings. Family businesses, it was argued in the popular press, were the bedrock of the UK economy and taxes, that constituted a disincentive to businesses being passed from one generation to the next, risked undermining that bedrock.

Our simplistic view in the proposal to Leverhulme was that we might be able to throw a little light on this thorny problem. If we were able to demonstrate that family businesses, in general, outperformed otherwise comparable non-family businesses, then this would provide supporting evidence for those seeking to lower these taxes. If the non-family businesses outperformed the family businesses, then the case for an inheritance tax was very difficult to make.

The simple empirical question of whether or not family businesses did or did not outperform non-family businesses was dogged by the difficulties associated with defining what was meant by 'a family business'. It has always seemed to me that the last refuge of the scoundrel is to keep changing definitions until one emerges that yields the 'right' answers. But in this case it was genuinely tricky – as is shown in Chapter 1 by myself, Paul, Marc Cowling and Carole Howorth.

Even so, despite devising a cornucopia of definitions, we found the relationship between family ownership and business performance a very difficult link to make. In bald terms, whether a business was family-owned or not did not seem to influence its performance. Hence justifying the lowering of inheritance taxes on these grounds was difficult. This finding failed to endear us to those wishing to demonstrate that family businesses were in some sense 'special' or 'different'. But the finding that the performance of family- and non-family-owned businesses did not differ did not mean the factors influencing the performance were the same – or that, in some sense, family business was an uninteresting subject of study.

For those interested in the internal organisation of businesses the family ownership component adds an important extra dimension. Denise Fletcher makes this point clearly in her editorial overview to this volume. She is at pains to ensure the readers 'don't take this (family) special quality for granted'. So, just what is it that makes family businesses special? Being a small business owner, of almost any sort, is clearly different from being an employee or from being a shareholder in a large business. In comparison with large businesses, small firm owners have more internal certainty than large firm managers but more external uncertainty (Storey and Sykes, 1996). But the addition of family, as Denise Fletcher argues, leads to additional 'tensions and contradictions' because of the 'social and emotional relations'.

Conventionally the family component is defined in terms of ownership – that is, having the shares of the businesses owned by family members – but what the literature seems to imply, but not make explicit, is what difference that ownership makes. In my view what makes family businesses 'special' is not the fact that the shares are owned by family members *per se*, but the implication of this for the way the business is organised internally. The 'special' quality derives from a 'closeness' that only families can provide. At its most simplistic, the Chief Executive Officer/Chairman of large companies never meets the vast majority of their shareholders. At best they might come face to face with a (probably unrepresentative) sample of them at the AGM, so their relationship is 'arm's length'. In contrast, the CEO of the family business regularly looks into the eyes of the key shareholders, possibly every Sunday lunchtime.

But does 'closeness' really influence behaviour? The economists' response to the 'closeness' argument is that business is so fundamentally competitive that a failure to implement profit-maximising practices puts at risk the very existence of the firm. In a competitive world the distinction that Hollander and Elman (1988) make between the rational business motivation having to take second place to the irrational family motive is unrealistic. Instead, all businesses, whether family- or non-family-owned, have to perform in the same way if they are to survive and prosper; our own performance findings on family/non-family businesses are certainly compatible with this proposal. The Hollander and Elman distinction therefore exists only in imperfect markets. But such markets are surely the norm, and only the purest of economists believe them to be the exception. So, let us assume that such imperfect markets do exist and that family businesses are present in these markets. How, then, does 'closeness' influence behaviour?

The obvious way is that the family would be expected to be better informed about what is happening in the business than 'anonymous' shareholders. Since they frequently work in the business, and discuss its performance and prospects, information is likely to circulate more freely. However, in practice, as shown by several chapters in this volume, the key figure in the business often takes steps to ensure that information about the business is restricted. Family shareholders, in fact, can be less well informed about what is going on than the 'anonymous' shareholders in large companies who are, by law, provided with a minimum level of information. Nowhere perhaps is this more clearly illustrated than in the quotation in Denise Fletcher's chapter by the second-generation chairman of the small electrical engineering company.

This issue of 'closeness' seems to encapsulate issues relating to family business. However, because the subject is, comparatively, in its infancy, equally plausible, but wholly contradicting, *a priori* arguments may be presented. Denise Fletcher in her overview is highly sympathetic to such 'mixed results'. In her view, this new area of study would be ill-served by seeking to deliver a unified paradigm, which would risk closing off potentially promising areas of development. What she and her fellow authors have certainly done is to demonstrate that 'the relationship between family and small business organisations is complex, ambiguous and shaped by contradictory discourses of control and nurturing'. I am sure that readers of this volume will find a similar therapy which the (family) small business owner claimed to feel when discussing these issues with Denise.

David J. Storey
21 November 2001
SME Centre, University of Warwick

Introduction

'Family' as a discursive resource for understanding the small family business

Denise E. Fletcher

Introduction

In this chapter, a route map is laid out to provide the reader with a set of signposts and directions with which to journey through and explore the dominant antecedents and approaches that have shaped understanding of the work–family–small business relationship. A substantial literature has emerged over the past thirty years concerned with raising the profile of family businesses as a special area of study. Studies have focused on: definitional issues and the contribution of family firms to national employment and gross domestic product (Donckels and Fröhlich, 1991; Cromie *et al.*, 1995; Daily and Dollinger, 1993; Litz, 1995; Poutziouris and Chittenden, 1996; Shanker and Astrachan, 1996; Westhead, 1997); strategic management practices in family firms (Beckhard and Dyer, 1983; Gersick *et al.*, 1997) and the complex nature of the business–family–work relationship (Holland and Boulton, 1984; Dyer and Handler, 1994). In the following sections, the reader is introduced to the contributors to this book and also to other scholars who are enhancing understanding of the small family business sector. In embarking on this journey, the reader will become familiar with current research interests and how support or policy initiatives may be directed in the future.

The journey, however, is not always a smooth one. The aim of the book is not to produce a family business research monograph that re-produces (and reinforces) what is already known about family business. In contrast to Wortman (1994: 3), who laments that there is no 'unified paradigm for the field', it is not the intention here to argue that there should (or could) be a unified paradigm for the study of family business. Such a unified paradigm, which might privilege common methodologies and ways of theorising the family business, is unhelpful for a dynamic and growing area of study. Also, the very complexity of the institution of 'family' (Holland and Boulton, 1984: 16) and its role/meaning in different socio-economic contexts means that a unified paradigm is not only senseless but also untenable. The notion of 'family' in society refers to groups of people bound together by blood and marriage ties (Muncie and Sapsford, 1997) and can include the traditional nuclear form of family, extended families, kin groups, clans and single-parent families. Such a unified paradigm, therefore, would risk closing off new perspectives and insights that explore the complex relationship between work–family and the small business.

In contrast, therefore, the aim of this book is to examine the relationship between work and family in the context of the small business. As approximately 70–80 per cent of small firms are family firms (see Matlay, this volume), it is important to explore the relationship between family ties/roles and organisation of the small business. One aim of the book, in particular, is to draw attention to the tensions and contradictions that are created within the small business as a result of this distinctive work–family relationship. These tensions are examined through a wide variety of theoretical and methodological perspectives including quantitative and in-depth case analyses using interpretive techniques. These tensions are also examined through three dominant discourses which are identified as shaping the development of family business research. As the reader approaches this collection of writings, it is hoped that the journey through the book will be an enjoyable and informative one. At times the reader will be reassured when their assumptions and expectations of family business practices are confirmed. At other times, readers' assumptions might be challenged. Also, the reader should be prepared to ignore the signposts (or discard the route map) when a new (theoretical or methodological) perspective, seen for the first time, looks more promising and inviting. Thus, the reader is invited to consider some of the approaches that have enhanced family businesses as a distinctive area of study and at the same time be introduced to the variety of perspectives put forward by the contributors to this volume. Before this, however, narrative from a second-generation chairman of a small manufacturing company is presented in order to give space and voice to the people who are continuously negotiating the 'special' and distinctive features of small family businesses:

> *I can remember walking into this place and I'd walked away from a job where I had to fill a time sheet in and account for my hours and that was a shackle, if you like. I came in here and, OK, I got paid every week and I didn't have to account for my time but I worked twice as hard as I did before but I found myself obligated because it is a family company. You just can't walk away from this place. You can't slam the door and think, sod it, I'll go and work somewhere else, which I've done many times. It's so frustrating because you know as soon as you get one bit of the business right, there's another bit going wrong. So you know you are going to go from one problem to another and after twenty years you get a little bit fed up of it and so it is a bit of a prison as well. At one time I always used to say I didn't like this job and one aspect I haven't, I've never enjoyed it, but on another plane I have. I enjoy coming in here and opening the post because you don't know what's going to be in the post or the next phone call.*

> (Second-generation chairman of small electrical
> engineering company in the UK)

The 'special' quality of small family businesses

In the above quote the voice of this chairman is made prominent to highlight how working in the family business is distinctive. In reflecting on his life in the business from when he joined the family firm as a qualified electrical engineer, he comments that while there is less accountability and more secure wages, there is also hard work, constant problems, forever commitment and both the frustration and satisfaction of 'being obliged' to continually keep on working to get the business right even when the temptation is to walk away. For this owner and many others like him, the family business is special and distinctive. Also, the now extensive literature concerned with highlighting the family business as a special area of study, is evidence of this. For example, Gersick *et al.* (1997) argue that the family business is an extraordinary, 'special' form of organisation and this special quality brings both negative and positive consequences. It is not the intention in this book to challenge the aspirations behind this dominant assumption of family business research, training and consultancy. At the same time, however, this special quality and distinctiveness should not be taken for granted. It needs to be made explicit, to be evaluated, explored and justified using different methodologies and theories. The aim of this book, therefore, is to bring together a collection of works from leading and developing scholars who are researching, exploring and writing about the special quality and distinctiveness of family firms. I want now to return to the case of the small electrical-engineering company to explore this notion of 'special' quality.

The company was started in 1948 by two brothers. One brother left the business and Fred, the remaining brother, continued to run the electrical-engineering business. On Fred's retirement, he distributed ownership of the company's shares equally to his four daughters. None of the daughters wanted to be involved in day-to-day management of the company. However, two of the husbands did come in to run the business (Robert, first – now chairman; followed by the younger Stewart as managing director). In 1999, Robert and Stewart were faced with a serious dilemma. Robert tells the story:

> *Fred was very secretive with his daughters and whatever. He gave them shares but they were never given accounts or anything. They were asked to sign bits of paper but never knew what they were, you know. As I was when I was made a director. I never had accounts for five years even though I was a director. I was taken to meetings with the accountants and told sit there and don't say a thing, you know. But luckily after one year, I ended up doing all the talking because I knew what was going on and nobody else did you see but, anyway, Stewart and I decided it's a family company, the shares are pretty much divided between the family. We would have a meeting with the family to explain to them what they have inherited, what the company was, how it was formed and its good things and bad things. So obviously, Stewart and I married the two daughters and there's the other two daughters. We all get on socially and as a family fine. So we sat down in Stewart's house and we said, we'll make it very informal. We said, right, we'll tell you about the company. How much we do and how many people we employ, and they sat and nodded and at the end of it, Peter, the leading brother-in-law, said, 'Well, we'd like out.' 'What do you mean, Peter?' 'Well, you know, business is not really us, we've got no involvement in it whatever, you and Stewart are obviously there and we'd like out.'*
>
> *So they said, we'd like out. So I said, what do you mean Peter? He said, well, you know, buy our shares whatever. It knocked me back a little bit I must admit. So we left it*

there, we came away and I thought, well, hang on a minute, if we pay them out, buy their shares off them, how are we going to finance it? If we do it personally, we'd have to borrow money and I thought I'm coming up for sixty, I'm not borrowing any money. I've got a pension as well and I don't need to do that and Stew said, I'm the same, I'm not putting my house at risk and whatever. The company could buy its own shares back. We had a chat to the accountant. Yes, you can do that. We thought, well, but no way we've got cash reserves but I'm certainly not letting them walk away with assets and leaving us with all the debts and going into having overdrafts and God knows what and mortgages. Fred's shares had to be valued by an accountant in this formula. So we told them, which started a massive family row because it was substantially less than the realisable value and, God, it caused no end of problems. Until at the end I then said, enough of this, I'm not having any of this. We called a formal meeting. We had a meeting in here and we went round the table and said, does anybody want to buy the shares? Nobody wanted to buy any shares. I said, right, the company doesn't want to buy any shares and everybody, and even all of us, agreed that it had gone too far. So we more or less said, right, enough is enough. Obviously it brings the problem up, how do we all realise our potential in this company? I'm not bothered. You see, I've got some shares but I started out with no shares. They've been given to me over the years and I'd gladly give them to the lads to be honest but I'm sure the daughters won't. So how do we, then, I've got six to eight years to sort something out, say to Chris and Tony, look, do you want to buy these shares? Do you want to do a management buy-out? You've seen what we can make over the years and whatever. They're still young enough and they're hungry enough perhaps to do it or maybe even bring the other people in as well. If that doesn't happen, then the only alternative is to go to a competitor and say, do you want to buy us, but we won't get a lot of money for it because they can quite happily sit and let it go. So, yes, we could liquidate the company which Stew, myself, our two wives – and we have overall control of the company – are all adamant that that will not happen. You know, I've found myself caring more about this company than I thought when that happened. But the trouble is when Stewart and I go, what will happen? I don't know there'll be a younger man, shares will be left to families that have no understanding of the company and whatever but I don't know. But this is a thing of family companies, isn't it?

The 'special' nature of family firms can be seen very clearly from this short case extract. During his narrative, the chairman speaks about complex issues and processes which influence his understandings and persuade him to act in particular ways. In addition to the hard work, frustration and obligation to always be there, owner-managers not only have to deal with day-to-day product/market/employee/growth/marketing/training issues that all managers face, but also they have to carefully manage and negotiate a complex set of social and emotional relationships involving family and non-family members who have different expectations and motivation for involvement in the family business. Thus, day-to-day issues of management are combined with issues of ownership (shares, buy-outs, cash reserves, personal borrowings, equity and capital). Such concerns are stimulated by age, thoughts of retirement, ill health, succession and the need for good leadership to realise the potential of the business. Also, there is a voicing of concerns that all the shares might be left to the daughters who do not understand the business and recognition of the need to bring good, loyal non-family members into the management team with a view to, and eventually giving them, ownership. Thus, kinship ties, nepotism, hereditary management and emotions are special features of the family business. But also, strategic concerns of growth, finance, leadership, succession and in-house training/development of non-family managers are woven into the chairman's comments.

'Family' as a discursive resource for understanding small business organisation

From this short account a number of discourses can be identified. 'Discourses are a connected set of statements, concepts, terms and expressions which constitute a way of talking or writing about a particular issue, thus framing the way people understand and act with respect to that issue' (Watson, 1994a: 113). Therefore, an interest in discourse is revealed, whereby human beings draw upon a set of linguistic resources to give voice to and express aspects of their organisational lives (Watson, 2002). A focus on family as a discursive resource is important for understanding small business organisation for two reasons.

First, the concept of family is multi-dimensional and interpretively dynamic in that 'family discourse ... assigns meanings to the actions we take on behalf of the social ties designated as familial' (Gubrium and Holstein, 1990: 14). From this perspective also, the key research focus becomes not 'what is family' but in what ways 'family' becomes a resource for specifying individuals' relations with others (ibid.). McCollom (1992) takes a similar perspective in her research where she concludes that talk, interaction, relationships and discourse in the business are dominated by family issues and that through this 'family discourse' meanings (of family, organisation, business) are 'managed' in the system (ibid.: 19). Ram (1991, 1994a) also refers to the concept of 'negotiated paternalism' to draw attention to the way in which meanings are 'managed' through social/family relations within ethnic firms. In addition, Ram and Holliday (1993a) and Holliday and Letherby (1993) explore 'family culture' and the 'familial analogy' in small firms in order to examine why people in small firms refer to themselves as 'one big happy family'. A focus on family as a discursive resource is therefore important for understanding small businesses.

A second reason relates to the close relationship between discourse and processes of social construction. A social constructionist perspective is emerging in entrepreneurship research (Steyeart and Bouwen, 1992; Bouchiki, 1993; Fletcher, 1997; Chell, 1998). Social constructionist ideas invite researchers into new worlds of meaning and action (Alvesson and Sköldberg, 2000: 16) and the opportunity to challenge dominant assumptions, discourses and ideologies. Social constructionist ideas provide for a critical stance towards taken-for-granted knowledge (Burr, 1995) and provide a means of understanding how small business 'reality' is interpreted or constructed. On the one hand, there is an emphasis on the meanings (of family–work, business–families) generated by people as they collectively engage in descriptions and explanations in language

(Gergen and Gergen, 1991: 78). Also, people bring to their interactions previous cultural, historical and political understandings that contextualise and shape further interactions. Therefore, social constructionism is used by people in the process of relating (Gergen, 1999). In relating to each other, there is an emphasis on language and the discursive resources (for example, family concepts) that people use or draw upon to provide meaning in their organisational contexts.

In the chairman's account above, discourses relating to hereditary management, kinship ties and family responsibilities are made explicit. Also, discourses referring to the special needs of family firms in terms of business development (succession, leadership, training, finance) are expressed in order to indicate how family firms are different from non-family firms. Reference is made, on the one hand, to how the family influences can impede strategic business development and therefore need to be isolated and contained. This can be made sense of in terms of a rationality discourse. At the same time, attention is drawn to how the family can provide important resources in the form of nurture, support and emotional labour to support the development of the business or provide opportunities for self-expression and realisation for family business members. Here, reference is made to ways in which the small business is tightly embedded and interwoven within a complex set of emotional, kinship and household ties which yield special obligations and commitments. This can be made sense of in terms of a resource-based discourse. However, a critical discourse can also be identified which highlights how commitment to family can also mean suppression or inhibition of individual freedom of action or self-expression/realisation. This discourse relates to issues of control, oppression and inhibition that can be seen to some extent in the earlier quote from the chairman when he refers to the family business as a 'prison'.

These contradictory but overlapping discourses which are inferred interpretively from the chairman's short account relate to and reflect the ambiguity of the family–work relationship. The discourses show how the concept and meaning of 'family' are complex and ambiguous in that the dynamics at work will be socially constructed and negotiated according to gender and ethnicity (Ram, 1991; Ram and Holliday, 1993a; Holliday and Letherby, 1993; Fletcher, 2002). Focusing on the ambiguity of the work–business relationship provides a means of enhancing understanding of small business organisation. Also, research, policy direction, government support and private consultancy can be targeted more appropriately to respond to these special needs. The discourses are now used to provide a rationale for making sense of the family business literature on the one hand, and for structuring the chapters in the order that they appear in this volume, on the other.

Part I: A rationality discourse in studies of the small family business

The emotional aspects associated with the family business such as hereditary management and attention to kinship ties or responsibilities identified above are often referred to in the family business literature as 'irrational'. Family ties and emotional issues are often seen as competing with the demands of the organisation and that commitment to family clashes with the ability to be loyal, efficient and totally committed to the work organisation. The rational approach, according to Hollander and Elman (1988), sees two organisations co-existing within the family business – the family, non-rational component and the business rational component – and when the two parts clash, the 'business' side (i.e. structure, functions, purpose) loses out to the power, sentiment and emotional issues of the family. As a result, therefore, early writers lamented the fact that family firms were not operated in a more "business-like" way. The solution [for which] was to excise the family (Calder, 1961; Donnelley, 1964). Their solutions tended to be highly normative, prescribing how the emotional issues involved in running a family business could be smoothed away by preventive or corrective strategies. Attempting to separate the 'family' from the 'business' issues was espoused as the guiding principle for developing a successful business and this view has also permeated a number of family business texts (see Leach, 1994) and is very dominant in short training and consultancy programmes.

One important consequence of rational thinking, however, is that it has encouraged the development of useful classificatory schemes of the family business that have applicability in different socio-economic contexts. Such schemes are important for providing common frames of reference for research teams who aim to evaluate the characteristics and processes that strongly differentiate family from non-family firms (Daily and Dollinger, 1993; Poutziouris and Chittenden, 1996; Westhead, 1997) and in so doing highlight the special quality of family firms. Initially, Holland and Boulton (1984) delineated between the husband–wife or large family business in order to make a distinction based on the participation of family members in ownership and day-to-day management (i.e. pre-family, family, adaptive family, post-family). Also Leach (1994) defined a family business as any firm which was influenced by a family relationship. Furthermore, Litz (1995), taking forward Barry's (1989) framework, identifies nine categories of family firms derived from two structural considerations: ownership and managerial control. Within this typology three categories characterise family firms. The first type is a more 'pure' definition: firms involving family members in both ownership and management of the company. Other categories include those firms with non-family ownership but with family managers involved in day-to-day management (for example, a first generation company preparing for succession). Third, other categories include the family business that has gone public but where family members are still in senior management positions. Importantly, Litz emphasises the 'intentionality' within the business (i.e. to become, remain, erode or displace the family). This avoids a static perspective of the family business and provides a framework for analysing the role of family relationships at different levels and stages within both large and small organisations (cf. Dyer and Handler, 1994). Also, Gersick *et al.* (1997) proposed a three-dimensional view of the family firm in order to draw attention to the complexity of family firms in their different guises from single entrepreneur moving into second-generation, to 'cousin consortiums' faced with maturity market/product/business life cycles.

The definitional issue is taken up in Chapter 1 of this book. Paul Westhead, Marc Cowling, David Storey and Carole Howorth take forward their earlier work in this area and assert that if the family business is associated with more superior business performance than non-family businesses, then strong arguments are needed to support this. Otherwise these 'special' quality claims are always definition dependent. In their chapter, these authors present their extensive family business classificatory scheme using a range of criteria. This definitional framework is helpful to policy-makers/support agencies in targeting particular client groups. However, Westhead *et al.* state that a problem with wider definitions is that the proportion of firms classified as 'family business' can vary from between 15 and 81 per cent depending on the narrowness or extensiveness of the definition selected. As such, they make a case for selecting a fairly broad definition (whereby 50 per cent of ordinary voting shares are owned by members of the largest single family group related by blood or marriage and where the company was perceived by the chief executive as a family business). In taking this definition, their findings show that family firms represent 63.7 per cent of all businesses surveyed in their sample. Also, these family firms tend to be older and smaller in terms of employment size and sales revenue. They also did not find any statistically significant differences between family and non-family with regards to performance indicators, non-financial objectives (including the need to ensure independent ownership and retain employees). The only significant difference was that family firms tended to be more concerned with lifestyle and securing family jobs in the management team. These findings were in line with research by Poutziouris and Chittenden (1996) but contrast with the research undertaken in the early 1990s that showed that family firms considerably outperformed non-family firms.[1]

What can be highlighted from this is that while many business practices are similar in family and non-family firms, certain aspects such as hereditary management and family lifestyle influences are the distinguishing features – particularly if they have undergone an inter-generational transition. What is needed, then, is further, in-depth research on the complementary and contradictory processes through which family and business discourses interact in the small business organisation and this is where this book makes a major contribution.

In summary, therefore, rational discourse has highlighted the special nature of family businesses. On the one hand, as is also seen throughout this book, it is effective in isolating the special situation and needs of family firms as they attempt to achieve succession (Fox *et al.*, 1996; Kimhi, 1997), manage culture (Hall *et al.*, 2000), manipulate product, business, family life cycle changes (Davis and Stern, 1988; Gersick *et al.*, 1997) and professionalise their businesses (Dyer, 1989). It has also encouraged greater understanding of those features which characterise family from non-family firms (Daily and Dollinger, 1993; Poutziouris and Chittenden, 1996). At the same time, however, a number of writers are critical of the influence of rational thinking in family businesses. These criticisms are now discussed.

Kepner (1983) argues that a rational perspective and the desire to isolate special problems and challenges created by inter-generational transition, emotional-kinship aspects and hereditary management have encouraged unhelpful polarity within studies of family business. This 'business versus family' dualism manifests itself in a number of studies, which have created polar assumptions of how family businesses behave and thus how they can be categorised. For example, family firms are often characterised as less entrepreneurial, professional, and more risk-averse or closed in terms of culture. For example, Daily and Dollinger (1993) found that small family-managed firms tend to be smaller, younger, less formalised and growth-oriented and tending towards a 'defender' strategic typology. This is also shown in Gartner (1990) and Hoy and Verser (1994) in which 'family state' and 'entrepreneurialism' are depicted as separate (although overlapping) domains. However, as identified above, the relationship between family and small business organisation is an ambiguous one producing many tensions and contradictions. The following two chapters, therefore, explore the tensions produced by rational discourses and the implications of this for an understanding of small family businesses.

In Chapter 2, Annika Hall questions the usefulness of a rational perspective in family business research. However, rather than arguing that family firms are rational or non-rational, she puts forward a multi-rational perspective to explore the ways in which individuals working in family firms engage in multiple rationalities at different times. She explores a multi-rational perspective in the context of a small Swedish company and shows how multiple rationalities (from genuine to expressive) shape strategic change processes during inter-generational transition.

In Chapter 3, Bengt Johannisson is also critical of the tendency to see family business life as irrational and introverted. He argues that entrepreneurship is absent in many family business debates and accounts for this partly because of the dominance of rational thinking but also because of managerialist perspectives which focus on recipes for growth or success. Taking forward Dyer and Handler's (1994) work, which examines how family and entrepreneurial dynamics intersect in the life of a small business, Bengt posits that it is important to inquire into the differences between family, managerial and entrepreneurial ideologies because these ideologies create both complementary and contradictory tensions which can energise medium-sized organisations as they grow.

The roots of rational thinking, Kanter (1989) argues, can be traced back to the rise of industrial capitalism and a movement towards scientific management, whereby firms became larger and work became less craft-like, more mechanised with better-trained workforces. The result of this was that the worlds of work and family came to be separated. The need for loyalty from workers and their family networks, Kanter (1989) argues, became less important to employers and family influence and control were seen as best isolated from the workplace. Family ties and emotional issues were seen to compete with the demands of the organisation and ties to the 'family' clashed with the ability to be loyal, efficient and totally committed to the organisation. As a result, Kanter argues that during the post-Second World War period the separation of family from work to ensure the smooth functioning of both family and economic institutions became accepted as the conventional wisdom for the organisation of work. This also meant that the institutions of 'economy' and 'family' as 'connected organisers of experience and systems of social relations, are virtually ignored' (1989: 77). She argues that in pre-industrial societies 'family' and 'working life' were highly integrated and the family unit was seen as important for imposing some control over daily tasks.

> The family was an important work unit in city factories in England ... spinners in textile mills chose their wives, children and near relatives as assistants, children entering the factory at eight or nine worked for their fathers, perpetuating the old system of authority and the traditional values of parents training children for occupations ... it was the family system that made possible the transition from pre-industrial to industrial ways of life.
>
> (Kanter, 1989: 79–80 referring to the work of Hareven, 1975; Nelson, 1975)

Muncie and Sapsford (1997), however, provide an alternative perspective. The issue was not so much that the family became separated from work but that the nature of the family unit changed. They remind readers of the work of Talcott Parsons (1959) who argued that the pre-industrial family, which was characterised by a large-scale kinship unit providing a mixture of economic, educational, social and political functions, changed to a more nuclear form during industrialisation because it was more adaptive to the functional necessities of an industrial economy. However, Muncie and Sapsford review historical and contemporary evidence to conclude that there is no simple pattern of a shift from extended to nuclear families during industrialisation. Instead, the nuclear unit was always prominent as a key domestic grouping (1997: 16). From this, it is possible to argue that it is not that the worlds of work and family became separated (as is reflected in the rational discourse) but that the nature of their relationship is more ambiguous and becomes less transparent. This ambiguity is explored further in the following section, which examines the 'resourcing' relationship between families and working life.

Part II: A resource-based discourse in studies of the small family business

Many studies of the small business have emphasised the important resourcing function provided through the mass of inter/intra-organisational connections and interdependencies that are drawn upon to shape small business emergence and growth. In the context of the smaller business, these interdependencies are often explored through a network perspective of personal and social network contacts (including family linkages) which are seen as a 'resource' through which small business owner managers gain access to important social, cultural, emotional, financial information, resources and capital (cf. Mitchell, 1969; Boissevain, 1974; Tichy *et al.*, 1979; Aldrich and Zimmer, 1986; Johannisson, 1987a, 1987b; Curran and Blackburn, 1991; Butler and Hansen, 1991; Larson, 1992; Ibarra, 1993; Ram, 1994b).

Also, other studies emerge in the form of business history accounts of family firms and industries (Crossick *et al.*, 1996; Grell and Woolf, 1996; Muller, 1996; Hareven, 1975; Nelson, 1975; Chapman, 1996; Cookson, 1997) to examine how family ties and networks have important regional economic development potential (Lombardini, 1996; Muller, 1996; Weidenbaum, 1996; Brogger and Gilmore, 1997; Heuberger and Gutwein, 1997). Furthermore, discussed in terms of social capital, gender, and family (Whatmore, 1991; Rosa, 1993; Stafford, 1995; Salaff and Hu, 1996) other accounts emphasise the important role of women's emotional labour in 'resourcing' enterprise development and also ethnic or immigrant labour (Ram, 1994a; Sanders and Nee, 1996, Fletcher, 2002) or household labour (Whatmore, 1991; Wheelock, 1991).

This research is important for understanding the small business sector on three counts. First, it highlights the social embeddedness of business activity within a broader social context incorporating family, kinship and social relations (Granovetter, 1985; Grabher, 1993). Second, this research led to closer examination of the relationship between family and organisation of the small business workplace and consideration of the complexity, ambiguity and multiple directions of the business–family, family–business relationship (Kepner, 1983; Wheelock, 1991; Ram and Holliday, 1993a; Poutziouris and Chittenden, 1996; Fletcher, 2000). This argument has much value for understanding the organisation of the small business. It also provides some background and context to the remaining chapters of the book which are concerned with exploring the contradictory relationship between work–family–small business organisation and the complex ways in which the 'family' is a resource providing both supportive/buffering and controlling/inhibitive functions.

In family business studies during the 1980s and 1990s, resourced-based ideas were centred on a 'developmental' view of the family firm which acknowledged how the different elements of the family business system (comprising market place, industry, technology, stakeholders, founder issues, family issues) come together to shape the organisation of the family business (Kepner, 1983; Hollander, 1984; Ward, 1987). Taking this perspective forward, Hollander (1984) and Beckhard and Dyer (1983) began to draw attention to the interdependency of business, family and environmental components and examine how the family business 'system' operates according to rules which are derived from the conflicting needs and demands of the components of the system. At the same time, Kepner (1983) highlighted the need for a 'co-evolutionary' perspective of family business based on a more interactive understanding of family and firm. McCollom (1988) also explores how the family system can perform a key integrating role for the business and at the same time meet the needs of the family. She sees the relationship as a dynamic one in terms of dominant–subordinate positions (with the family goals as dominant). The middle section of the book contains chapters that combine or take forward developmental perspectives in order to examine particular strategic processes faced by family businesses. These contributions are now discussed.

In Chapter 4, Kosmas Smyrnios, Claudio Romano, George Tanewski, Paul Karofsky, Robert Millen and Mustafa Yilmaz examine how and why work–family domains are interrelated by comparing owner-managers of family and non-family firms in Australia and the United States. In particular, they test owner-managers' ratings of their anxiety and work stress in order to examine how individuals intentionally create, modify or eliminate work–family links. This emphasis is distinctive in that few studies have researched this in the context of family business owners who constantly manage work and family tensions. They conclude that high levels of work to inter-personal conflict and business dissatisfaction have an adverse effect on family cohesion. But the strength of association between work to family conflict and family cohesion is stronger for non-family than family firms. This is because family supports have a buffering effect for family business owners.

In this chapter, therefore, the authors acknowledge the supportive or 'buffering' role of the family in helping individuals to realise opportunities for self-expression. This perspective is also highlighted in Chapter 5, where Barbara Murray examines the 'Emotional Dynamics of Family Enterprises'. Barbara adopts a grounded theory and case study approach to report on fieldwork undertaken over a five-year period in which she explores how emotional dynamics are realised in family businesses facing inter-generational succession. Through in-depth analysis of two Scottish case studies, Barbara combines family life cycle and adult development theory to show that anxiety and emotional issues provide different (complementary and contradictory) outcomes in terms of organisational action. Emotional dynamics have the dual effect of often accelerating and, at other times, slowing down decision-making processes.

What is emerging from the contributions, so far, is an understanding of the special nature of small firms in which there are family relationships. From these analyses, it can be seen how the family can often provide a locus for emotional support and fulfilling relationships – a protected enclave against impersonal and rational world of capitalism (Zaretsky, 1976). In this sense, the family can sometimes provide a nurturing context in which business developments are enacted.

The 'family dynamics' theme is further elaborated in Chapter 6 in which Mattias Nordqvist and Leif Melin combine institutional theory with concepts from corporate governance and strategic change in order to examine why certain changes in the corporate governance process occur. Using a case study approach, they analyse the empirical results of strategic change and succession in two small, third-generation, family firms in Sweden. They conclude that the relationship between corporate governance and strategic processes is complex and unique to each family firm. As such, they should be examined in conjunction with each other. However, internal political dynamics and family values are identified as important in shaping the institutionalisation of governance which in turn has implications for the processes of strategic change and the structuring of the corporate governance system.

In Chapter 7, Panikkos Poutziouris discusses the 'Financial Affairs of Smaller, Family Companies'. Here Panikkos examines the finance gap and principles of the 'pecking order' framework to explore how these restrict survival and long-term growth of smaller, privately held companies (including family firms). Evidence is drawn from 150 owner-managing directors of small family businesses to establish their views and experiences about venture capital financing and other capital options. Panikkos shows that the financial development of family businesses adheres to the pecking order philosophy whereby smaller family companies tend to be more dependent on internally generated funds for survival/development (i.e. share capital plus retained profits and internally generated equity) and are governed by a 'keep it in the family' tradition. Also, they are not enthusiastic about parting with venture capital which risks losing family business control. So they also tend to build a stronger equity base over time through retention of profits. They are also sceptical about fast growth as this might entail relinquishing control and dependence on external investors. Panikkos concludes by arguing for tax-based schemes to offer an allowance for corporate equity.

Continuing the business development theme, Chapter 8 is entitled 'Training and HRM Strategies in Small Family-owned Businesses'. Here, Harry Matlay discusses the lack of attention to training and human resource management practices in small family firms. Using data from triangulated telephone, survey, and case research he identifies that there are differences between family and non-family business in terms of the ways in which human and financial resources are allocated. Harry found that there is a positive link between management progression and career development of owner-managers in small firms but there were some differences in the way non-family members were approached in terms of training. Also, employing close relatives secures against managerial or supervisory skills shortages and trust/commitment provided by family members mitigates against the need for training.

The issue of leadership development in succession processes which has not received widespread attention in family business research is the focus of Chapter 9. Here Jill Thomas explores some of the issues raised in the previous chapter through in-depth case analysis of Australian small firms. She examines the influences on leadership and explores whether attributes of succession can be developed. In contrast to Harry Matlay, she finds that there is no evidence of formal development plans matching successor skills with development opportunities although some informal strategies for leadership development were evident. She finds that genuine choice of entry to the family business is a valuable indicator of subsequent leadership potential (although leadership skills could also be learned). Also, low expectations in joining the family business and extensive exposure in other companies lead to excellent leadership skills. Likewise, evidence of formal education is found to be complementary to leadership development of succession (although less so for older generation CEOs).

In contrast to earlier chapters which have focused on the more dynamic (and sometimes supportive) features of the 'resourcing' relationship between family and small business organisation, the last three chapters of the book approach the notion of family from a perspective which is being made sense of here in terms of a 'critical' discourse. This is now discussed.

Part III: A critical discourse in studies of the small family business

A critical perspective of family business research is explored by Fletcher (2001) in which ideas from critical theory are drawn upon to acknowledge some of the quieter and more divergent voices/actors/practices involved in the small family business contexts. A critical discourse refers to issues of control and the suppression of individual freedom of action, self-expression and realisation. A critical perspective also seeks to draw attention to underlying social, historical, cultural issues and expressions of dominance that give rise to particular ways of working (Alvesson and Sköldberg, 2000). From this perspective, family can be seen as a site of exploitation from which small business developments grow.

Taking a critical stance towards the dominant discourses and approaches used to evaluate the family business, Part III identifies some of the conflicts and difficulties that owners and workers from family businesses find themselves in when attempting to balance work and family lives. Each chapter in this Part problematises the notion of family and challenges the tendency to over-glamorise the role of family in business development. Ram and Jones are critical of the positive association usually made between family and ethnic minority small business development and the assumption that the family yields a wealth of social capital and resources. For Baines *et al.* the family becomes the means through which small business creation is realised. For Katila, the family is exploitative and controlling through the way in which it draws upon a moral code in order to sustain its use of unpaid and underpaid labour.

The role of the family as a notable feature and vital support mechanism of ethnic minority enterprise in terms of providing business resources and competitive advantages which enable ethnic minority groups to transform social/family capital into entrepreneurial enrichment, is critically challenged in Chapter 10. Here Monder Ram and Trevor Jones explore the dominant discourse that makes a strong link between family and ethnic minority enterprise and argue that this assumption needs to be qualified in several ways. While ethnic minority businesses are often deeply embedded in family processes, this relationship is ambiguous and conflictual, often characterised by gender and generational tensions that needs careful consideration. They posit that the family influence and the use of social capital (trust, mutual obligations) may not always be positive, operating for the common good of the ethnic group. Also business resources derived from social capital and networks are not the exclusive preserve of any national origin or religious groups. Indeed, 'family' is much more ethnically generalised than is often portrayed and there is a need therefore to link aspects of ethnic minority enterprises and families to broader academic discourses which are not restricted to a cultural approach.

In Chapter 11 Sue Baines, Jane Wheelock and Elizabeth Oughton suggest that there has been a return to a 'traditional' organisational form for the business family, with parallels a shift from a single bread-winning wage to a family employment model with all adults earning. This means that the new micro-businesses emerging in the 1990s are a reinvented form of the traditional business family that both Kanter (1989) and Muncie and Sapsford (1997) referred to. Baines *et al.* take the 'household' as the economic provisioning unit for small business because, they argue, the world of micro-business should be understood in the context of changes in labour markets and household livelihoods. They present a conceptualisation of the 'household livelihood jigsaw', which takes account of the (gendered) interrelationship between market, household and state. They provide evidence that micro-businesses (0–9 employees) are often sustained through contributions from a variety of household members in ways that are reminiscent of older ways of working. Modern small business families, in other words, may be exploiting themselves and their household members as they struggle to compete in the market. Thus, Baines *et al.* posit that the emergence and shape of business-families are more an indicator of survival rather than enterprise and entrepreneurship in local economies.

In a similar vein, in Chapter 12, Saija Katila discusses 'Emotions and the Moral Order of Farm Business Families in Finland'. She conceptualises the family as a social construction whereby families are representatives of their cultural communities that adhere to, embody and enact particular moral codes. This perspective is important because it highlights the rights and obligations ascribed to family members within a community and how the moral order shapes the way families do business. Through ethnographic research and the use of biographical accounts she explores how the norm of unpaid family work and the use of labour are regulated with regard to the community's moral order in one Finnish farm family. This focus is particularly interesting given that farming in Europe is dominated by familial units. Saija shows that in Finnish agriculture monetary incentives in farms are irrelevant because of the social obligations to kin and promise of future succession. However, the price to pay for these family and social obligations is a lifetime's commitment to hard work which begins at a young age. Also, the family, she argues, is still often the legitimate site for unpaid and underpaid work (involving children).

In summary, the discourse emerging from these chapters is that in the context of the smaller business, notions of family often reflect a discourse of control where family ties, social capital and kinship obligations suppress and inhibit the personal freedom of owners and managers to act in ways in which they otherwise might. What can be identified also is a move away from a closed and non-problematised idea of 'family' and its relationship with 'business' (Levin, 1993). This is seen also in the quote earlier from the chairman who uses words such as 'prison' or 'shackle' to indicate the ways in which his obligations to the family business constrain and inhibit his opportunities for individual freedom. This perspective is also seen in small business studies which emphasise the paternalistic role of the small business owner-manager who keeps a tight and controlling rein over the workforce and strongly influences the employment relationship (Newby, 1977; Rainnie, 1989; Scott *et al.*, 1989; Curran and Stanworth, 1979a, 1979b, 1981a and 1981b; Scase, 1995). It can be argued, then, that the family can also be seen as an ideological construct – a stereotype produced and maintained for the purpose of exerting certain kinds of social control (Gittins, 1985). From this perspective, the family is associated with a discourse of control that helps to define the roles people should play and the power structures within which these roles are worked out.

Understanding the small family business

This introductory chapter has been concerned with discussing the dominant antecedents, approaches and discourses that have shaped approaches to studies of the family business over the past thirty years. As can be seen from the summaries of each chapter, the relationship between family and small business organisation is complex, ambiguous and shaped by contradictory (and yet complementary) discourses of control and nurturing. The intention has not been to provide a 'unified paradigm' for the study of family business as Wortman (1994) proposed. Instead, the aim has been to examine the theoretical and conceptual issues which have shaped the study of family firms. In reviewing a range of conceptual and methodological approaches, the complexity and ambiguity of the institution of 'family' (Holland and Boulton, 1984: 16) and its role/meaning in different socio-economic or organisational contexts are highlighted. This book and the contributions therein highlight how the concept of family is interpretively dynamic (Gubrium and Holstein, 1990). An emphasis on discourse is important because through language and discourse people realise interpretations and meanings of family in a small business context (Bourdieu, 1996). As can be seen from some final words from the chairman introduced earlier in this chapter, family is a concept that is socially constructed, is multidimensional and is constantly being realised through rational, resource-based and critical discourses:

> *It's funny but talking here now, it feels like therapy ... a sort of counselling. You know, I have a brain tumour, it's benign, and I am not going to die from it or anything but it's left me with only 60 per cent of what I was and that does concern me, it really does. While I was able to keep lots of balls in the air, always have done ... but now I can only do one thing at a time. But this company, you know ... I've gone along thinking it's a prison. But yes, I'm really pleased with the way the company has gone. I'm quite proud of what we've done. I really am.*

I welcome you to the book and hope that your journey through the chapter contributions is an enjoyable one.

Note

1   London Business School/BDO Stoy Hayward and BBC 2 *Business Matters*/BDO SH.

Part I

A rationality discourse in studies of the small family business

1 The scale and nature of family businesses

Paul Westhead, Marc Cowling, David J. Storey and Carole Howorth

Introduction

A key objective for owners of family businesses is to pass their businesses on to the next generation of family members (Morris *et al.*, 1997). Many family business owners are concerned that the fiscal regime, particularly capital taxes, can put at risk the inter-generational transfer of businesses (J.L. Ward, 1987). Policy-makers and practitioners can introduce policies that encourage the survival of family businesses. They are, however, reluctant to introduce new policies or change the tax regime without reliable information about the scale, nature and economic contribution of family business activity. There is, therefore, a need for academics, practitioners and policy-makers to carefully define, identify and understand their target group of analysis. Policy-makers are interested in reliable information that indicates whether family businesses report superior levels of performance than non-family businesses (Shanker and Astrachan, 1996). If family businesses were associated with superior business performance than non-family businesses, this would be a powerful argument for lowering capital taxes, because of the benefits to the wider economy. Further, if the transfer of businesses between generations of family owners were to lead to enhanced performance (i.e. faster sales revenue and employment growth), then it could be argued that inter-generational transfers are in the interests of the national economy as well as family business owners. If family businesses transferred from one generation to the next performed no better, or worse (i.e. 'clogs to clogs in three generations'), then there is no clear case for seeking to lower/abolish capital taxes.

Of particular relevance to policy-makers and practitioners is reliable information relating to the following questions:

*   Is the reported scale of unquoted family company activity influenced by the family business definition selected?
*   What proportion of unquoted companies are family businesses?
*   Are unquoted family companies over-represented in older business age bands?
*   Are unquoted family companies over-represented in small employment size bands?

- Are unquoted family companies over-represented in lower sales revenue size bands?
- Are unquoted family companies over-represented in any industrial sectors?
- Are unquoted family companies over-represented in any regions?
- Do family businesses report superior levels of financial performance than non-family businesses?
- Are family businesses more likely to stress non-financial performance objectives than non-family businesses?

In this chapter, it is emphasised that the scale of the family business phenomenon is definition dependent. Demographic differences as well as similarities between family and non-family businesses are discussed. Evidence from studies focusing upon the performance of family and non-family firms is also reported. In the final section, conclusions and implications for policy-makers and practitioners are discussed alongside directions for additional research attention.

Family business definitions

There is a lack of consensus surrounding the theoretical and operational definition of a family firm (Handler, 1989b; Litz, 1995, Chua *et al.*, 1999). Researchers have frequently used four key issues when defining family firms. First, whether a single dominant family group owns more than 50 per cent of the shares in a business (Donckels and Fröhlich, 1991; Cromie *et al.*, 1995). Second, whether members of an 'emotional kinship group' perceive their firm as being a family business (Gasson *et al.*, 1988; Ram and Holliday, 1993b). Third, whether a firm is managed by members drawn from a single dominant family group (Daily and Dollinger, 1992, 1993). Fourth, whether the company had experienced an intergenerational ownership transition to a second or later generation of family members drawn from a single dominant family group owning the business (Gasson *et al.*, 1988). In addition, some researchers have considered multiple conditions when defining family firms.

Studies in which the numerical dominance of family businesses is greatest have used the widest definitions, by asking respondents whether their business satisfied one specific criterion. Westhead and Cowling (1998) argue that two or more of the above elements in combination need to be considered when identifying family businesses. It is, however, appreciated that there is no single definition of a family business that is widely acceptable.

Using the four criteria highlighted above, several operational definitions of an independent unquoted family company were identified by Westhead and Cowling (1998) as follows.

1 The company was perceived by the Chief Executive/Managing Director/Chairman to be a family business (categories a, b, c, d, e, f and h combined in Figure 1.1).

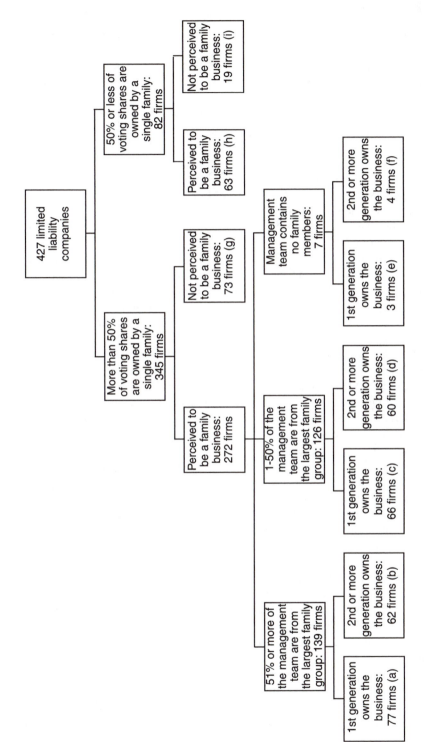

Figure 1.1 Numbers of family and non-family companies as classified by Westhead and Cowling

Source: Westhead and Cowling (1998).

2   More than 50 per cent of ordinary voting shares were owned by members of the largest single family group related by blood or marriage (categories a, b, c, d, e, f and g combined).

3   More than 50 per cent of ordinary voting shares were owned by members of the largest single family group related by blood or marriage and the company was perceived by the Chief Executive/Managing Director/Chairman to be a family business (categories a, b, c, d, e and f combined).

4   More than 50 per cent of ordinary voting shares were owned by members of the largest single family group related by blood or marriage, the company was perceived by the Chief Executive/Managing Director/Chairman to be a family business and one or more of the management team was drawn from the largest family group who owned the company (categories a, b, c, and d combined).

5   More than 50 per cent of ordinary voting shares were owned by members of the largest single family group related by blood or marriage, the company was perceived by the Chief Executive/Managing Director/Chairman to be a family business and 51 per cent or more of the management team were drawn from the largest family group who owned the company (categories a and b combined).

6   More than 50 per cent of ordinary voting shares were owned by members of the largest single family group related by blood or marriage, the company was perceived by the Chief Executive/Managing Director/Chairman to be a family business, one or more of the management team were drawn from the largest family group who owned the company and the company was owned by second generation or more family members (categories b and d combined).

7   More than 50 per cent of ordinary voting shares were owned by members of the largest single family group related by blood or marriage, the company was perceived by the Chief Executive/Managing Director/Chairman to be a family business, 51 per cent or more of the management team were drawn from the largest family group who owned the company and the company was owned by second generation or more family members (category b).

Westhead and Cowling used these stated family business definitions to measure the scale of family business activity. Data were gathered from a stratified random sample (by broad industrial categories and by standard region) of independent unquoted companies that were at least ten years old located throughout the United Kingdom. Evidence from a postal survey of 427 respondents was analysed.

In Table 1.1, the 427 independent unquoted companies surveyed by Westhead and Cowling were subdivided with regard to majority share ownership of ordinary voting shares, perception by the Chief Executive/Managing Director/Chairman of being a family business, family members involved in the management team and the generation of family business ownership. Table 1.1

shows the proportion of businesses classified, as 'family businesses', is highly sensitive to the definition used. Using the widest definition 81 per cent of companies sampled could be viewed as 'family businesses'. Whilst using the narrowest definition, this fell to only 15 per cent.

All four elements are potential influences upon definitions of what constitutes a family business. Some elements, however, are more central than others. While it is important for the Chief Executive/Managing Director/Chairman to view the enterprise as a family business, i.e. definition (1), this can be regarded as a necessary, but not a sufficient, condition. If it were a sufficient

Table 1.1   Numbers of surveyed family and non-family unquoted companies in the United Kingdom

Family company definition	Family companies		Non-family companies	
	No.	*(%)*	*No.*	*(%)*
(1)	335	78.5	92	21.5
(2)	345	80.8	82	19.2
(3)	272	63.7	155	36.3
(4)	265	62.1	162	37.9
(5)	139	32.6	288	67.5
(6)	122	28.6	305	71.4
(7)	62	15.0	365	85.0

Notes:

(1)   The company was perceived by the Chief Executive/Managing Director/Chairman to be a family business (categories a, b, c, d, e, f and h combined in Figure 1.1).

(2)   More than 50 per cent of ordinary voting shares were owned by members of the largest single family group related by blood or marriage (categories a, b, c, d, e, f and g combined).

(3)   More than 50 per cent of ordinary voting shares were owned by members of the largest single family group related by blood or marriage and the company was perceived by the Chief Executive/Managing Director/Chairman to be a family business (categories a, b, c, d, e and f combined).

(4)   More than 50 per cent of ordinary voting shares were owned by members of the largest single family group related by blood or marriage, the company was perceived by the Chief Executive/Managing Director/Chairman to be a family business and one or more of the management team was drawn from the largest family group who owned the company (categories a, b, c, and d combined).

(5)   More than 50 per cent of ordinary voting shares were owned by members of the largest single family group related by blood or marriage, the company was perceived by the Chief Executive/Managing Director/Chairman to be a family business and 51 per cent or more of the management team were drawn from the largest family group who owned the company (categories a and b combined).

(6)   More than 50 per cent of ordinary voting shares were owned by members of the largest single family group related by blood or marriage, the company was perceived by the Chief Executive/Managing Director/Chairman to be a family business, one or more of the management team were drawn from the largest family group who owned the company and the company was owned by second generation or more family members (categories b and d combined).

(7)   More than 50 per cent of ordinary voting shares were owned by members of the largest single family group related by blood or marriage, the company was perceived by the Chief Executive/Managing Director/Chairman to be a family business, 51 per cent or more of the management team were drawn from the largest family group who owned the company and the company was owned by second generation or more family members (category b).

condition, then the definition would be totally subjective and, as outsiders, we would have no clear idea upon what basis the categorization was made. Broad all-embracing definitions of a family company, such as definition 1, have, however, been questioned on the grounds that they are too inclusive. As a result, definition (1) cannot be regarded as the most appropriate definition. Similarly, definitions with multiple conditions, such as those associated with definitions (6) and (7), have been questioned on the grounds that they are too restrictive. It may be overly restrictive to require that all family businesses have to be at least 'second generation businesses'.

The elements that most closely encapsulate the concepts of a 'family business' are 'perception', 'share ownership by family members' and 'management of the business by family member'. Definitions (3), (4) and (5) in Table 1.1 best incorporate these concepts, with definition (3) being the most expansive and definition (5) being more restrictive. Westhead (1997) argued that 'ownership' rather than 'family management' is the crucial family element that distinguishes family companies from non-family companies. As a result, Westhead favoured definition (3) rather than definitions (4) and (5), which, in fact, are very similar.

Characteristics of family businesses compared with non-family businesses

In this section, demographic differences between family and non-family firms are discussed with regard to business age and size, principal industrial activity of the business and the location of the business.

Business age

The Stoy Hayward (1992) survey of family and non-family unquoted and quoted companies in the United Kingdom found family companies were longer established than non-family companies. With regard to several family firm definitions, Westhead and Cowling (1998) also detected that independent unquoted family companies were much more likely to be older than non-family companies.

Business size

Daily and Dollinger (1993) found professionally managed independent manufacturing firms with less than 500 employees in the United States were significantly larger in terms of number of employees than family-owned and family-managed firms. Furthermore, Donckels and Fröhlich's (1991) study focusing upon independent manufacturing firms with less than 500 employees in eight European countries noted the highest proportions of family firms were found in the smallest employment size bands. Cromie *et al.* (1995) and Westhead and Cowling (1998) also detected that Irish and British family firms were smaller in terms of employment size and sales turnover than non-family firms.

Principal industrial activity of the business

In the United States, Reynolds (1995) found new family firms were less likely to be engaged in manufacturing and business services. Stoy Hayward (1992) detected that a larger proportion of service businesses were family companies in the United Kingdom. Gasson *et al.* (1988) also noted the majority of farms in the United Kingdom are family businesses. More recently, Westhead and Cowling (1998) detected that family businesses were more likely to be over-represented in agriculture, forestry and fishing as well as in the distribution, hotels and catering industrial sectors. Family businesses were, however, under-represented in the banking, financing, insurance and business services sectors.

Location of the business

Westhead and Cowling (1998) explored whether family unquoted companies were over-represented in particular locations. They detected that family businesses were over-represented in rural locations (i.e. in areas with less than 10,000 people). Moreover, family businesses were slightly over-represented in the East Midlands of England. Conversely, they were markedly under-represented in the South East of England (associated with the Greater London agglomeration). Reynolds (1995), however, found family firms were significantly over-represented in urban areas.

The performance of family and non-family businesses

Because of their numerical importance, the performance of family businesses is of critical importance to the development of an economy. Family business performance is also of importance if such firms seek to obtain 'special' fiscal treatment from government, for the reasons outlined earlier. Poutziouris and Chittenden (1996) explored the performance of family and non-family businesses in the United Kingdom. They failed to detect any significant differences between the two groups of firms.

Westhead and Cowling (1997) also explored the performance of unquoted family and non-family companies in the United Kingdom with regard to several performance indicators. They used family firm definition (3). Two 'matched paired' sub-samples of unquoted family and non-family companies were identified. Family and non-family companies were paired/matched on four criteria: age of the company since receiving its first order, location type (i.e. a rural or an urban location), location of the company by standard region and the main industrial activity of the company. Companies were simultaneously perfectly matched on the latter three criteria. In essence, the matched paired design held these three elements constant, during the performance comparisons of matched family and non-family companies. Ultimately, two matched paired sub-samples of family and non-family companies were identified, each containing seventy-three companies.

The financial performance indicators selected by Westhead and Cowling (1997) are detailed in Table 1.2. Table 1.2 shows the two matched groups of companies were compared with regard to nine performance indicators. They found between 1991 and 1994 both family and non-family unquoted companies contributed to wealth creation and job generation. Row 1 in Table 1.2 shows the average gross sales revenue sizes of family and non-family companies in 1991, while row 2 shows their average gross sales revenues in 1994. In the 1991 to 1994 period, family companies, on average, recorded higher levels of absolute gross sales revenue growth (means of £791,000 and £406,000 for family and non-family companies, respectively), although not in a statistically significant direction (row 3). On the surface, it appears that family companies, on average, recorded faster growth in sales over the 1991 to 1994 period. However, it must be appreciated that absolute gross sales revenue growth was concentrated in a small number of family as well as non-family companies. Because the variations within the two groups of companies (i.e. the standard deviations for the family and non-family samples) were so large, the absolute and percentage gross sales growth difference between family and non-family companies were not statistically significant. With regard to gross sales revenue growth as a percentage, a difference was detected between the two groups of companies but not in a statistically significant direction. Family companies over the 1991 to 1994 period, on average, increased their gross sales revenues by only 27 per cent, compared with a 55 per cent growth recorded by non-family companies (row 4).

The job generation performance of family and non-family companies over the 1991 to 1994 period was compared. Family companies were not significantly larger than non-family companies in employment size in 1991 (row 5) or 1994 (row 6). Family companies, on average, recorded slightly lower levels of absolute (means of 2.4 and 3.1 employees for family and non-family companies, respectively) as well as smaller percentage employment growth (means of 17 per cent and 19 per cent for family and non-family companies respectively) over the 1991 to 1994 period (rows 7 and 8). These differences between the two groups of companies were, however, not statistically significant.

A weighted performance score was calculated for each company (Naman and Slevin, 1993), based upon the importance respondents attached to six selected performance indicators (i.e. sales revenue level, sales revenue growth rate, cash flow, return on shareholder equity, gross profit margin and net profits from operations) and the level of satisfaction their business had achieved with regard to each of these indicators. No statistically significant difference was recorded between family and non-family companies in terms of reported weighted performance scores (means of 12.4 and 12.2 for family and non-family companies, respectively) (row 9).

Westhead and Cowling (1997) also tested, although it is not shown in Table 1.2, for differences between family and non-family companies with regard to the propensity to export outside the United Kingdom, as well as the percentage of gross sales exported. No statistically significant differences between the two groups of companies were identified.

Table 1.2   Performance contrasts between matched-paired family (*n* = 73) and non-family
(*n* = 73) unquoted companies in the United Kingdom

Performance variable	Family companies[a]	Non-family companies	Student's 't' test statistic	Degrees of freedom
	Mean	Mean		
1. Gross sales revenue for the financial year ending in 1991 (£'000s)[b]	2,800	1,551	0.93	132
2. Gross sales revenue for the financial year ending in 1994 (£'000s)[b]	3,591	1,957	0.92	132
3. Absolute change in gross sales revenue, 1991–4 (£'000s)[b]	791	406	0.92	132
4. Percentage change in gross sales revenue, 1991–4[b]	27.3	55.2	−1.20	132
5. Number of people employed at the end of 1991[c]	20.8	18.9	0.42	141
6. Number of people employed at the end of 1994[c]	23.2	22.0	0.22	141
7. Absolute change in the number of people employed, 1991–4[c]	2.4	3.1	−0.29	141
8. Percentage change in the number of people employed, 1991–4[c]	16.9	19.4	−0.24	141
9. Weighted performance score[d]	12.4	12.2	0.36	142

Notes:

[a]More than 50 per cent of ordinary voting shares were owned by members of the largest single family group related by blood or marriage and the company was perceived by the Chief Executive/Managing Director/Chairman to be a family business (categories a, b, c, d, e and f combined in Figure 1.1).

[b]Seven family companies and five non-family companies were excluded from the analysis because they failed to provide gross sales revenue data for 1991 and 1994.

[c]One family company and two non-family companies were excluded from the analysis because they failed to provide employment data for 1991 and 1994.

[d]A weighted performance score was calculated for each company surrounding the 'importance' and 'satisfaction' respondents reported with regard to six performance indicators.

Westhead and Cowling (1997) concluded that it is difficult to attribute a clear performance impact purely due to family ownership. They suggested that where such attribution had been made in the past, it might have reflected sampling bias differences between samples compared in previous studies. Most notably, family ownership contrasts may have been contaminated by other influences upon business performance such as age of the company, or main industrial activity of the company or location of the company.

Different prioritising of objectives between family and non-family companies

Family businesses may have different priorities of objectives to non-family businesses. In particular, family businesses are associated with several non-financial objectives. Binder Hamlyn (1994) noted that family companies were much more likely to be concerned with stability and continued independent ownership of the business by family members. They were less likely to seek rapid business expansion by selling equity privately or on the stock exchange.

Westhead and Cowling (1997) compared the non-financial objectives reported by family and non-family unquoted companies. A matched sample methodology was used (i.e. companies were matched with regard to age of the company since it received its first order; location of the company in a rural area; location of the company by standard region type and the main industrial activity of the company). Family firm definition (3) discussed above was used to identify family companies. Westhead and Cowling noted some differences in non-financial objectives reported by family and non-family companies. They were, however, more struck by the similarities than the differences between the two groups of companies. Non-financial objectives of matched paired family and non-family companies are summarised in Table 1.3. Family and non-family companies sought to: 'ensure the survival of the business'; 'ensure that our employees have secure jobs in the business'; and 'ensure independent ownership of the business'. To a lesser extent, both family and non-family companies sought 'to enhance the reputation and status of the business in the local community'. These objectives are generally long-term objectives, which might have been expected to be more characteristic of family companies, yet non-family companies emphasised them equally. Only two statistically significant differences emerged between family and non-family companies with regard to their non-financial objectives. Table 1.3 shows family companies were markedly more likely to have reported that they sought 'to maintain/enhance the lifestyle of the owners'. They also identified the provision of employment for family members within the management team as being a prime objective.

Conclusion

This chapter has highlighted the need for researchers to justify the criteria used to define family firms. The presentation of clear and justified family firm definitions would allow the results from one study to be compared with those using the same definition in another industrial, locational or cultural setting. Policy-makers, practitioners and researchers must be aware that the scale of family firm activity is highly sensitive to the family firm definition selected. Westhead and Cowling (1998) showed that the proportion of surveyed companies classified as family companies varied between 15 per cent and 81 per cent depending on the family firm definition selected.

Evidence presented in this chapter will interest policy-makers and practitioners. Individuals concerned with encouraging the survival and development of family firms must carefully consider and identify the 'target group' for assistance. Agencies wishing to assist a broad spectrum of firms may prefer to select a broad all-embracing family firm definition. They may, however, select a tighter family firm definition in order to limit their 'target group' for support.

Before introducing new policies (e.g. policies that lower inheritance or estate taxes) to assist the survival and development of family firms, the economic case

Table 1.3   Non-financial objectives – contrasts between matched-paired family (n = 73) and non-family (n = 73) unquoted companies in the UK

Non-financial objective[a]	Family companies[b] (Mean score)	Non-family companies (Mean score)
1. A prime objective is to ensure the survival of the business	4.7	4.6
2. A prime objective is to ensure that our employees have secure jobs in the business	4.3	4.2
3. A prime objective is to ensure independent ownership of the business	4.1	3.8
4. A prime objective is to enhance the reputation and status of the business in the local community	3.6	3.7
5. A prime objective is to maintain/enhance the lifestyle of the owners[c]	3.9	3.6
6. A prime objective is to provide employment for family members of the management team[c]	3.2	2.3[d]

Notes:

[a] Measured on a scale where strongly disagree = 1, disagree = 2, neutral = 3, agree = 4 and strongly agree = 5.

[b] More than 50 per cent of the ordinary voting shares were owned by members of the largest family group and the company was perceived by the Chief Executive/Managing Director/Chairman to be a family business.

[c] Statistically significant difference recorded between family and non-family companies at the 0.05 level of significance.

[d] It may seem curious that non-family companies would consider employment of family members to be a prime objective. However, this reflects the definition of family companies used in this study; under this definition, it is perfectly feasible that individuals from within non-family companies would have an objective of bringing members of their family into the management team.

for supporting the family firm sector needs to be clarified. Policy-makers need to know whether family firms generally perform better than non-family firms. Evidence reported by Westhead and Cowling (1998) suggests that in making these assessments policy-makers and practitioners must be aware of the demographic differences that exist between family and non-family firms. They detected the following important demographic differences between family and non-family companies with regard to several family company definitions:

- Family businesses were much more likely to be older than non-family businesses.
- Family firms were significantly smaller in employment size as well as sales revenue size with regard to family company definitions (5) and (7) but not family company definition (3).
- Family businesses were more likely to be over-represented in agriculture, forestry and fishing as well as in the distribution, hotels and catering industrial sectors.
- Family businesses were under-represented in the banking, financing, insurance and business services sectors.
- Family businesses were over-represented in rural locations.
- Family businesses were slightly over-represented in the East Midlands of England. Further, family companies were under-represented in resource-rich

'core' regions (associated with high levels of new firm entry as well as high business closure rates), for example, the South East of England (associated with the Greater London agglomeration).

This review has shown that demographic sample differences may distort the results of bivariate studies that try to identify a 'family firm' impact relating to the performance of family and non-family firms. Further, this review has suggested that several demographic influences (i.e. age of the company, location in a rural area, location by standard region type and the main industrial activity of the company) need to be controlled if the aim of a study is to compare family with non-family firms. Reluctance to address this important methodological issue will lead to the perpetuation of myths surrounding the economic contribution of family firms. More importantly, biased empirical evidence may lead to the introduction of inappropriate policies.

The matched paired sample technique was used by Westhead and Cowling to detect 'real' differences between family and non-family companies rather than demographic sample (i.e. contextual) differences between the two groups. Business performance differences (and similarities) between matched paired family and non-family companies have been reported in this review to highlight important differences (as well as similarities) between the two groups of companies. While no single definition of a family company addresses all concerns, definition (3), which included two conditions, was used in the study conducted in the United Kingdom.

It might have been expected that the performance of family companies would have been markedly poorer than that recorded by non-family companies which did not have to deal with 'family agendas'. Evidence presented by Westhead and Cowling (1997) failed to isolate clear differences between family and non-family unquoted companies with regard to several performance indicators. They also found a greater similarity than expected between the non-financial objectives specified by respondents in family and non-family companies. Family and non-family companies sought 'to ensure the survival of the business', 'to ensure that our employees have secure jobs in the business' and 'to ensure independent ownership of the business'. These similarities almost certainly reflect the market imperatives of being in business, in the sense that any business which deviates from these conventional objectives is unlikely to survive. However, as anticipated, Westhead and Cowling did find respondents in family companies were more concerned with maintaining/enhancing the lifestyle of the owners and with providing employment for family members of the management team.

Evidence presented in this chapter will interest researchers. If researchers decide to use a single family firm definition, there is a case for selecting the reasonably broad family firm definition (3). Researchers using only one family firm definition must appreciate that this decision may lead to the development of definition-sensitive conceptual and empirical models. Individuals concerned with developing more widely acceptable models and frameworks should consider developing a 'familyness' scale along which each business can be placed. A more abstract 'familyness' scale (i.e. a composite scale composed of information derived from several questions or indicators using techniques such as factor analysis) may encourage more comparative research to be conducted surrounding business performance, management practice and strategic orientation differences between types of firms.

In order to develop more appropriate public policies to support the independent family firm sector, additional theoretical and conceptual work needs to be conducted surrounding the role played by owners and managers in family firms. There is a need for researchers to broaden the range of research methods used to collect and analyse data surrounding family firms (and the owner-managers of family firms). Qualitative studies need to specifically focus upon the important 'how' and 'why' questions. Additional bivariate and multivariate quantitative questionnaire studies will bear further fruitful information and confirmatory evidence. A matched paired methodology that controls for key demographic influences should be considered by researchers doing bivariate comparative studies. The opportunity exists for researchers to use more multivariate statistical techniques to explore the business performance, management and ownership structures and strategic orientation differences reported by independent family and non-family firms. Additional quantitative longitudinal research could identify the management and ownership structures associated with enhanced business survival and superior financial and non-financial business performance.

Acknowledgements

The authors would like to express their gratitude for generous financial support from the Leverhulme Trust and the BDO Stoy Hayward Centre for Family Businesses. Our views do not necessarily coincide with those of the sponsors.

2 Towards an understanding of strategy processes in small family businesses

A multi-rational perspective

Annika Hall

Introduction

> As both owner and leader you don't always behave the way you would have if you had been only a leader ... you don't take as rational decisions, you are too influenced by the family.
>
> (Family business owner-manager)

Are family businesses irrational? The literature on family business sometimes gives this impression (Hollander and Elman, 1988). This is not the least the case in relation to strategy processes which is the focus of this chapter. In many respects, strategy processes are the same in all businesses, family dominated or not (Sharma *et al.*, 1997). The key difference is that, in the family business[1] all stages of the process are likely to be influenced by family values, goals and relations (Holland and Boulton, 1984). Moreover, the close inter-relationship between family and business often leads to a mix up of issues from the different contexts (Davis and Stern, 1996). Since relatively little research has been conducted on family business strategy (Harris *et al.*, 1994), the understanding of how these influences affect strategy processes in family business is quite limited (Sharma *et al.*, 1997). Even so, the fact that family relations do impact upon strategy processes in family businesses seems to be enough to label them 'irrational'. The meaning of rationality is, however, seldom discussed. Instead it seems to be implicitly taken for granted.

What is thought of as 'rational' is most often calculative[2] rationality (Sjöstrand, 1997), referring to actions that are the most 'efficient means for the achievement of given ends' (Hargreaves Heap, 1989: 4). This account of rationality originates from economics (Simon, 1976) and builds on the notion of 'economic man'. Starting with a well-defined goal the economic man evaluates all possible alternatives from which, the one that maximises his utility, is chosen. This mode of rationality has its main focus on the outcome of action and requires an analytical, calculative agent who has consistent preferences, perfect information, is able to cope with extreme complexity, and who is not socialised into any traditions/norms but is totally free to act (Granovetter, 1985; Mäki *et al.*,

1993; Hollis, 1994; Sjöstrand, 1997). 'With perfect information and correct computing, preference is automatically transmitted into outcome so as to solve the maximizing problem. The agent is simply a throughput' (Hollis, 1983: 250).

Even though the assumptions of economic man can be accused of unrealism (Simon, 1947; 1976; Hargreaves Heap, 1989; Flyvbjerg, 1991; Sjöstrand, 1997; McCloskey, 1998), the calculative account of rationality still dominates the literature on strategy and management (Whittington, 1993; Sjöstrand, 1997; Mintzberg *et al.*, 1998; Eriksson, 2000). Traditionally, strategy has been viewed as the sequential formulation and implementation of an organisation's long-term goal to achieve profit maximisation. This is the essence of economic rationality. Strategy has typically been portrayed as a plan, a rational search for the most efficient way of achieving this goal based on objective responses to environmental demands – formulated by top managers. This perspective on strategy, often referred to as the 'Classical' (Whittington, 1993) or 'Rationalistic' (Johnson, 1986), does not put much consideration on the implementation phase. Instead, the accomplishment of the intended strategy is implicitly taken for granted (Whittington, 1993; Mintzberg *et al.*, 1998) and the process behind the realised strategy is, by and large, ignored.

Considering the domination of the mono-rational, classical perspective on strategy, the condemnation of family business as 'irrational' is perhaps not so surprising. It does, however, limit understanding of strategy processes. Therefore, scholars in the field of strategy have pointed out the importance of understanding strategy processes from other perspectives which are 'concerned less with prescribing ideal strategic behavior than with describing how strategies do, in fact, get made' (Mintzberg *et al.*, 1998: 6). These perspectives represent a contextual and processual view on strategy. Far from being planned, strategies emerge as a pattern in a stream of actions (ibid.). This view is close to the one held by economic sociologists who argue that economic action, like any other form of action, is socially situated. It is embedded in ongoing networks of personal relationships and is expressed in interaction with other people (Granovetter, 1985; Mäki *et al.*, 1993). A focus on the outcome of action (calculative rationality) is thereby insufficient and has to be complemented by non-calculative, social accounts of rationality with a focus on process and meaning (Sjöstrand, 1997; McCloskey, 1998; Eriksson, 2000).

The questioning of economic rationality has led to an increased interest in the notion of multi-rationality among strategy researchers (Whittington, 1993; Sjöstrand, 1997; Regnér, 2001; Volberda and Elfring, 2001). Doubtful about the empirical relevance of the classical perspective on strategy, Regnér (2001: 44) argues that strategic development is better understood as 'an interweaved process involving diverse rationalities and strategies simultaneously rather than individual rationalities and strategies as distinct lumps in a process of episodic stages'. Relating rationality to degrees of complexity he further claims that the more complex the strategic process, the more important are rationalities that take context and process into account. Moreover, each strategy process has to be understood in terms of its specific composition, or configuration of rationalities:

'A strategy process could involve all sorts of complexities and, thus, rationalities and therefore it does not make sense to analyse it according to a single rationality view' (ibid.: 47).

In line with the criticism of the mono-rational, classical view of strategy, the aim of this chapter is to contribute to a better understanding of strategy processes in family businesses through a multi-rational perspective. In order to investigate how accounts of rationalities are interrelated and shaping strategy processes in a small, family business, the case of ACTAB is presented and analysed. A business in the second generation was chosen in order to capture the complexity, role integration and multi-rationality that are likely to be present when members of two generations together own and manage a company.

Research methodology

ACTAB is a manufacturing, 130-employee, second-generation family business, located in a small town in the south of Sweden. Over time, the company has faced a number of turning points, dividing its development into four main periods. During the first period, 1937–70, the company went through a rather modest and unstructured development under the sole leadership of the founder. Between 1970 and 1994 the company was jointly run by the two oldest brothers who managed to further expand and develop the company. The third period, 1994–9, begins with the unexpected death of the younger brother, forcing the company, for the first time in its history, to rely on external middle managers. The starting point of period four (1999 to present) is the bringing in of an external CEO which then led to rather radical changes in structure and management philosophy. During these periods, different accounts of rationality stand out as influencers of the decisions taken. This highlighted the relevance of the multi-rational perspective for understanding the shaping of strategy over time.

Methodologically the research is conducted as a qualitative, in-depth case study. McCollom (1990) argues that qualitative field research is especially adapt to the study of family businesses. Characterised by a complex structure, an emotionally coloured culture and diffusion of roles, research on family businesses requires methods that are capable of exploring these aspects. The qualitative field study has the capacity to capture the richness of the family business and also enables the researcher to develop a relationship with the people studied and achieve depth over breadth,

For the fieldwork, twenty, 1.5-hours, in-depth interviews with leading family members, external managers, board members, and employees were conducted. The respondents were asked to give their view on the development of the company, with a special focus on how critical incidents and relations had been dealt with and why.

The description of the strategy process in ACTAB in the next section is based on the transcribed interviews. In order to enable the reader to come close to the empirical material the description is fairly rich in quotations. The aim is to allow the reader to hear the voices of respondents and to show how the interpretations

have been reached. Since there is always the possibility of differing interpretations, this is important for the trustworthiness of the results. Only if judged as
trustworthy, will the interpretations offered make a scientific contribution as one
of many possible ways of understanding strategy processes in family businesses.

The chapter aims to frame ACTAB within a multi-rational perspective.
Different accounts of rationality are identified, and concepts are suggested for
describing the relations between them (and their configuration). It is suggested
that the categories reinforcive–contradictive, and dominant–submissive, are
fruitful for operationalising such configurations. Through this conceptualisation,
the influence of different rationality accounts on the strategy processes is made
more 'visible', thus enabling a better understanding of these processes as they
unfold in the family business.

In the concluding part of the chapter it is argued that an understanding of
strategy processes does benefit from a multi-rational perspective. Strategies
develop under the influence of context-specific rationality configurations
(Regnér, 2001). For efficient management of family businesses knowledge of
these configurations and their possible impact on strategy processes is important.

The ACTAB case study

ACTAB was founded in the late 1930s by Albert, who, for many years, was the
only family member working full-time in the company. As the children grew
older, they occasionally helped out, although not in any leading positions. The
situation did not change much until 1970, when Albert's wife died. With the loss
of his wife, Albert more or less stopped caring about the business. Until then, he
had been the sole manager of the company, but now he totally let go and sold it
to his children. 'I have done my duty, now the time has come for you to do
yours,' he told Steve and Martin, the two oldest sons. It was not without regret
that Steve joined the company full-time. He had lots of other interests that he
would have liked to develop, but felt he had no alternative but to obey his father.
'Not taking over the company had probably meant breaking with my family, and
my feelings for them were too strong to do that.'

As the oldest brother, Steve had always had the feeling of having to earn the
approval of both his father as well as other people working in the company, and
taking over the business became part of that.

> *Our father was, one might say, successful ... he had an idea to which he held on, he
> pushed it and he succeeded ... And when we took over everyone questioned whether we
> would succeed or not ... and we have worked incredibly hard to prove that ... for that was
> the requirement ... and this is part of everything I do, that I may not do worse than my
> father ... failures are not allowed. Everyone had their eyes on us, but today I can look back
> and say, 'We didn't do so bad after all.'*

Together, the two brothers ran the company for many years with Steve as CEO
and sales manager and Martin as production manager. Apart from them, no one

took any active part in the strategic running of the company. Under the joint leadership of the brothers the company started to expand in a more structured way. New products and techniques were developed and customer relations were intensified. Through systematic work, the quality of products was increased and on time delivery improved. Thanks to Steve's skills in English and German, the company also started to expand on the international market. All these efforts changed the position of the company from a small, local manufacturer to a well-recognised actor in its field.

Although the leadership might best be characterised as joint, there were also conflicts between the brothers.

> *Their discussions were very fierce. Initially, they almost never had the same opinion, but somehow they always reached an agreement. But the discussions were very tough.*

> *Steve worked to get a lot of orders, and sometimes he was really frustrated when Martin, as the production manager, argued: 'We do not have the time to do this, you have to reject this, we simply do not have the capacity.' This situation repeated itself over and over again.*

In spite of being an individual with a very strong will, Steve never really took this matter to the extreme:

> *That would have meant losing my brother … we had very close family relations.*

> *I have been the one that has done most of the travelling and I have met other managers and seen other ways of organising … and the advantages with this … and sometimes I wanted to implement some of this into my own organisation. But that has turned out to be difficult because of different opinions of other family members … and when emotions are strong, reason has a hard time winning … And this was the case even under my joint leadership with Martin … I wanted to do things differently and we argued about it and finally we reached some kind of compromise … and I settled with that, in order to keep the family together.*

Sometimes the many, intense discussions hampered the development of the company:

> *They got stuck in an argument and nothing happened, there was no decision but lots of delays … but on the other hand … these discussions could also be rewarding because the best suggestion won … one of them always backed down if the other suggestion was better for the company, the well-being of the company was always central … But the problem was that these discussions could also lead to no decision being made.*

(work colleague)

Twenty-five years after the succession, Martin died after just a few month of illness. For Steve, this was of course a very difficult blow. With only two years between the brothers, their relationship was very close. 'We were inseparable, we had grown up together, sharing a bedroom, and we did not let go even when we had families of our own.'

Apart from growing up together, the brothers had managed the family business for more than twenty years, and now Steve was left alone to do the job. He worked day and night, trying to do both his own job and that of his brother:

> *During a period I of course worked very hard with both tasks … I took all the decisions, I went straight ahead, … I was blinded … and I must say that I used all the strength I had had, there was no one to stop me, I was deeply affected by the death of Martin. Once again I had the feeling 'this should not wreck us'. It was the same thing … when we took over from our father we, his sons, should prove that we were just as capable as him, and when Martin died I wanted to prove that the company would do all right, that it was solid enough … It was exactly the same thing.*

After six months the workload got too much and Ron, a sales manager, was hired with whose help Steve was able to develop the company faster than ever before. The company's economic statistics show, for instance, that the rate of returns was doubled during the period 1994–2000. Different reasons have been put forward as an explanation of this development. One is that this was due to many years of hard work, the result of which happened to come at this time:

> *It was very well prepared, tremendously well prepared … we had had a breakthrough as a recognised supplier, our name was known, we had taken part in trade fairs, we had made commercials, I had held lots of lectures and been deeply engaged in local and national business issues. To a great extent the expansion was due to this.*

Another reason put forward for the expansion is the new ideas and perspectives brought in by Ron:

> *The bringing in of Ron really meant a lot. He represented something completely new, something completely different … It was really letting a stranger in; you could almost say he represented another part of the world, coming from Gothenburg [Sweden's second largest city, author's comment]. He came from another culture … he was member of another communion … he was a constructional engineer, with no experience of our kind of products. And he was a tremendous shot in the arm.*
>
> (work colleague)

A final explanation proposed is that, as the sole manager, Steve was able to drive the company in a direction and with a speed that he found appropriate, without having to negotiate with anyone:

> *Once Steve was alone by the rudder … Martin was a bit more careful, he wanted to investigate things to be sure before taking action … but once Steve was alone, things exploded … we were supposed to do everything.*
>
> (work colleague)

> *Since the death of Martin, the investment rate at ACTAB has been very high … Martin was a bit more careful, as I see it … and Steve is more … he has been pushing investments and such things quite hard.*

(work colleague)

Over a four-year period, Steve and the external sales manager ran the company. Leaving the sales manager to build up a sales department, Steve was both CEO and production manager. Further, he did all the purchasing of machines and still devoted much time to customer relations. All this meant a lot of work and travelling, and Steve simply could not manage the production department the way his brother had. With time, the work of that department, therefore, became rather unstructured. In spite of this, Burt, the external production manager, was not hired until late 1998. According to Steve, the reason for this was that 'I simply did not do it, and, after all, we did all right anyway.' Other explanations have, however, been suggested:

> *Since Steve took over Martin's tasks and hired someone to take over his own … Ron never replaced Martin, no one ever replaced Martin. When Martin was ill, it was a natural thing for Steve to take over his tasks besides being the CEO, and when Martin died it was natural for Steve to continue that way, you don't replace an individual, emotionally, you simply just don't. In this way, the wounds had time to heal. And then Steve realised that he simply couldn't do all the jobs, he couldn't be both CEO and production manager and sales manager. And then Ron was hired as sales manager. And Steve kept on as head of the production. Later when Burt (the production manager) became part of the company he did not replace Martin. No one ever replaced Martin.*

The event that triggered bringing a new production manager was a period of illness, which made Steve end up in a hospital bed with strict orders to slow down.

> *This was an alarm clock … after that I started to think of what to do … and I realised that I had to have a production manager and, moreover, someone taking care of the restructuring of the company, because I had far too much to do … you know there were heaps of papers on my desk … I have heaps now, but at that time they prevented me from seeing someone on the other side of the desk.*

The 'someone to take care of the restructuring' was an external CEO. The idea to hire such a person was first introduced by the chairman of the board. The final decision was, however, long in coming. Not until one more year after the entrance of the production manager was the external CEO appointed. Emotionally, it was not a very easy decision, but with time, Steve realised that his way of running the business was more suited for a small company than for a business with 130 employees and that time had come for a change of management style:

My way of running the business ... I had it all in my head. And to a certain extent that is applicable, but you reach a point when it just does not work any more. Now I have the feeling ... and that was the feeling I had when I started to think of changing the organisation and bringing in an external CEO ... that my methods do not apply in a company of this size, but instead of trying to change myself I could bring in someone who could change the whole organisation.

One further reason for bringing in an external CEO was that, with the third generation growing up, it had become more and more obvious that Steve and his siblings differed in opinion regarding whether, and if so, under what circumstances, the cousins were to enter the family business. Steve did not share the view of his siblings, that all cousins should have a place in the family business. To Steve this was not merely a question of family membership but one of ambition and competence level. To Steve this had, over the years, given rise to a lot of agony. On the one hand he was head of, not just his nuclear, but also the extended family, which he loved very much. On the other hand, as CEO of the business he experienced how the bringing in of family members regardless of competence could be a problem both for the family and the business. Steve was hopeful that, by hiring an external CEO, this would be less of a problem for him:

He is the oldest one in the family, and he has to ... he has a certain role, everyone looks up to him. To the cousins he is, one could say, like a godfather. And then, it's not easy to be head of the company at the same time. So I think it is sort of a relief for him to have an external CEO for whom the separation of these roles is no problem.

Bringing in an external CEO has not meant a change of vision for the company. In this respect the thinking of the former and present CEOs is much the same. What differs is, however, the management philosophy. Much more than his predecessor, David focuses on efficiency, productivity and profitability. To Steve these things have never really been of any high priority. Traditionally, maximising profit has never been the overriding goal of the company. Instead, running the company has enabled Steve to develop his technical interest and to get an outlet for his entrepreneurial vein.

Many times it has cost us far more than we have had in return, ... for our father it was a much bigger success to have a machine to admire in the factory, that was the recipe for success, if we had a lot of money in the wallet was of less importance. And this is part of not having maximised profits, of not having tried to financially get the most out of everything ... that has been our way of doing things. To me, it is a tremendous satisfaction having new machines in this house. Over the years I have realised that I should perhaps do more careful calculations ... not just go out buying, but you know, I am kind of impulsive: 'Wow, this is a great machine, we have to have this one, this is something for ACTAB.'

> *I have been to trade fairs with Steve, and he can get so excited just by looking at a machine, observing its operations ... The case is, I think, that if he doesn't have a need for the machine they like, he makes sure he finds such a need ... he's just got to have it.*

The technical interest, and the pride in having new machinery have resulted in ACTAB having a very modern assembly of machinery:

> *That has been their niche, they have always had the latest ... they have never hesitated to invest. In other businesses, where money is more important, it is perhaps a natural thing that the owners are benefited by the returns. But this has never been the case here, returns have always been used for buying new machines.*

Having existed for more than 60 years, the company has hardly ever given anyone notice, and the family has always taken pride in keeping promises to customers and suppliers, sometimes to the extent of financial disadvantages.

> *I have continued this tradition ... I know the whole industry. I know several of my competitors, and I know all suppliers. And that has been a tremendous advantage, but, of course, also a disadvantage, because friendship makes you a less tough negotiator. In these situations I say to myself: 'It's OK, we'll do alright', and that deepens the friendship. In the end there are two winners if you are humble and reasonable. I have always felt I have what I need ... the relationships have been built on the ambition to always keep a promise ... that is central.*

With the arrival of the external CEO a new management philosophy is introduced. Joking about it David says that the change in the company could be described as 'a move from dictatorship to democracy'. Building on the work of Steve, David focuses on providing clear structures and goals. Much effort is being made to decentralise decision-making, budget responsibility, etc., to middle managers. In line with this, much time is devoted to reaching an agreement on, and implementing, the core values, managing philosophy and future strategy of the company. The company has partly been restructured which has led to changes in the composition of the management team. Profitability has been put in focus, and decisions concerning investments, supplier and customer relations, are to a much larger extent based on economic calculations. Further, for the first time in the history of the company, David has brought up the issue of dismissing employees.

Framing the case within the multi-rational perspective

Although a great deal of importance is attached in the strategic management literature to the calculative/economic, rationality, framing the ACTAB case, it is difficult to find situations which have been dominated by calculative/economic considerations. As illustrated by the case, this rationality account therefore has to be supplemented by rationalities that consider the processual, social and contextual dimension of human life. Over time, consideration of relations to family members, but also employees, customers and suppliers, have been shaping strategy processes in ACTAB to a considerable extent. Steve's decision to take over as CEO, despite the fact that this meant giving up his own interests, was, for instance, influenced by fear of rejection and break with the family. The tendency of the brothers always to reach consensus, and Steve's adaptation to his brother's more cautious way of running the company, are further examples of the impact of family relations. The order in which the external sales and production managers was brought in, leaving the company without a formal head of production for a period of four years, can be interpreted as a desire not to replace a deeply beloved brother. Consideration of customer and supplier relations, in spite of potential financial shortcomings, is a further example of how personal relations shape business decisions. Finally, bringing in an external CEO was partly due to Steve's problems of balancing concern for family relations with the increase in 'rational' decision-making which he felt was needed in the business.

From a mono-rational (calculative) perspective the influence of these considerations on business decisions would be described as irrational. However, when interpreted as an expression of *genuine rationality* they make more sense. 'In the course of more lasting relationships with known others, exchange acts will have meanings that extend beyond the actual objects involved in the particular transaction' (Sjöstrand, 1997: 23–4) and tend to be influenced by genuine rationality. Genuine relations could be biologically determined, such as the parent–child relationship, and thus, are based on certain roles and positions. But genuine rationality could be important even in the absence of a biological connection, when the interaction between individuals is characterised by love or friendship. In either case, the interaction is emotionally coloured and the people involved are not easily replaceable. This account of rationality is based on reciprocity, and it aims at obtaining or preserving confidence and trust (ibid.).

Another explanation is the need for individuals to prove their own ability, to live up to the expectations of others, as well as to find an outlet for one's own personality and interests. One of Steve's main driving forces in running the company seems to be the desire to prove his own ability in developing the company, something that became rather evident after the death of the brother. Another reason for owning and managing the company seems to be the possibility of pursuing his technical interest, of which the modern assembly of machinery is an example. Profit maximisation *per se* has never been a goal. Instead, money has been a means of realising other objectives. This reason for action also relates to the need to say something about oneself, to manifest one's own personality, and is labelled *expressive rational* (i.e. the need to express ideas about what is worthy in our selves) (Hargreaves Heap, 1989). Not often explicitly considered, this account of rationality seems to have been rather influential in shaping strategy processes in ACTAB.

In the light of the case, therefore, at least three different accounts of rationality can be recognised: genuine, expressive and calculative/economic. The notion of rationality configuration (Regnér, 2001) is useful for understanding the relationship among the rationalities as well as the relationship between strategy and rationality. The rationality accounts are not exclusive; instead one and the same decision could be based on different kinds of rationalities. The decision to hire an external manager was, for instance, based on both economic and genuine rationality. Moreover, the relationship between the rationalities varies. They can be supportive of each other, in which case they together push a decision in a certain direction. This would be an example of a *reinforcive* relation. Again, the decision to hire an external manager applies here. But rationality accounts might also be in opposition to each other, pushing a decision in different directions. In this case, the relation is *contradictive*. Had the relation to the brother not meant as much to Steve (genuine rationality), he would probably have been able to develop the company faster (expressive rationality).

It is argued that in this case both genuine and expressive rationality have been far more important than economic rationality. In no situation has economic rationality been the sole basis for a decision. In situations characterised by a contradictive relation between the multiple rationalities involved, economic rationality has had to give way to the genuine, procedural or expressive accounts. Examples of this are the tradition not to dismiss any employees and to keep customers or suppliers in spite of financial disadvantages (i.e. genuine and procedural rationality). Profit maximisation (economic rationality) has never been an overriding goal for the owners, instead running the business has been a way of self-expression (expressive rationality). Hence, in the company, economic rationality has been *submissive* to social rationality accounts.

In contradictive situations it seems as if genuine rationality has had the strongest impact. The expressive account of rationality is important, but in this case, it has been used only to the extent of not jeopardising family relations. Again, the example of the joint decision-making of the brothers is illustrative. Another example is the fast expansion after the death of Martin. Without (explicitly) having to consider the relationship with his brother, Steve's actions were no longer dominated by genuine rationality. Instead, the expressive rationality came to the forefront. Moreover, if it had not been for family relations, Steve might very well have refused to take over the company. In ACTAB, genuine rationality has tended, therefore, to be a *dominant* rationality account.

Finally, what on the surface might appear as an expression of economic rationality is, on closer inspection, often caused by a social rationality account. The expansion after the death of Martin is explained both as the result of careful preparations (economic rationality) and as the result of not having to take family relations into consideration (expressive rationality comes to forefront). Thus, economic rationality is not just bounded by the limited calculative ability of the individual. To a large extent it is also restricted by the social contexts of which the individual is a part.

Conclusion

The aim of the research presented in this chapter has been to contribute to a better understanding of strategy processes in family businesses. Understanding something implies seeing it *as* something, from a certain perspective (Ödman, 1991; Burr, 1995). Depending on the perspective used, images will be created which 'selectively highlight certain claims as to how conditions and processes – experiences, situations, relations – can be understood and in so doing suppressing alternative interpretations' (Alvesson and Sköldberg, 2000: 6). Different perspectives, thus, give rise to different understandings of the same phenomenon.

Beginning with a critique of the dominance of calculative rationality, and of the mono-rational, classical view on strategy, this chapter has proposed an alternative perspective of family businesses as not irrational but multi-rational. An understanding of strategy based solely on economic rationality runs the risk of being partial or superficial. As pointed out by Regnér (2001), strategy derives its meaning in complexity, and the higher the degree of complexity the more important are rationalities that take context and process into account. One of the most distinguishing features of family businesses, the integration of systems and roles (Gersick *et al.*, 1997), can be assumed to add to the complexity normally characterising strategy processes. If this is the case, a multi-rational perspective would be especially relevant to the study of these organisations. To understand family business strategy, it is important to go beyond a mono-rational perspective, and supplement the calculative rationality with social rationality accounts. This is evident in the ACTAB case, where the genuine and expressive accounts of rationality have had a dominant influence on the strategic development of the company by either causing or preventing the realisation of intended strategic actions. These aspects would not have been taken into consideration, or they would simply have been categorised as 'irrational', if the analysis had been conducted solely according to the calculative rationality account. For a deeper understanding, the social rationalities have to be acknowledged as equally legitimate. Further, through a multi-rational perspective, attention is paid to the processual, social and contextual dimension of strategy. Thereby, focus is put on the stream of *inter*actions (cf. Mintzberg *et al.*, 1998), in which strategies gradually take shape.

Overall, an analysis of the strategic development of ACTAB within the framing of multi-rationality leads to the conclusion that many strategic moves can be better understood if the process, and hence, the non-calculative, social rationalities are taken into account. Strategies develop as the result of context-specific rationality configurations. It is here suggested that the categories *reinforcive–contradictive* and *dominant–submissive* might be fruitful for operationalising such a configuration, and, thereby, for understanding the specific logic behind the strategic development of a particular family business.

Implications for family business owners and managers

For family business managers, it is important to understand the specific logic, or rationality configuration, of the organisation. Objectively, there are no better or worse accounts of rationality on which to base a decision, there are only different ones. Different rationalities imply different goals and priorities. Therefore, the dominant one will to a large extent influence the strategy of the business. To be able to manage the family business effectively it is, thus, important to be aware of the interplay between these rationalities.

This is particularly the case when external management is brought in to change the organisation. If the external management tries to introduce a different business logic manager too abruptly, the change process might be delayed, or even get stuck, because of contradictive rationalities. An awareness of the specific rationality configuration should help (external) managers of family businesses to handle the dynamic of these organisations. In a change process it is important to identify the dominant rationality and to avoid violating it to the extent of getting stuck in situations of contradictive rationalities. Gradually, competing rationality accounts might be introduced, which, over time could lead to changes in the rationality configuration, and, thereby, also strategic change. This can, however, only be achieved by repeated interaction and communication between key individuals. For change to be successfully implemented, the processual, social and contextual dimensions of strategy must be fully recognised.

Suggestions for further research

Also, these results are based on an analysis of the strategic development of a small, family business. However, there is nothing to indicate that multi-rationality should be a typical small business phenomenon. The research presented in this chapter is part of a larger project involving two large, family businesses. A preliminary analysis of strategy processes in these companies shows that, irrespective of size, the processes have been shaped by multiple accounts of rationality. Calculative rationality has not played a prominent role in the larger family businesses. Perhaps, similarity in governance structure is more important than size for the logic behind the shaping of strategy. Research focusing on the relation between governance structure, rationality configuration and strategy processes would, therefore, be of interest.

Applying Regnér's notion of rationality configuration to the ACTAB case resulted in genuine rationality turning out as the dominant rationality account, while calculative/economic proved to be submissive. Expressive rationality was found to dominate the calculative/economic rationality, but to be submissive in relation to genuine rationality. As this rationality configuration is specific to ACTAB (cf. Regnér, 2001), the question is whether it would be relevant to regard genuine rationality as typical for family businesses. In the literature, arguments could be found for the likelihood of this being the case (Becker, 1993; Sjöstrand, 1997). From only one case study, such a generalisation is, however, not possible to make. Therefore, further research is needed to explore the impact of genuine rationality on strategy processes in family businesses.

Notes

1 A family business is defined as a business in which 'one family group controls the company through a clear majority of the ordinary voting shares, this family is represented in the management team, and the leading representatives of the family perceive the business to be a family firm' (Westhead *et al.*, 1996).
2 There are many labels for this account of rationality, including calculative rationality (Sjöstrand, 1997), instrumental rationality (Hargreaves Heap, 1989), analytical rationality (Flyvbjerg, 1991), outcome rationality (Mäki *et al.*, 1993), Zweckrationalität (Weber, in Hollis, 1994), and substantive rationality (Simon, 1976).

3 Energising entrepreneurship
Ideological tensions in the medium-sized family business

Bengt Johannisson

Introduction

In the beginning was entrepreneurship. However, while all novice private firms materialise entrepreneurial processes, most, if they overcome the liabilities of newness, stagnate and remain small firms in which family concerns dominate. Only a minority of family businesses nurture growth ambitions and expand to become, first, medium-sized companies and then, possibly, evolve into global corporations. Most authors adopt Penrose's (1959/1995) view that while entrepreneurship is needed to trigger the original growth process, its continuation calls for more professional management and less family involvement.

In the family business, family concerns blend with entrepreneurial forces and managerial technologies. Research into family business also recognises the tensions between family life and business life, cf. e.g. Davis and Stern (1980); Dyer (1986); Leach (1994); Kets de Vries (1996); Brunåker (1999). In this research entrepreneurship is, however, ignored and family life is usually associated with the irrational and introvert, creating problems for the business when it struggles for growth. Davis and Stern (1980) are especially clear on this point whereby they argue that a major objective of management is to neutralise the problems created by family involvement in the business.

The argument presented in this chapter is that entrepreneurship, management, and family concerns are all aspects of organised (economic) life and therefore important to every family business. Their co-existence becomes especially obvious in medium-sized firms that have experienced an inter-generational succession. Hoy and Verser (1994) and Lansberg (1996), for example, both discuss how the interfaces between the three systems 'family', 'ownership', and 'management' determine the outcome of the succession. Entrepreneurship again is left out and use of the notion of 'system' signals a functionalist/consensus approach with little concern for recognising, let alone nurturing, the tensions between proposed aspects of the family business.

This chapter, in contrast, argues that the very tensions between entrepreneurship as passion for change, the family as a social institution, and management as a profession, may energise the medium-sized family business. In the second section, the available family-business literature is briefly reviewed with respect to how it deals with entrepreneurship, management and the family respectively. The next section presents entrepreneurialism, paternalism, and managerialism as co-existing and competing ideologies. Then, the features ('dimensions') of the three ideologies are operationalised and the research design presented. Searching for differences and similarities as regards ideological profiles, this model is explored in the context of six, successful, medium-sized Swedish family businesses. In the concluding section the basic arguments are summarised and some implications for further research, practice and policy are presented.

Dominant perspectives in family-business research

A review of family-business research, mainly that published in the *Family Business Review*, results in four major conclusions. First, there is little concern for differentiating between entrepreneurship and management – only the business/management and family perspectives are contrasted (cf. Dyer, 1986; Kets de Vries, 1996; Brunåker, 1996, 1999). Also 'ownership' is sometimes included as a third 'system' (Handler, 1994; Hoy and Verser, 1994; Lansberg, 1996; Gersick *et al.*, 1997). Second, the comparative analysis is often made within a cognitively biased (and frequently normative) framework that considers emotional processes and structures (where they are paid attention to at all; Donckels, 1997) to be highly problematic (Sharma *et al.*, 1997). Consequently the vocabulary used is quite vague, indicating the co-existence of various (value) subsystems (e.g. Dyer and Handler, 1994; Gersick *et al.*, 1997). Stafford *et al.* (1999) are especially elaborate when adopting this perspective, proposing a model where the family and business systems always co-exist but how much they intermingle remains an empirical question. All these approaches, though, have a consensus bias – in that subsystems are assumed to 'fit', a managerial ambition indeed. Third, following the previous argument, it is usually argued that, as the firm grows, it takes/should take on managerial attributes at the expense of family influences (e.g. Davis and Stern, 1980; Brunåker, 1996, 1999) or entrepreneurial contributions (Watson, 1994b). James (1999a), however, certainly provides a slightly different view by arguing that there has to be a balance between informal personal (family) ties and formal contractual (business) relations within and across the family business boundaries if the business is going to stay viable. Fourth, there is little concern for constructive tensions between the business and family perspectives in the family business. On the contrary, conflicts between the family system and the business system typically are considered to be dysfunctional from the point of view of the firm. In his normative text, Leach (1994) ascribes the family system weaknesses such as 'inward-looking' and 'minimising change' while the business system by definition is alert and change-oriented. His conclusion is that the two systems should be kept as much apart as possible. Lansberg (1996), Cosier and Harvey (1998), on the other hand, state that (cognitive) conflict may be productive. However, they mainly use the family-business context as a convenient setting for their general argumentation for dialogue as a strategy for organisational development.

This brief review of the family-business literature generally suggests that there is little acknowledgement in the family-business literature of the need to explore the friction energy that is produced when the different ideologies interface and how these may contribute to family-business vitality. Instead, the literature supports a managerial view at the expense of entrepreneurship and family involvement as potential contributors to business development. A framework that pays attention to all three forces is much needed.

Ideological tensions in the family business

The taken-for-granted need for management hegemony in the medium-sized, family firm seems to be a premature and unfortunate conclusion. Our research into successful Swedish family businesses suggests that such enterprises have to be kept within the family in order to stay viable. In a follow-up of twenty-four successful family businesses fifteen years on, the most successful firms were those that had remained genuine family businesses (i.e. they had not invited, or if so, had eroded their dependence on external equity, Johannisson, 1992). This more broadly designed research inquiry into fast-growing European family businesses shows that external venture capital, a hallmark of management, does not significantly contribute to growth (Roure, 1998). In order to make sense of these observations and to supplement present family-business research, a framework is proposed that is concerned with forefronting entrepreneurialism, paternalism and managerialism as co-existing and competing ideologies that contribute to growth

Ideology is defined as *a consistent and permanent way of perceiving and appreciating the world that, charged by emotional commitment, generates a specific mode of conduct.* An ideology is a lens through which its members see reality and make it intelligible, furnishing them with confidence and self-enforcing norms (cf. van Dijk, 1998: 8). Such sense-making and self-confidence trigger action that in turn confirms the assumed interconnections between events in the environment – in that the environment becomes enacted (Smircich and Stubbart, 1985). An ideology tells its adherents what aspects of society are desirable and how they may be enacted. Ideologies, thus, are societal phenomena that embed economic, goal-directed organisations. In that respect ideologies resemble institutions. The latter, however, whether informal or formal, provide general rules of the game (North, 1990). The medium-sized family business is assumed to accommodate different ideologies in order to achieve legitimacy among different stakeholders.

Ideology is different from 'world-view' and 'perspective'. The latter concepts, and even more so the notion of 'logic' (Prahalad and Bettis, 1986), have a cognitive bias. This especially disfavours entrepreneurship and the family as phenomena since they also thrive on social mechanisms and sentiments. Sentiments, as emotional structures (Berg, 1979), encompass sources of competence and energy which are beyond reason (e.g. intuition and improvisation, feeling and empathy, passion and commitment). Scandinavian research has also shown that in managed organisations, commitment is needed for action (Brunsson, 1985) and that 'irrationalities' as much as reason and routine guide action (Sjöstrand, 1997). However, these authors look upon different rationalities as complementary, rather than competing, as is proposed in an ideological framework.

As indicated, there are three ideologies of special interest to business in general and family businesses in particular. The growth into a medium-sized firm calls for continued entrepreneurship and professional management as well as for sustained family involvement. Each of these phenomena represents an ideology addressed here as *entrepreneurialism*, *managerialism* and *paternalism* which feature respectively in the proposed framework. These ideologies are as much political as socially constructed ideologies and are different in kind. Figure 3.1 presents the medium-sized family business as embedded in these three ideologies. However, it should be noted that ideology is different to (intraorganisational) 'politics', where dysfunctional conflict concerns struggle between factions representing different interests and the pursuit of power over resources.

Although societal phenomena, ideologies differ with respect to what institutional support they receive in society in general and on the market in particular. In decreasing order the family (with paternalism as the associated ideology), managerialism and entrepreneurialism are recognised by well-established institutions in contemporary society. The family represents a universal system of norms, unquestioned in few cultures. Obviously family values remain extremely important in the small family business, where a working family life seems to be a condition for business creation and development. Schumpeter (1934) considered the creation of a (family) empire as one of three major motivators for entrepreneurs (beside the need to create and compete). By way of organising, the family business very much reproduces the family structure. As indicated in the previous section, the family, in spite of this, is far more established in society at large than in the business community. The paternalistic leadership style in

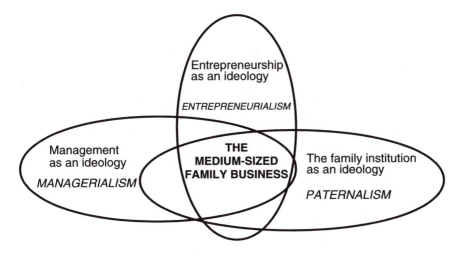

Figure 3.1   The medium-sized family business at an ideological intersection

owner-managed firms is rather considered as an obstacle for development (Scase and Goffee, 1982). Gambetta (1993) sees the Mafia as an extreme application of this ideology. Introducing the 'clan' as a generic form of governance, Ouchi (1980), however, indirectly gives credit to the family way of organising.

Managerialism as an ideology not only dominates the market but has invaded all spheres in society (Deetz, 1992). Managerial vocabulary and ways of organising (economic) life are enforced by management schools and consultants and uncritically conveyed by mass media in public discourse. Its rhetoric, which refers to growth and profits as the main measurable indicators of success, is appealing to both the stock market and to politicians. Formal and informal institutions within both the private and public sector thus reflect management ideals with respect to both objectives and forms of organising.

Entrepreneurship which practises 'creative destruction' as a basis for genuinely new activity obviously challenges existing structures. Regardless of whether we have the enterprising child or the innovative entrepreneur in mind, playfulness, curiosity, and experiential learning are needed for frame-breaking. While management means taking care of what is available (in terms of resources), entrepreneurship envisions that which does not yet exist but that which is becoming (Gartner *et al.*, 1992). Management and entrepreneurship are thus contrasting phenomena (Stevenson and Gumpert, 1985; Bygrave, 1989). This is especially obvious as regards internal entrepreneurship, where the corporate management is assumed to be able to tame entrepreneurial passion in the interest of the organisation (cf. e.g. Stopford and Baden-Fuller, 1994).

However, no single ideology can guarantee any firm viability in the global, complex, and turbulent post-modern society. Even large corporations, which are often creators of their own markets, may run into crises if they deny the need for entrepreneurship and renewal (Miller, 1990). Stagnant micro-firms pay a high price for independence declining both entrepreneurship and management. Many family businesses, though, import needed management technology through their hired accountants and absorb ideas about renewal through peer exchange. The only paternalistically run family businesses that seem to be able to maintain and even organically enhance their entrepreneurial capabilities are localised clusters of firms in so-called industrial districts. As a collective of traditional owner-managed firms, the business community in such contexts appears to be highly entrepreneurial due to local dynamics (Johannisson, 2000).

The research challenge taken on here is to inquire into differences between ideologies and how their interplay may help medium-sized family businesses to maintain their entrepreneurial drive. Since previous research is lacking, an empirical investigation is needed to explore the conceptual arguments.

Operationalising ideology and research design issues

In order to provide a basis for empirical research, the three ideologies have to be modelled and decomposed in a way that makes description and comparison possible. The joint dimensions assumed to reflect each ideological profile were quite impressionistically generated out of received knowledge about what matters in organised endeavours. Altogether eleven dimensions were generated as a basis for the empirical study (see Table 3.1). Some of these dimensions will briefly be commented upon. One dimension, for example, concerns *the dominant world view*. It is assumed that entrepreneurs thrive on ambiguity since that provides the space for realising visions: both opportunities and resources needed to enact them can be more freely sculptured in less structured environment. To managers an intelligible world means predictability and certainty which can be created, for example, by way of benchmarking and partnerships. Owner-managers search a place of refuge where family life and a business career can combine. *Resource control* within entrepreneurialism means combining flexibility and access to resources by way of personally enforced, long-term and co-operative relations. Managerialism, safeguarding for malfeasance, recommends the (formal) contract as the major road to resource acquisition. Paternalism is closely related to property rights which means that ownership control is favoured. *Pivotal competencies* within the realm of entrepreneurialism means experientially acquired knowledge that, once sedimented into tacit knowledge, can be used intuitively for pattern-breaking action. Managerialism promotes formal and standardised education while local, idiosyncratic knowledge is respected within paternalism. As regards the *success criterion*, availability of cash is crucial for upholding entrepreneurialism. Managerialism suggest that the principals' (i.e. the owners') expectations must be met, which usually means that (short-term) profitability defines success. Paternalism preaches continued ownership within the family as the major success criterion.

Table 3.1 Ideologies in the family business context – dimensions and meanings

Dimension	Entrepreneurialism	Managerialism	Paternalism
Focal agent	**The entrepreneur**	The CEO	The family head
Secondary agents	External actors	**Managers**	Family members
Dominant world view	Ambiguous potential space	**Uncertain, risky space**	Familiar, screened-off space
Temporal order	**Emergence**	Present and future	Past, present, and future
Spatial order	**Glocal**	Global	Local
Organising	Organic (continuous networking)	**Mechanistic (functional hierarchy)**	Clan (emotional hierarchy)
Internal relationships	**Trust and commitment**	Formal position	Loyalty
Business relationships	Personal	**Professional**	Confidential
Resource control	**Trust relationships**	Formal contracting	Ownership
Pivotal competencies	**Holistic, tacit knowledge**	Formal education	Local knowledge
Success criterion	Cash resources for continued venturing	**Return on investment, quantitative growth**	Survival as a family business

Note: The most frequent ideological choice over all cases is marked in bold italics, the second most frequent in italics.

Sharma *et al.* (1997) in their review of more than 200 articles published in thirty-two journals over the period 1980–94 found that only slightly more than a third of them included empirical data. In particular, qualitative research is much needed in family-business research (Dyer and Sánchez, 1998). For this reason, this study uses a multiple embedded case-study approach without any ambitions to undertake statistical generalisation. The research aims to explore the feasibility of the suggested framework.

The basic proposition, thus, is that the three proposed ideologies co-exist in medium-sized, successful family businesses. In order to test for variation in origin, firms with presumably different original ideologies were approached. In the founder-managed firms entrepreneurialism was assumed to be (still) prominent and in the second-generation family business, paternalism was expected to be strong. Managerialism was considered to be the originally dominant ideology in family businesses that had been created through management buy-out. In each of these three categories two firms were studied using a standardised questionnaire with semi-structured questions. Previous research and/or personal recommendations provided privileged access to the firms and the interviewees. Table 3.2 provides some basic information about the six family businesses, all within the manufacturing industry. The study was carried out in Spring 1998. Besides the two management buy-outs (E and F) the firms are well-established family businesses. Two of them (A and B) are still run by the founder while one business (C) was involved in an extended succession process at the time of the study. In one company (D) the second-generation owner-manager took over

Table 3.2 The family businesses – some basic facts (end of 1997)

Indicator/family business	A	B	C	D	E	F
Founding year	1949	1967	1947	1943	1991	1993
Family business status	Founder management	Founder management	First/second generation	Second generation	MBO	MBO
Products – industrial (I), consumer (C) markets	C	I	I	I	I	I
Size (number of employees)	104	219	362	201	162	65
Turnover (million ECU)	14.1	17.1	33.0	22.5	24.0	4.8
Growth 1994–7 (per cent)						
– employees	42.5	50.0	3.7	21.8	26.6	25.0
– turnover	49.4	60.2	18.5	46.0	68.5	59.9
Equity ratio (per cent)[a]	70.6	28.9	31.8	68.1	30.3	35.3
ROI (per cent)[b]	33.1	2.0	7.0	11.2	3.7	2.8

Notes:

[a] 'Equity ratio' is calculated as the quotient between equity and total assets.

[b] 'ROI' is calculated as quotient between result after financial items and total assets.

about three decades ago. All firms but A operate in business markets and all but E are located in small towns outside metropolitan areas.

In each company individuals assumed to embody each ideology were approached. Thus, the still active founder was invited as a presumed representative of entrepreneurialism and their spouse as representing paternalism. Professional managers, as well as outside board members, were tentatively classified as the medium for managerialism. In the second-generation family businesses and in the management buy-out firms, *a priori* identification of ideology exponents turned out to be especially difficult.

Altogether twenty-five people, four or five in each company (although in one of the two buy-out cases only two people), were interviewed face-to-face for between one and two hours. The interviews, most of them carried out jointly by two researchers, were audio-taped and completely transcribed for subsequent interpretation. The narrative accounts were analysed both within (i.e. embedded) and across cases (Yin, 1989). The study remains qualitative and explorative which means that no attempt was made to create indices reflecting ideological rating concerning firms or individuals. Along each ideology dimension interviewees were simply classified as associated with either ideology and individual business ideology profiles were made out of aggregated individual classifications. The summary qualitative ranking of the ideologies on each dimension according to Table 3.1 is based on the distributions of ideological choices over all firms (six) and respondents (twenty-five). Thus, the interpretation of the findings adopted an 'abductive' mode which here means that the findings were used for affirming and qualifying the tentative framework as a sense-making construct. Details concerning this design are reported in Johannisson and Forslund (1998). Elsewhere we presented two more empirical studies which adopted the framework presented here. These are discussed in the context of the recruitment of outside directors to the board (Johannisson and Huse, 2000) and spatial small-firm clusters (Johannisson, 2000).

Findings: an ideological kaleidoscope

Analysing our interview data we found that in four (out of six) cases our assumptions about 'core' ideologies were confirmed. This means that the two founder-managed firms were still dominated by entrepreneurialism and the two management buy-outs were framed by the management ideology. In the two second-generation family businesses presumed to be dominated by paternalism, entrepreneurialism as well as managerialism were, however, aggressive challengers. For at least three reasons this must not, however, be taken as a justification for expelling paternalism from the family-business arena as new generations enter. First, the presumed representatives of paternalism were under-represented in our study. Second, although under siege family involvement was still strong. Third, the two researchers were by training biased towards managerialism and entrepreneurialism respectively. Our vocabulary and theories, as well as the methodology adopted, may have been less able to trace family influence in (family) business operations. One entrepreneur's wife also reprimanded us: our interview guide in her mind both underestimated the degree of impact of family on business and left out important intrinsic family issues (partly because of our methodology).

Analysing the six cases we found that all the successful family businesses nurtured at least two ideologies along the majority of proposed ideology dimensions. Managerialism and entrepreneurialism represent the dominant ideological forces in the medium-sized family business. In six out of the eleven dimensions entrepreneurialism predominated most often. In the remaining five dimensions managerialism was represented. Along two dimensions paternalism was dominating management, along one dimension entrepreneurship. For the three ideologies and their dimensions presented in Table 3.1 the most frequent ideology along each dimension is marked in bold and second most frequent in italics.

The outcome of the empirical study, which was concerned with attributing dominant ideologies to interviewees according to achieved or ascribed position in the firm/family, provided some surprises. For example, in one case paternalism was not primarily represented by the founder, nor by his wife, but by the controller with no kinship ties whatsoever to the owner family. In yet another case the one external member of the board, in our design representing managerialism, was recruited not just because of his professional competencies as a manager. Due to his local roots, he shared the owning family's paternalistic concerns for the community in which the firm played an important role as an employer. This board member embodied a constructive tension between paternalism and managerialism. Another experience was that medium-sized family businesses can be looked upon as a habitat for shifting personal ideologies over individual careers. One of the companies had recently recruited a new production manager from a global corporation in the engineering industry. This professional manager explicitly stated that he was looking for a organisational setting where he could satisfy his emerging need for entrepreneurial action.

The somewhat ambiguous findings reflect a challenging and experiential research setting. Medium-sized family businesses were addressed because of their special status. On the one hand, they have left the scale of operation and time when the memory of the firm's pioneering times still was fresh. On the other, they have not yet reached the size where ownership and control might have become separated. There are several theoretical and methodological lessons to be made from the empirical study. First, an individual's dominant ideological domicile is not defined by origin and formal position alone. The person may be attracted to or influenced by the family business as a domicile of alternative ideologies. Second, individuals, for various personal or other reasons, may, with diverse urgency, shift ideological domicile. Third, an individual is not necessarily guided by one ideology alone. Due to the transparency of the medium-sized family business, individuals may have developed a capability to combine several ideologies without losing their own identity. For example, both keep the entrepreneurial spirit and demonstrate the managerial qualities that external legitimacy demands. Fourth, this probing research called for interviewing quite a large number of persons at the expense of more in-depth inquiries into individual life stories. Further research should use a more sensitive methodology and address more specific issues.

Conclusion

This study suggests that medium-sized, privately held enterprises can be depicted as strongholds for different ideologies. An 'abductive' approach was adopted to deal with the propositions. Previous research into successful (medium-sized) family business was used to organise semi-structured interviews in six successful firms where altogether twenty-five people, each for periods of between two and three hours, were interviewed and represented the three different ideologies.

'Paternalism' and 'managerialism' as ideologies penetrate all aspects of social life and are both well supported by formal and/or informal institutions. In contrast, entrepreneurship and 'entrepreneurialism', as an ideology, has only weak support from societal norms and rules. On the one hand, entrepreneurship as a basic human faculty is taken for granted and therefore hidden. On the other, it is epitomised by passionate heroes or unreliable villains. In the medium-sized family business, it is proposed that (1) all three ideologies have to be accommodated; (2) entrepreneurialism must be especially safe-guarded; and (3) the tensions between the ideologies as they appear within the firm can and should be constructively exploited to energise the organisation.

Successful medium-sized family businesses materialise continued entrepreneurship. The organisations all turned out to simultaneously accommodate each of the three ideologies. The ability to actively exploit tensions between different ideologies may be identified as the unique quality needed to energise entrepreneurial processes also under the pressure of institutionalisation (DiMaggio and Powell, 1983) and a fading original entrepreneurial spirit in the multi-generation family business. It should not be surprising that co-existing ideologies vitalise organisations. A living democracy is constituted by multiple and contrasting ideologies. It is rather the dominance of functionalistic and normative managerial approaches in previous family-business research that makes the proposed ideological approach stand out.

An ideological perspective may deepen academic understanding of family business in general, and the successful medium-sized firm in particular. Two additional research challenges include, first, an elaboration of the basic approach suggested here. All three ideologies must be practised by the individual firm in unique configurations. Also, additional qualitative longitudinal research is needed to elaborate our understanding of what constitutes such configurations. Second, each ideology provides learning strategies that are much needed in contemporary environments in constant flux. Entrepreneurialism encourages experiential learning (Schön, 1983), paternalism rationalises social learning (Bandura, 1986), and managerialism justifies explicit knowledge and formal education. It is also suggested that an understanding of organisational learning can be further expanded through confronting the different learning modes once they have all been mutually recognised as contributory factors to business development.

This perspective also has practical implications. As pointed out, a unique feature of the medium-sized family business is intergenerational succession. According to Kets de Vries (1996), succession in the family business rather accentuates problems: the firm is often seen as a refuge for succeeding generations. The ideological framework presented here suggests that such a crisis may as well become a turning point towards an ossifying structure with languishing entrepreneurship and unchallenged paternalism. The successor, if furnished with a formal education, may become the very injection that spurs an ideological dynamism take-off. A formal education at a business school may create a springboard for the offspring both inside the firm and in its business context. This does not necessarily mean physical co-existence in the business. In one of our cases, the son in the family, as a globally recognised scientist abroad, operates an academic laboratory in the same technical field as the family business. Father and son have a continuous exchange of formal and tacit knowledge that keeps the business at the technological cutting edge.

A second practical lesson from the study is that the board may be used as an institutionalised arena for mobilising and exploiting ideological tensions. The introduction of an outside member to the board may radically change the constellation of forces in the family business. Since the recruitment of an external board member usually favours managerialism, it is no surprise that traditional, defensive family businesses, dominated by paternalism, hesitate to invite outsiders in. Genuinely entrepreneurial firms may, in contrast, consider managerial competencies as just another resource to exploit when growth is aggressively promoted. In one case the third-generation family business had a nepotistic structure turned into a market-oriented professional organisation. In another case, the very dynamic entrepreneur engaged his former employer at a listed company to tame himself and control the high growth of the business (Johannisson and Huse, 2000). Orchestrating the board as a meeting place for several ideologies seems to be a major challenge for the leader in the family business.

Paternalism remains an ideology that makes indispensable contributions to society and to the making of a viable (family) business. This underlines the importance of an institutional framework (e.g. with respect to taxes and legislation) that makes the continuation of owner-management over generations possible. The case material provides examples of initiatives which reflect interrelationship between family, economic and community concerns. A daughter, giving up a career as a teacher in order to join her father's company, not only successfully took charge of a niche product but bridged her previous career by creating a small library within the personnel premises. In a family business created through a buy-out, the buyer's wife changed her sales representative duties to a position in sales and promotion, thereby presenting a role model for other women. Family concerns may also release entrepreneurial energy. In one company, the wife's need for computer services in her new accounting agency triggered the husband into starting his own software company. Its success, in turn, prompted the wife to leave her company to become first controller in his company and later take charge of renewal projects. Business and family life thus remain tightly intertwined also in the medium-sized family business where its size calls for more managerial attention.

From a policy perspective it is especially important to prevent the provision of often needed additional professional managerial competencies in family businesses at the expense of family concerns and/or continued entrepreneurship. Knowledge associated with each ideology must be made available, a responsibility of policy-makers indeed. Owner-managers and their descendants should be able to feel proud of their mode of conduct and priorities, and not given a bad conscience because of lacking managerial training. Consultants in both the public and private sectors must be made aware of the role of entrepreneurship and family concerns when advising owner-managers. Ultimately it is a challenge for the educational system, from the secondary school to the university, to present a more varied image of why most firms emerge and continue as family businesses and why attitudes and knowledge associated with each ideology are needed to keep them viable. As indicated, the institutional support for managerialism is elaborate, not the least in the educational system. However, a recent review of the field of entrepreneurship studies at Swedish universities indicates that institutionalised support for entrepreneurialism is gaining ground (Landström and Johannisson, 2001). This is good for (family) business.

Part II

A resource-based discourse in studies of the small family business

4 Work-to-family conflict

A comparison of American and Australian family and non-family business owners

Kosmas X. Smyrnios, Claudio A. Romano, George A. Tanewski, Paul Karofsky, Robert Millen and Mustafa R. Yilmaz

Introduction

For many people, work and family roles have become notable sources of conflict, as the demands associated with each domain affect each other (Kanter, 1977). Indeed, balancing work and family demands is a major challenge for many organisations (Ingram and Simons, 1995). Given that both work and family factors are potent contributors of stress as well as significant sources of emotional well-being, a number of models have been developed to explain the interface between work-to-family conflict and well-being (e.g. Frone *et al.*, 1997; Parasuraman *et al.*, 1996). These models depict linking mechanisms or causal connections between specific work and family constructs (Edwards and Rothbard, 2000). Although these models differ in many respects, it appears that none have focused on cross-national phenomena nor examined, quantitatively, owners of family-controlled businesses.

A unique feature of family business is its inherent multiple and interdependent roles, and examining a stress-based model of work conflict among owners across two nations in this context provides important insights into the interface between work and family. For example, members of family businesses are affected by an overlap of family, business, and ownership subsystems, with owners playing simultaneous roles among these three subsystems. These roles can be complementary, but they can also lead to confusion and create role conflict owing to differences in values between the family and business subsystems (Hollander and Bukowitz, 1990). Moreover, overlap between family and business can impede effective role performance and decision-making because of difficulties separating business decisions from family objectives.

In light of the unique features associated with family firms, the aim of the present study was to test a causal model of stress-based conflict and family cohesion to family role performance across American and Australian family and non-family business owners. In order to establish parameters for this study, we further elaborate on factors relating to family businesses, provide an operational definition of family firms, and then discuss linking mechanisms between work and family domains. The following section explains linking mechanisms used in different conceptualisations such as spillover and work–family conflict theories, particularly in relation to family enterprises. This section is followed by a discussion of variables comprising a stress-based model of work-to-family conflict tested in our study. The Methods section provides a description of participants and measures. Model evaluation and discussion of results follow. Specifically, findings demonstrate significant relationships between work-to-interpersonal conflict, business dissatisfaction, and family role performance. The present model highlights that different types of work-to-family conflict indirectly and differentially affect family role performance. This chapter ends with a brief discussion of the implications of our research findings, particularly the importance of specific mediating factors associated with different types of work-to-family conflict.

Stress-based work–family conflict model and family business

Over the previous two decades, researchers (e.g. Burke and Greenglass, 1987; Zedeck, 1992) have identified inter-relationships and linking mechanisms between work and family domains. Edwards and Rothbard (2000) defined linking mechanisms as directional, causal or non-causal relationships that span work and family constructs. Linking mechanisms also describe why and ways in which work and family domains are related. That is, the extent to which individuals intentionally create, modify, or eliminate work-to-family links. Linking mechanisms have been translated into different theoretical conceptualisations including *spillover* (see George and Brief, 1990), *compensation* (see Zedeck, 1992), *segmentation* (see Lambert, 1990), *congruence* (see Zedeck, 1992), *resource drain* (see Small and Riley, 1990) and *work–family conflict* (see Burke and Greenglass, 1987). These models have been used to articulate connections between work and non-work lives.

Owners of family businesses offer an exceptional vantage point from which to examine not only the impact of work-to-family conflict on family role performance, but also the mediating effects of one's perceptions of overall psychological well-being and family processes (Frone *et al.*, 1992). Owners of family businesses face challenges not only from operational business areas such as competitive markets, planning, financing, and marketing, but also from issues associated with ownership and family. Given these systems, it has been argued that family business owners require special characteristics and experiences to maintain an appropriate balance between business interests and those of the family (Neubauer and Lank, 1998).

Family firms offer possibilities for exploring unique patterns of work–family conflict dependencies not necessarily found in other work–family situations. Family enterprises often involve multiple and interdependent roles (Beehr *et al.*, 1997), and owners in these businesses can be susceptible to greater inter-role conflict than non-family business owners. Indeed, family businesses have been described as involving *high levels of role and inter-role conflict* (see Kahn *et al.*, 1964), which culminate in stress and adverse family role performance outcomes. A number of authors (e.g. Ward, 1987; Kanter, 1989) have reported on effects of family on work roles, and vice versa, in particular internal conflict associated with differences between family and business cultures (Hollander and Bukowitz, 1990; Rosenblatt, 1991). Role pressures can be particularly intense when work and family roles are central to an individual's self-esteem or self-concept (Greenhaus and Beutell, 1985). This can be particularly the case for family business owners who are also founders, managers, entrepreneurs, mentors, and parents.

In line with these distinguishing characteristics, a family business was defined as one in which owners regard their enterprises as a family firm and when any one of the following three criteria held true: 50 per cent or more of the ownership is held by a single family; a single family group is effectively controlling the business; and a significant proportion of the senior management is drawn from the same family (Stoy Hayward and the London Business School, 1990).

For the present investigation, a stress-based work-to-family conflict model was adapted from Edwards and Rothbard (2000) owing to the high likelihood of inter-role conflict being experienced by members of family businesses (Guzzo and Abbott, 1990). In line with this decision, Beehr *et al.* (1997) suggested that inter-role conflict often existed in these enterprises because of different role expectations associated with the family and business subsystems. Thus, the model adopted suggests a negative statistical relationship between work stress, anxiety, and family functioning. Furthermore, the effects of work stress on family role performance are viewed as being mediated by family functioning (Edwards and Rothbard, 2000). The remaining discussion presents an explanation of linking mechanisms between stress-based conflict, family cohesion, and family role performance, and elaborates on the present stress-based model tested.

A hypothesised stress-based model of work-to-family conflict

Edwards and Rothbard (2000) outlined a number of considerations that influence work-to-family linkages and assist in the development of more complete models of the work-to-family interface for further research. One such consideration involves the extent to which 'work–family linkages operate differently for different types of work and for different [cultures and] family structures. For instance, work–family segmentation is perhaps … more difficult for family-run businesses' (ibid.: 197).

Consistent with recommendations for a re-evaluation of models in different contexts, we undertook this investigation principally to determine whether American and Australian family and non-family firms differ in mechanisms linking work and family constructs as hypothesised by stress-based work-to-family conflict paradigms. Another reason for carrying out this study relates to the restricted research in the family business area and the importance of investigating whether work-to-family mechanisms operate differently for different types of work. A further reason concerns the hitherto focus on employees rather than business owners.

We chose to compare Australian family business owners with their American counterparts as both cultures are similar, yet distinct. On the one hand, both cultures have federal government systems, are multicultural, involve Anglo-Saxon heritages and possible sharing of common family values, and use English as their primary language. Indeed, Hofstede (1991) maintained that the source of a society's values may be the legal system in which it operates, and both the USA and Australia share similarities in this regard. Furthermore, both cultures share masculine traits and individualistic values that may be the result of emigration policies that have fostered a spirit of competitiveness and assertiveness (Hofstede, 1991). On the other hand, both cultures are distinct owing to the roles they play in the global economy. The USA has evolved into a global superpower, whereas Australia is an emerging developed country. The roles of these two cultures in the global economy have an effect on how business owners perceive themselves and their interaction with their immediate business environment. These interactions and perceptions, in turn, might further impact on work strain and stress levels experienced by owners.

Family role performance

At the core of this conceptualisation is our measure of family role performance, representing the extent to which business owners perceive that they are meeting family expectations and experience inter-role conflict between family and business. Inter-role conflict can be the direct result of family business owners giving preference to business needs and demands over those of the family. Inter-role conflict also occurs when work-related problems and responsibilities interfere with family-related obligations, and vice versa.

Work-to-family conflict research posits that attitudes and behaviours spill over from one role to another (e.g. Leiter and Durup, 1996). Indeed, work is a significant predictor of job and family distress (Frone *et al.*, 1992). In comparison, role-related dissatisfaction has been found to be associated with work-to-family conflict and family distress (Frone *et al.*, 1997). Moreover, research demonstrates a positive statistical association between family distress and work-to-family conflict (Frone *et al.*, 1994). Another paradigm of the work-to-family link suggests that work and family roles are incompatible owing to role overload and competing time constraints. Notwithstanding, Cooke and Rousseau (1984) stated that social support functions of a family can temper effects of inter-role conflict.

Family cohesion

We chose a measure of family cohesion to represent the conceptual domain of a family-related variable in order to extend the work of a number of investigators. For example, Adams *et al.* (1996) reported a negative relationship between family instrumental support and family-to-work conflict. Similarly, Frone *et al.* (1997)

found a significant, negative, direct relationship between family and spouse supports and family distress, and a significant indirect effect on family-to-work conflict by reducing family distress and parental overload. Thomas and Ganster (1995) noted a negative relation of supervisor support to work-to-family conflict.

Collectively, direct and indirect evidence suggests that sound family and social supports can contribute significantly to ameliorating work-to-family conflict. That is, family members have the capacity to reduce role pressures and mediate or buffer relationships between work-to-family conflict and psychological well-being (Greenhaus and Beutell, 1985). Consistent with these views, systems theory posits a dynamic, systemic, and circular feedback loops connecting work and family domains. Furthermore, the recent findings of Frone *et al.* (1997) demonstrate an indirect reciprocal relationship between work-to-family and family-to-work conflict (p.162). Thus, the proposed directions in Figure 4.1 seem reasonable given that family cohesion involves skills and characteristics demonstrated to be effective in dealing with individual and family conflict.

Anxiety

Evidence relating indirectly to this study shows that interpersonal conflict at work can culminate in anxiety, frustration, physical symptoms, and dissatisfaction (Spector, 1987). For example, Barnett and Baruch (1985) indicated that poor fitting work–family roles contribute to stress. Similarly, Bacharach *et al.* (1990) reported that excessive workloads and ambiguous or conflicting role demands produced emotional distress. Workload and role conflict are also positively associated with hypertension, angina, and ulcers (House *et al.*, 1979). Other research in this area demonstrates that role ambiguity is positively related to high blood pressure (van Dijkhuizen and Reiche, 1980). Job pressure is positively associated with higher risks of dying (House *et al.*, 1986), and interpersonal conflict at work is positively associated with angina (Medalie and Goldbourt, 1976). Furthermore, reported levels of work complexity, challenge, and autonomy have been found to be associated with emotional well-being (Loscocco and Spitze, 1990).

Work stress

A further key feature of our model is the construct of work stress, as measured by business dissatisfaction, work-to-household conflict, and work-to-interpersonal conflict. Although recent investigations have focused on the bidirectional nature of work–family conflict (e.g. Adams *et al.*, 1996; Greenhaus and Beutell, 1985 and Parasuraman *et al.*, 1996), this model focuses on only the magnitude and direction of associations between work stress and owners' ratings of their anxiety, family cohesion, and family role performance. In keeping with research in the area, we acknowledge the importance of the bidirectional nature of work-to-family conflict and that each type of conflict is associated with unique family- and work-related antecedents and outcomes (Frone *et al.*, 1997: 148).

Consistent with Frone *et al.* (1997), our conceptualisation also makes a distinction between proximal (i.e. direct) and distal (i.e. indirect) predictors. Proximal predictors (i.e. family cohesion) mediate the impact of distal predictors (i.e. business dissatisfaction, work-to-household conflict, work-to-interpersonal conflict). As an example of our current model, work-to-interpersonal conflict is regarded as an indirect predictor of family role performance and is mediated by the extent of family cohesion.

The following sections of this chapter describe our methodology, report our findings, and discuss our findings in the light of previous research in the area. The implications of our findings are also presented.

Method

Participants

In Australia, a stratified random sample of 2,000 family firms was employed. This sample was obtained from the AXA Australia Family Business Research Unit and Family Business Australia databases and 2,000 businesses (obtained from Dun and Bradstreet, 1999) based on state, turnover, and industry. The response rate for Australian firm owners was approximately 33 per cent ($N =$ 1,320), which compares favourably with national (Smyrnios *et al.*, 1997) and international (Dunn, 1995b; Nager *et al.*, 1995) surveys.

For the USA, a sample of 850 family firms from the New England region was used. Approximately 300 firm owners in this group are members of the Center for Family Business at Northeastern University. The remainder of the sample was selected randomly from directories of businesses in New England. The overall response rate for this cohort was approximately 18 per cent ($N =$ 156). Table 4.1 provides a profile of business and owner background characteristics.

Measures

All measures formed part of the Australian Family Business Lifestyle Audit (AFBLA) questionnaire (Smyrnios and Romano, 1999) which was developed by a team of experts including academic researchers, and family business owners and practitioners. Development of the AFBLA proceeded through focus group discussions and pilot testing on 100 family business owners. The 150-item AFBLA comprises seven sections: business impact, family, health, leisure/recreation, personal and work harmony, business background, and respondent characteristics. Where appropriate, all items were measured on 7-point Likert scales (see Table 4.2 for reliability coefficients)

Table 4.1 Family business background characteristics

	Aus (%)	US A (%)
Family business		
yes	63.0	62.8
no	37.0	37.2
Ownership		
>50% ownership one family	63.7	70.1
>50% ownership two or more families	15.9	15.9
family has control or provides management	14.0	6.5
family business publicly owned	0.5	3.7
none of the above	5.9	3.7
Generation managing business		
1st generation	65.7	48.2
2nd generation	24.8	26.3
3rd generation	6.6	18.4
4th generation	2.9	7.0
Primary original objective of business		
accumulate wealth	32.2	20.6
employ family members	1.9	1.4
provide family with careers	3.1	2.1
pass on to next generation	3.1	2.8
increase value of business	18.1	25.5
sell at opportune time	3.8	0.8
improve lifestyle	25.0	31.9
other	12.9	14.9
Primary objective still current		
yes	85.4	80.3
no	14.6	19.7
Industry		
retail and wholesale trade	27.6	21.1
manufacturing	26.6	22.4
technology	10.4	7.5
primary	2.1	2.0
recreational	1.8	7.5
personal and other services	2.4	4.1
transport and storage	2.8	0.7
construction	11.0	2.7
other	9.8	8.8
Scope of operation		
local	18.2	29.7
regional	28.4	28.4
national	35.4	25.0
international	18.1	16.9
Marital status		
single	8.7	12.8
married/relationship	91.3	87.2

Table 4.2   Correlations[a] between measures, reliabilities, means and standard deviations

	1	2	3	4	5	6	α	Mean	SD
1. Family role performance	1.000						0.79	4.32	1.26
2. Family cohesion	−0.369	1.000					0.89	5.23	1.16
3. Anxiety	0.216	−0.188	1.000				0.79	3.68	1.37
4. Business dissatisfaction	0.308	−0.334	0.295	1.000			0.83	2.73	1.05
5. Work-to-household conflict	0.362	−0.185	0.373	0.182	1.000		0.78	4.00	1.45
6. Work-to-inter-personal conflict	0.362	−0.409	0.272	0.297	0.329	1.000	0.81	4.07	1.18

Note: [a] All correlations significant at $p < 0.0001$ level.

Endogenous variables

Our model specifies three endogenous variables. *Family role performance* was adapted from Beehr *et al.*'s (1997) inter-role work–family conflict measure. Four items (e.g. My family expects me to do things at work that conflict with my own judgement) gauge the extent to which a business owner views meeting family expectations and experiences inter-role conflict between family and business. Our measure of *anxiety* was adapted from the Health and Lifestyle Inventory of the Australian Living Standards Study (ALSS: Australian Institute of Family Studies, 1997). Three items, *tense*, *restless*, and *angry*, measure anxiety. *Family cohesion*, adapted from the Strong Families Inventory (Stinnett and DeFrain, 1985), comprises five items (e.g. have effective communication) which gauge levels of family cohesion.

Work–family conflict

Three constructs measure work–family conflict. *Business dissatisfaction*, which forms part of the ALSS, comprises four items (e.g. relationship with employees) assessing extent to which owners are satisfied with various aspects of their business. *Work-to-household conflict* has two items, 'meeting responsibilities you have for members of your family' and 'keeping up with household chores', which assess effects of work on household obligations. *Work-to-interpersonal conflict* has four items (e.g. What effect does working in your business have on your relationship with your spouse/partner?) which assess effects of work on interpersonal relationships (Frone *et al.*, 1992).

Results

Model evaluation

Table 4.2 presents bivariate correlations between measures, reliabilities coefficients, means, and standard deviations. The hypothesised structural equation model was examined using covariance matrices and LISREL's (7) maximum likelihood procedures. Covariances, using listwise deletion of missing data, were computed. The full structural equation model encompasses both measurement and structural relationships. The measurement component of the model shows that family role performance is assessed by four indicators, family cohesion by five items, anxiety by three, business dissatisfaction by four, work-to-interpersonal conflict by three, and work-to-household conflict by two indicators.

Structural components of our model (see Figure 4.1) suggest that family role performance is significantly and negatively related to family cohesion, which in turn is negatively but non-significantly associated with owners' reported levels of anxiety. Work-to-interpersonal conflict, work-to-household conflict, and business dissatisfaction are associated significantly and negatively with family cohesion, but positively and significantly with anxiety. Relationships between our three exogenous variables and family role performance are mediated significantly by family cohesion, but not by anxiety.

Three criteria (i.e. absolute, incremental, and parsimonious fit measures) assess the acceptability of the hypothesised model (see Figure 4.1). The independence model that tests the hypothesis that variables are uncorrelated with one another is rejected, χ^2 (231, $N = 1,205$) = 10,616.51, $p < .000$. A chi-square difference test indicates a significant improvement in fit between independence and hypothesised models, with the hypothesised model yielding the following results: χ^2 (178, $N = 1,205$) = 970.16, $p < .000$, GFI = .926, AGFI = .904, χ^2/df = 5.45. These findings indicate acceptable fit to observed data and provide sound support for hypothesised model relationships. Figure 4.1 shows results for the hypothesised structural equations model.

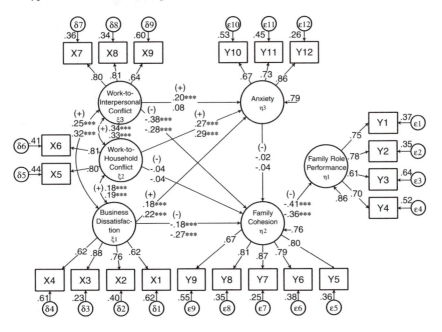

Figure 4.1. Results of hypothesised work–family conflict model

Table 4. 3   Summary of goodness of fit information for between-group comparisons

Group	χ^2	df	p	NFI	CFI
Family versus non-family business					
Unconstrained between-group model	1168.09	365	0.000	0.901	0.921
Constrained between-group model	1204.47	401	0.000	0.899	0.916
χ^2 difference (constrained–unconstrained)	36.38	36	0.114		
USA versus Australia					
Unconstrained between-group model	1294.57	365	0.000	0.890	0.911
Constrained between-group model	1501.16	401	0.000	0.870	0.885
χ^2 difference (constrained–unconstrained)	206.59	36	0.000		

As a primary aim of this study was to examine whether findings are invariant across family and non-family businesses, and between Australian and US data, two between-group models were specified using LISREL's multi-sample feature (see Table 4.3). Multi-sampling analyses are used to address issues relating to levels and to assess whether structural relations estimates differed significantly across groups (see Klein *et al.*, 1994). As such, we imposed equality constraints on both factor loadings and structural paths across Australia versus the USA, and family versus non-family firms.

Comparisons involving family versus non-family firms

Direct effects

SEM indices reveal that the model fits well for family versus non-family enterprises. A non-significant chi-square value ($\Delta\chi^2_{(17)} = 36.38$, $p > .05$) pertaining to family versus non-family businesses indicates statistical equivalence when conducting a global test of the equality of covariance structures (i.e. measurement and structural model) across both business groups. However, tests focusing on structural regression paths failed to observe equality of variances across family and non-family enterprises ($\Delta\chi^2_{(17)} = 182.19$, $p < .000$), indicating that work–family conflict dynamics differ for different business structures. In particular (see Figure 4.1), results indicate that owners of non-family enterprises are more likely to associate work-to-interpersonal conflict with anxiety than family business owners, suggesting that work-to-interpersonal conflict is a stronger stressor for owners of non-family businesses. In contrast, family business owners report that business dissatisfaction is a stronger contributor of family disharmony than their counterparts. These comparisons provide evidence of differing dynamics across family and non-family enterprises.

The direct significant inverse relationship between (a) work-to-interpersonal conflict and family cohesion and (b) business dissatisfaction and family cohesion are also enhanced by significant covariations among business dissatisfaction, work-to-interpersonal conflict, and work-to-household conflict. However, there is a non-significant association between work-to-household conflict and family cohesion for both family and non-family businesses. The significant direct effect that work-to-household conflict and business dissatisfaction has on owners' reported levels of anxiety highlights the importance of inter-role conflict and satisfaction to overall perceptions of anxiety.

Associations between work-to-interpersonal conflict and family cohesion and between business dissatisfaction and family cohesion provide support for the hypothesised directions in our work–family conflict model and suggest that high levels of work-to-interpersonal conflict and business dissatisfaction have an adverse effect on family cohesion. However, the magnitude of the association between work-to-interpersonal conflict and family cohesion is stronger for non-family than for family businesses, suggesting sound family supports have a buffering effect particularly for family business owners. Indeed, this finding for non-family businesses provides support to Beehr *et al.*'s (1997) finding that inter-role conflict is not necessarily more heightened in family businesses. In contrast, because of issues relating to centrality of work to one's life and an all-encompassing business domain, family business owners seem to be less able to deal with business dissatisfaction than their counterparts.

Figure 4.1 also shows that family cohesion has a direct negative impact on family role performance, providing support for the hypothesised direction that higher levels of family harmony are related to lower levels of inter-role conflict. Surprisingly, the magnitude of the association between family role performance and family cohesion is stronger for non-family businesses than for family businesses, suggesting that there are potential benefits working in a family business environment. However, anxiety's direct negative but non-significant impact on family cohesion suggests that personal stress levels do not have an adverse effect on family cohesion.

Indirect effects

Findings of the present study also reveal significant indirect effects between work-to-interpersonal conflict and family role performance, and between work dissatisfaction and family role performance. Work-to-interpersonal conflict has an indirect and positive structural effect on family role performance through family cohesion (standardised coefficient for family businesses $= .13$, $p < .01$ versus .16, $p < .000$ for non-family businesses). This finding suggests that family cohesion is a significant mediator between the effects of work-to-interpersonal conflict and family role performance. In contrast, business dissatisfaction has an indirect and positive structural effect on family role performance via family cohesion (standardised coefficient for family businesses $= .13$, $p < .000$ versus -.08, $p > .05$ for non-family businesses), indicating that a supportive family unit within a family business can culminate in lower levels of inter-role conflict. These findings support Greenhaus and Beutell's (1985) assertion that work and family role demands are mutually incompatible. Their work–family conflict argument maintains that meeting demands at work will make it difficult to meet family demands and vice versa, which in turn lead to greater stress-based conflict.

Comparisons of Australian versus US businesses

A poor fit was observed for the Australian and US groups. Regarding findings for Australian and US group comparisons, a chi-square value of $(\Delta\chi^2_{(17)} = 206.59, p < .000)$ exceeds the critical value associated with degrees of freedom, providing evidence for rejection of the null hypothesis of statistical equivalence between covariance matrices and model parameters. Despite differences between groups on magnitude of parameters, all direct and indirect effects are in the predicted direction. These findings suggest cultural equivalence between Australian and US business owners as items have similar patterns of correlations across cultural groups (Adler, 1983).

Discussion

In their discussion of directions for future research, Edwards and Rothbard (2000) recommended that investigators test existing models under different conditions, particularly differences in work and family arrangements. The present study adopted these recommendations providing a useful framework within which to develop and test a model of stress-based work-to-family conflict, incorporating anxiety, family cohesion, and family role performance in a selection of US and Australian family and non-family businesses.

The current findings demonstrate significant indirect relationships between work-to-interpersonal conflict, business dissatisfaction, and family role performance, providing support for the proposition that family cohesion acts as a buffer between inter-role conflict and family role performance. In other words, without the buffering effects of family cohesion, both work-to-interpersonal conflict and business dissatisfaction are associated with higher levels of family role conflict. However, the association between business dissatisfaction and family role performance is significant only for family business owners. On one level, this finding is not surprising given that our family role performance dimension taps role conflict between owners and family members (e.g. the extent to which family expect owners to do things at work that conflict with their own judgement or good work practices). On another level, this outcome demonstrates the important function family plays in ameliorating family role performance conflict and business dissatisfaction for family business owners.

This study goes beyond prior research by demonstrating that different types of work-to-family conflict indirectly and differentially affect family role performance. It appears that proximal and direct non-significant relationships reported in the literature (e.g. Frone *et al.*, 1997) can be attributed to the influence of a mediating variable such as family cohesion. Family role performance can be enhanced through family-related supports and, thus, reduce work-to-interpersonal conflict and business dissatisfaction.

This investigation clarifies mediating pathways linking work-to-family conflict, demonstrating a number of specific findings concerning the interface between work-to-family conflict and family role performance. First, as proposed, there is a positive reciprocal relationship between work-to-household and work-to-interpersonal conflict. This finding is to be expected given that owners who indicate that work has a negative effect on interpersonal relationships are more likely to report that working in the business interferes with household responsibilities. This finding also provides indirect support to Greenhaus and Beutell's (1985) assertion that work and family role demands are mutually incompatible. Their work–family conflict argument maintains that meeting demands at work will make it difficult to meet family demands and vice versa, which in turn lead to greater stress-based conflict. Second, work-to-household conflict is associated positively with owners' perceptions of anxiety, but negatively with family cohesion. These findings clarify relationships between different types of work-to-family conflict and mediating variables. That is, different types of work-to-family conflict might be associated with unique mediating conditions, and hence this investigation extends research in the area.

We acknowledge two main limitations. First, we use cross-sectional samples which limit the degree to which we can make causal references regarding hypothesised relationships. Our American sample is relatively small ($N = 156$) and may not be representative, thus placing constraints on generalisability. Second, our reliance on self-reports might suggest that the magnitude of relationships between variables is open to question owing to method bias or personality dispositions (see Brief *et al.*, 1988).

Future research

Future research could test, successively, parts of existing models by incorporating different types of family- and individual-based measures. According to Frone *et al.*, employing a broad range of family-related measures could lead to an in-depth view of the role of families in work–family conflict models (1992: 76).

Our finding of the importance of unique mediating processes underlying associations between variables suggests that these types of relationships should be examined in future research. For example, the proposed negative association of work-to-interpersonal conflict to family cohesion is based on the view that families who demonstrate sound communication and problem-solving capabilities will be able to resolve conflicts which might contribute to, or precipitate, feelings of anxiety or psychological distress. Thus, further examination of the influence of mediating processes underlying relationships warrants further investigation.

One implication of these findings for practitioners (e.g. business consultants, family therapists) is the importance of assisting family business families to deal effectively, and at an early stage, with conflicts involving the business. Disagreements that remain unaddressed may ultimately affect business performance and family relationships. From a systemic perspective, the interaction of family and business problems compounds the effect of conflict and calls for dispute resolution methods that target different sources of conflict (Harvey and Evans, 1994). Interventions include assisting family members to develop idiosyncratic markers for handling spillover of work–family issues.

Conclusion

The present study evaluated relationships between work-to-family conflict and family role performance as mediated by family and personal variables, across two cultures and two seemingly distinct firm types. Findings underscore the importance of specific mediating factors being associated with types of work-to-family conflict. Moreover, work-to-family conflict should no longer be regarded as broad-based. Distinct forms of work–family conflict should be identified and evaluated for their impact on overall measures of role performance.

Acknowledgements

The research assistance of Ms. Georgia Pashias is gratefully acknowledged. This research was partially funded by Family Business Australia and we gratefully acknowledge their support.

5 Understanding the emotional dynamics of family enterprises[1]

Barbara Murray

The enigma of family enterprises

As with all enigmatic phenomena, it seems that the more we seek to understand and learn about the family business, the more questions are uncovered. Family businesses are enigmatic because they embody the union of individual, family and organisational psychology along with organisational behaviour and economics. This leads to an uneasy marriage of emotionality and rationality acted out in businesses and in family homes throughout the world, and to issues that are connected to power, money and love. In family businesses that have clear sense of family mission and strategic direction, the emotionality–rationality dilemma is managed through the ability of the family to communicate its goals, and through a governance structure designed to manage the inevitable conflicts of self-interest that will emerge from time to time. But when self-interests clash, or when there is no shared dream for the business, then the family business can become 'stuck' or face strategic drift. In the family, individuals begin to sense that unless something changes, it may not be feasible for the family business to be the place where career goals and other life aspirations can be achieved. Most often, what appears to members of the business-owning family as a satisfactory solution to a given business problem may seem to others like a messy, sub-optimal outcome that could lead to undesired consequences for others in the system. This can happen, for example, when the owning family selects a family successor to lead the business in the next generation in order to solve problems regarding continuity of family control. Life in the family business is a life of compromises and negotiations for all concerned. It can often lead to a life of subordination of one's self-interest for the greater good of the family enterprise.

Families managing succession tasks

This chapter therefore aims to explore the influence of 'the family factor' in family enterprises by examining the importance of emotional dynamics in family business systems. The two case studies presented feature small family businesses going through structurally identical generational transitions from second to third generation. The cases are analysed to explore how each company managed the same tasks during the same five-year timeframe. The family in Case A have no problem dealing with the transfer of *managerial power and leadership* to the chosen successor in the next generation, but have a lot of difficulty dealing with the problem of deciding how to transfer *ownership control and wealth* to the offspring. Conversely, in Case B, arriving at the decision about *ownership control and wealth* transfer to the next generation is relatively easy, but the family get stuck when dealing with the transfer of *managerial power and leadership* to the chosen successor. The reasons for these differences are explored in the final part of the chapter. First, however, the following section outlines the literature that examines notions of rationality and emotionality in the family business during processes of inter-generational transition.

The influence of anxiety and its management during succession transitions

Following a brief description of the two case studies, some key questions will be posed regarding the centrality of family emotional factors, specifically the generation and management of anxiety in the decision-making processes used when formulating and arriving at such critical decisions in the business. A discussion will follow on the way in which anxiety affects these systems during transition times. The cases illustrate the circumstances under which anxiety, generated by the key individuals involved, accelerated the decision-making process about future ownership and leadership of the business. They also illustrate the circumstances in which anxiety appeared to slow down or stall the decision-making process, and in so doing, either held back progress within the succession process overall or led to the breakdown of the family business system.

The management of anxiety, therefore, is presented here as the central challenge facing the key individuals involved in the generational transition process. This is based on the evidence presented in the cases that anxiety functions as a mediating factor for either action or inaction within the system, depending on how it is managed by individuals within each of the family enterprise sub-systems and by the whole family enterprise system itself.

Family business systems: an uneasy marriage of the emotional with the rational

The developmental approach

The uneasy marriage of the emotional with the rational is often visible in the decisions and decision-making processes taking place within family enterprises. It has also been a key feature in the family business literature. Levinson's (1971) paper put forward the 'rational' view that family and business would be better kept apart. While Tagiuri and Davis (1982), Davis (1982), Hollander (1983), Lansberg (1988, 1999), Lansberg and Astrachan (1994), J.L. Ward (1987) and Herz Brown (1991) argued that family and business are inextricably woven together often by a legacy of ownership spanning one or many generations.

These authors highlighted that the owning family's fortunes depend on the extent to which they can perpetuate the ownership, control and long-term profitability of their enterprise while remaining emotionally connected and functional as a family. From these ideas came the conceptualisation of the 'family business system' as a complex, open system comprising three overlapping sub-systems: the family sub-system, the business sub-system and the ownership sub-system. Tagiuri and Davis's (1982) three-circles model has been universally accepted as the guiding theoretical framework for conceptualising family business systems.

In the years since the field of family business enquiry began, much of the published literature has explored in depth the conflicts and compromises that are engendered by the institutional overlaps of family, ownership and business (Davis and Stern, 1980; Lansberg, 1988). When there are different views among individuals within the system itself on how to manage the process of generational transition, the succession process can become slowed down, or immobilised. During generational transitions, people in the *family sub-system* have to deal with the anxieties they feel about the decline and mortality of the generation in power taking place alongside the rise to power of the junior generation (through the transfer of ownership and/or leadership). At the same time, the people in the *business sub-system* are anticipating and managing the consequences of changes that will unfold in the power, authority and control systems in the business when the succession is finally settled. Arriving at a decision in any one part of the system is usually contingent upon decisions having been made (and sufficient reliable data being available to enable these) in other part(s) of the system. The crux of the matter, and the factor that makes family businesses so enigmatic, is that most often it is the same people managing all these tasks and challenges.

The importance of respect throughout the life cycle

Handler (1989) identified mutual intergenerational respect and the management of family and business boundary issues as the key relational factors affecting the succession experience. When the overlaps of family and business issues were teased out, Handler identified 'separation strains' or pockets of resistance to the changes taking place in the relationships of the key players in the succession process, with strains principally emerging around changes being made in power relationships and changes in leadership styles. Mutual respect was also a key theme in Davis's (1982) doctoral study of eighty-nine father–son dyads reporting in a survey on the influence of life-cycle stage on the quality of work relationships. The respective stages of individual development (or 'life-stages') of fathers and sons was found to affect the quality of their work relationships. Harmonious, respectful relationships were found between the fathers' ages of 50–59 and their sons' corresponding ages of 28–32. However, relationships were relatively problematic when fathers' ages were 60–69 and sons' ages 34–40. The fathers in the study for this chapter were 59–64 and the sons were 28–33 during the five-year research period, and were therefore in and around this predicted problematic phase.

The influence of stages in adult development

These ages correspond to the developmental stages in men's lives described by Levinson (1978) and in women's lives in Levinson (1996), upon which Davis's (1982) study is largely based. Each stage has key developmental tasks to be attended to concerning the development of a 'life structure' comprising acceptable relationship, career and personal aspirations. Once a life structure is in place that the person feels is good enough or that they will settle for, a settling down period can ensue in which the structures obtained can be strengthened or capitalised upon. Having a less than satisfactory life structure impedes progress with the next series of developmental tasks to be faced, often causing tumultuous transition periods, or emotional crises especially around the age 30 transition (28–32), the mid-life transition (38–45) and the late adult transition (58–65).

Creating a 'life structure', however tentative, is the key task for young people entering early adulthood around the age of 18–22. This structure involves their first attempt at career and relationship building based on an identity that is forming separate from the family of origin. It also has a key component known as 'the Dream', signified with the capital 'D' to denote an exciting vision or imagined possibility of life aspirations during adulthood (Levinson, 1978: 91). The developmental task for a young adult is to find a clearer definition of this Dream, and a way to live it, before the time and opportunities to do so run out. For potential successors in family businesses, the opportunity to achieve at least some of their Dream in the family enterprise may seem more accessible, feasible and alluring. At the same time, it is possible that life in the family business may hold back the launching of children from parental authority (Kaye, 1996). Similarly, it may set back the young adulthood developmental task of forging an identity separate from the family of origin. For these reasons, spending time away from the family business and leaving the family home prior to joining the firm are strongly advocated (Lansberg, 1999).

Further along the life cycle, men entering late adulthood have the developmental task of re-visiting the Dream that emerged in their own period of young adulthood, and deciding what to do about any unfinished business in their life structure. Men who feel a sense of achievement about some of their Dream find it easier to integrate their feelings about the worth of their lives, while those who feel a sense of dissatisfaction about their lives can feel despair as they move forward into late adulthood (Erikson, 1950). Davis (1982) concluded that some consideration is necessary about when it may be expedient for father–son dyads to work on succession tasks together, and when it may be better to use other methods for developmental activity, such as mentoring or external experience.

The case studies: research method and design

Both of the case study firms selected for this study participated in the first comprehensive exploration of family enterprises in Scotland and Northern Ireland (Dunn, 1995a, 1995b). This involved a large-scale survey, interviews and focus groups, and reported on a general lack of readiness on the part of business-owning families and their advisers for generational transitions that were either under way, imminent or forthcoming. The case study family businesses were selected from this initial research data set (see Table 5.1) on the basis that they were at the same stage in the generational transition process, and were structurally identical in terms of the evolutionary development of the family business, and in terms of the life-stages of the key players in the system. A grounded theory (Strauss and Corbin, 1998) and case study method (Yin, 1984) was employed over a five-year period of fieldwork to examine the emotional context in the family enterprise system in which this activity was taking place. Each family business system was observed by twenty-three in-depth interviews with key stakeholders, dyads and families between 1994 and 1998. Interviews were transcribed and read many times reiteratively before being annotated extensively and the emerging themes noted. Secondary data in the form of company accounts, consultants' reports, media coverage and marketing materials were also collected. Primary and secondary data were collated to create a narrative account of the progress made by each case study family (Yin). Figures 5.1 to 5.4 outline more detailed descriptive details of the families and their companies. However, a brief summary is now provided.

Case A

- 100 per cent family-owned with a significant proportion of family in senior management.
- Second generation currently in control and transferring to third generation.
- Non-family in senior management but no non-family or advisers on the board.
- No documented succession plan; expects succession to be completed within five years.
- Last three years' average annual sales growth 10–25 per cent p.a.
- Sales £2m+ per annum; twenty employees.
- Would put 'business first' in event of conflict.
- Wholesale business selling parts to transportation industry.

Case B

- 86 per cent family-owned with significant proportion of family in senior management.
- Non-family in senior management and three non-family people on the board.
- No documented succession plan; expects succession to be completed within five years.
- Last three years' average annual sales growth 10–25 per cent.
- Sales £1–5m per annum; sixty employees.
- Would put 'business first' in event of conflict.
- Service industry operating in Scotland and England.

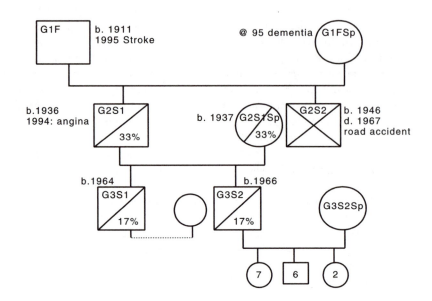

Figure 5.1   Case A: family genogram in 1994

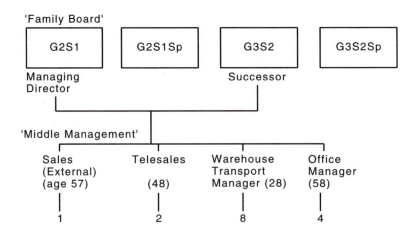

Figure 5.2   Case A: company structure in 1994

Notes: Key players in Figures 5.1 and 5.2.

G1F   The founder; first generation (G1).
G1Fsp   Founder's spouse.
G2S1   First son and eldest offspring of founder. Second generation (G2) successor.
G2S2   Second son and youngest offspring of founder. Killed in accident in 1967.
G2S1Sp   Spouse of G2 successor. Daughter of firm's accountant in G1, sister to firm's current (G2)
           accountant.
G3S1   Eldest sibling (son) of G2 successor. Works outside the business.
G3S2   Youngest sibling (son) of G2 successor. G3 successor.
G3S2Sp   G3 successor's spouse.

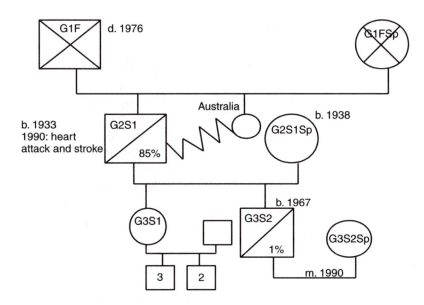

Figure 5.3   Case B: family genogram in 1994

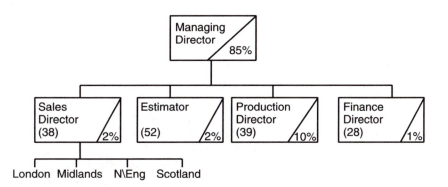

Figure 5.4   Case B: organisation chart in 1994

Notes: Key players in Figures 5.3 and 5.4.

G2S2   Present Managing Director, 85 per cent shareholder.
G2S2Sp   Present MD's spouse.
G3S1   Eldest sibling, female, not active in business.
G3S2   Youngest sibling, male, to be successor to MD – currently Finance Director, 1 per cent
        shareholder.
NF1   Non-family Director, 10 per cent shareholder.
NF2 &   Non-family directors, minority shareholders (2 per cent each).
  NF3

The fieldwork material and analysis is presented in two levels.

First level analysis: overall progress with succession tasks

The first level is concerned with the progress made by each family with its succession and ownership/leadership transfer. The absolute progress made by the families at the end of the research period differed in degree and quality. Case B failed to make any progress in the transfer of leadership, and the son left the family business. Case A completed the leadership and the transition of business leadership roles exactly as planned and in classic textbook style, but made no progress. In fact, it became entrenched with the ownership transition task.

Second level of analysis: family emotional factors impacting on business decisions

The second level of analysis explored the nature and characteristics of the activities carried out by the families that led to different outcomes for families undertaking the same tasks. For this, narratives and transcripts were analysed for key themes and insights into the relationship dimension affecting progress with required tasks in each case study family. It became clear that each family had its own story to tell containing complex family and business overlaps that were steeped in the families' histories and narratives.

Although the cases were structurally identical in terms of the individual, family, business and life-cycle stages and the stated aim of completing the succession in five years, it was not surprising that each family had a different culture, value system and regime. For example in Case A, religion was a very important feature of family life and behaviour. G2 in this case said religion meant to them a sense of spirituality about what they were trying to achieve in the business and a Christian outlook in their human relations. As a family, he said they were very grateful, and sometimes felt guilty that they had many resources and a good quality of lifestyle. The business had a healthy cash flow and had funds available for expansion. In Case B, G2 said that he was prudent and frugal, and did not believe in milking the profits from the family business. His son, however, said that G2 was spending excessively and was at a loss regarding what his father was doing with all the money. In the business, G2 prohibited borrowing or gaining access to external funding, and so future growth and expansion was constrained.

Patterns in emotional functioning within business families

The analysis also uncovered consistent patterns of emotional functioning in the families although the outcomes created by their functioning were very different. Tables 5.1 and 5.2 identify the key relationship events and themes and their emotional functioning responses emerging in the histories of Cases A and B respectively. It shows clearly that the tasks to be attended to in the family and in the business, life-cycle pressures and unexpected events all serve to mobilise emotional patterns of functioning in the owning family's key family–business relationships. The *outcome* of the task activity is different because each family has its own values and culture, but the *patterns of emotional functioning* that mobilise activity on the task in the first place are consistent. Multigenerational relationship dynamics, embedded in the emotional functioning of the families (Kerr and Bowen, 1988), were also uncovered. These were observable as patterns of emotional reactivity being repeated in the senior and junior generation as the system either got ready for ownership and leadership transfer decisions or resisted them. The patterns were often conducted just as the previous generation had done in its day.

Table 5.1   Family relationship themes and emotional functioning: Case A

Relationship themes	Emotional functioning in the family
1. Health / death in the family:	* Emotional shock-waves ripple out from this event: * – parents' and brothers' bereavement: founder's Dream is shattered.
Sudden death of (G1) founder's eldest son age 22, in 1967	* successor becomes an only child at age 11 (conflict avoidance pattern emerges). * founder loses key worker / successor? * mother joins the business: – as 'therapy' for herself; – as support for founder dealing with the gap left by his son; – and for support during difficult early trading years.
G2 angina attack in 1994	* Spouse panics and calls on their elder son for assurance about her long-term care and support if he dies. – elder son leaves home. – G2 sets about transfer of executive power/ major customers to successor: transfers title within 2 years when father age 60 and successor age 32. – two years later, spouse says G2 unreasonably fearful of relapse/paranoid. – successor occupies role in central triangle of parents–successor–business: i.e. so everyone gets taken care of by successor who then repeats family pattern and recruits his wife as bookkeeper/emotional caretaker.
2. Retirement: When to go; how spouses try to deal with time together, being useful/active. G2 retreats to business after holidays. No discussion about long-term healthcare despite founders now requiring full nursing care in home, financed by the family.	* Spouses find it hard to talk about mortality. Anxiety about this leads to avoidance/denial.

Continued

Table 5.1 Continued

Relationship themes	Emotional functioning in the family
3. *Conflict* between founder and G2 ('61–96): Conflicts blow up and soon blow over for founder; recipients left to deal with emotional backlash.	* G2's spouse recruited into business as bookkeeper; functions as emotional caretaker/buffer in triangle between G2, his wife and the founder.
4. *Successor's Dream*: G3 has less time for family and marriage as works on business growth and development to achieve his Dream.	* G3's spouse recruited as bookkeeper to take over from mother; functions in multigenerational central marital–parental–business triangle.
5. *Ownership / estate planning*: decision support e.g. how to divide up shares, whether to transfer before or after death; implications for balance of power between recipient siblings.	* Emotional triangles around ownership. Father seeks advice from accountant/brother-in-law and excludes son from discussions.
	* All function in 5 emotional triangles involving: Father-accountant (wife's brother)-successor.
No progress is made on this over 3 years.	Father-mother-accountant (her brother). Father-eldest son-successor. Parents-offspring-accountant. Father-accountant-accountant's father (who was the founder's original adviser).
6. *Board and governance*: board. Strategy and operational decisions made with successor; and the rest of the staff informed.	* Accountant/brother-in-law used as 'sounding board' for father only.
7. *Interaction with researcher* Relationship with researcher: no inconsistencies among narratives. Problems (and their inability to resolve them) are defined consistently.	* Indicative of open, direct communication in the family on topics of comfort only.

Examples are presented below of the consistency and impact of emotional functioning in these systems during task activities in the family, business and ownership sub-systems. Seven task-relationship themes were identified during the research that brought about emotional functioning responses and patterns in the case study families. These were to do with (1) health/death in the family; (2) retirement; (3) conflict management; (4) the successor's/successee's 'Dream'; (5) ownership and estate planning; (6) board and governance issues; and finally (7) how the family interacted with the researcher who became, temporarily, part of their system.

Emotional functioning in the family sub-system

To illustrate this in the family sub-system, the theme of death (when the families felt threatened by ageing, accidents or serious illnesses) mobilised activity by the senior generations to do what was necessary to secure the firm positioning of their successor in the business. For the successor in Case B, who was working

Table 5.2 Family relationship themes and emotional functioning: Case B

Relationship themes	Emotional functioning in the family
1. Health/death in the family: Row with G2's sister over mother's will: G2 made arrangements without sister's agreement. G2's heart attack/strokes in 1990 age 53, family relate this to the stress of 1984 financial crisis	* caused conflict and cut off; she returned to Australia with the conflict unresolved. * G2 seeks continuity solution and asks successor to join the business, leaving accountancy profession; he joins in same week as marriage age 23, same year as father's illness.
2. Retirement: G2 insists he cannot afford to leave having used his pension to finance the business in 1984. Son's account disputes this. Father achieves a balance between being at work and taking many long, expensive holidays. No healthcare plans.	* G3 son-successor in emotional triangle with parents: he is their 'insurance policy' securing their income and taking care of themselves as well as the business, where he brings his skills but has no power. G3 says father is 'living as if there was no tomorrow'.
3. Conflict between father and successor: son able to 'win' on tactical matters but lacks allies on the board to develop a sphere of strategic influence.	* G3 successor is emotionally isolated and personally 'stuck' in 1995–6: he misses his peers; has no support on the board and feels responsible for his father's health/parents' income.
4. Successor's Dream: stifled from a career and personal perspective during 1995–7.	* G3 successor's professional development is thwarted by father who can't risk giving son more power. Successor and spouse want a family but give priority to getting the influence of the family business on their lives under control.
1997: G3 successor makes a deal with father to get the business 'back on track' and then leave to return to the accounting profession.	* successor stands his ground; completes his plan. Joins firm's auditing company; starts a family.
5. Ownership/estate planning: G2 decides on estate plan leaving the business to son and other assets to daughter. Daughter has to accept any inequality, but says son will get at least equal and most likely more value. Father pleased with tax efficiency of plan.	* repeating gender pattern from G2's parents' estate
6. Board and governance: paper board: contentious issues (i.e. long-standing discipline matter) from consultant's report not taken up. G3 not able to create allies. G2 regards non-family managers as dependent on him to buy back their shares on retiral. Questionable handling of financial crisis if no legal case brought against auditors.	* G3 successor on outside position of triangle with: father-board-son. Non-family managers in triangle unable to separate their personal financial interests from the governance of the business. Hero worship of G2 by non-family staff, who never threaten his heroic status.
7. Interaction with researcher Inconsistencies among narratives throughout the system. Problems and their inability to resolve them defined inconsistently. Hero worship of father by non-family staff.	* father's narrative to validate his heroic stature; no access to extended family for research. Father upholds idealistic 'story'. Son debunks it in individual and father–son joint interviews.

elsewhere at the time in a different career, the family business offered a fast-track to the top, with pay above the market rates. This decision was made around some highly significant events that were unfolding in the family system (illness for the senior and marriage in the junior generation). Similarly, after the shock of the father's angina attack in Case A, detailed plans were drawn up between father and successor for an agreed time-scale to handing over the title. The transfer of ownership (or the legitimate expectation of controlling ownership) to ensure continuity of family control of the firm for the successor was also taken into serious consideration in both cases. The life-cycle process of ageing and the incidence of illness and nodal or emotionally significant events mobilised these developmental responses. There were different outcomes from these efforts (only part of Case A's plan has been seen through to fruition), but the relationship processes initiated were the same.

The senior generation men in both cases faced the task of handling the prospect of retirement and entering late adulthood. Their approaches to this task presented another example of identical emotional functioning processes taking place with different outcomes for both. The emotional functioning response in both cases was to shift the senior generations' spousal anxieties about what to do with each other, ageing and mortality in late adulthood, onto the junior generation. Each successor effectively become triangled-in between their parents when they perceived that part of the deal (the psychological contract) was to take on the emotional responsibility for the family by becoming positioned for leadership of the family and of the business. This means they absorbed and reacted to their parents' anxiety about the succession solution by assuming responsibility for the outcome. In a classic triangling process (Kerr and Bowen, 1988), the parents' anxious focus was shifted away from the imminent problem of how to cope as spouses together in retirement with no business to distract them, onto the successors' performance. By focusing on how well the successors were doing with the task of striving to attain worthiness for leadership as well as a satisfactory work–family balance in life, the parents could postpone, or at least buy some more time to prepare for a life that would be revolving around their relationship, rather than around the business.

Both fathers in the study intended to stay around the business in some form or other, so the purpose of the seniors' mobilising these dynamics was not necessarily to get the succession task of installing the new leader completed (only Case A did this). Remaining connected, even when there was no financial reason to (Case A), helped to reduce anxieties about retirement by getting an emotional insurance policy in place in case the marital relationship could not tolerate the change. In Case B, the successor was both an emotional and financial insurance policy to his parents, as the father has no viable income outside the business. However, G3 found himself in a bind because he had the title of Director but no strategic power. He found himself responsible for his parents' income and linked to their emotional well-being. Against this backdrop, he had no power to try to grow the business, and so he felt stifled and frustrated. In order to offset anxieties about retirement in these families, the same pattern of emotional functioning took place to draw in sons as successors and to position them as emotional buffers between the senior generation spouses. Whether the son attained the title and power (i.e. the succession task outcome) did not appear to make any difference to this motive: the priority was an emotional one: to achieve the emotional task of having someone else in the system to shift the focus of their spousal anxieties.

Emotional functioning in the business sub-system

In the business sub-system, both firms in the study stated their strategy was to grow (both had achieved significant growth in the three years prior to the study), and were evolving in the direction of expansion and formalisation of business operations. There were, however, internal struggles about what kind of growth, in what direction, and most importantly, who was to lead and be responsible for the growth? Both cases were analysed to compare how they handled the succession task of business planning. This led them into the issue of strategic choice, and the overriding question of the mission of the business. Underneath this lay the ultimate question of whether the owning family had a clear mission for the business.

Regarding the mission of these businesses, while the strategic outcomes turned out to be very different for each of the firms, what was consistent in all the families was the emotional processes with which they became engaged and its importance in the decision-making processes around strategic choice. Case A had been looking to make an acquisition for some time, and a potential deal had been on and off over the years of the study. The successor, who was 30 and married with two small children, had been working in the business eleven years when the acquisition fell through the second time. He comments:

> It is something I have wrestled with for maybe three or four years now. My grandfather started a business and made it from nothing into something, so he made his mark. My dad took it from where it was, greatly increased the turnover and made it a very profitable company. So he had made his mark. When it comes to the third generation, what am I going to do with it? ... I am not out in this life to build empires, I don't have a vision of ten years down the line, we've got twenty branches and I'm the sort of kingpin ... that doesn't ... it's not what I'm looking for. But I think if we want to keep the company successful and growing and able to provide the salary every month, then perhaps branching out in a wee bit of growth is necessary.
>
> (A1\V2\S\1 p. 11)

Clearly a big issue for this man entering middle adulthood is the developmental task described by Levinson (1978) of 'Becoming one's own man'. Having secure and satisfactory relationship and career structures in his life structure, he now felt the need to work on his Dream of taking responsibility for perpetuating the family business under his own leadership style.

In order to progress with achieving his Dream, after the acquisition fell through the second time, the son carried out an analysis of the market in England and recruited an agent to develop the business there. When the acquisition was finally completed a year later, he had certainly 'become his own man': by this time he had been given the title of MD, and he had made his mark by strategically positioning the business for market penetration throughout the UK by geographical expansion.

The successor's father was attending developmentally to the task of entering late adulthood and was actively working on building a life structure to help him cope with ageing, retirement and his relationship with his spouse. In this case, the personal, family and business developmental tasks were reasonably well aligned and led to productive, relatively harmonious working relationships for father and son on this matter. There was no board of directors in this firm and these decisions were very much the domain of the father–son dyad.

Things did not go as smoothly for the successor in Case B, where the outcome was quite different to Case A's approach to business development and expansion. In Case B, the stated business strategy was one of growth through expansion, but this had tailed off considerably in the last year. Throughout the study, the successor struggled in a number of ways to get the firm onto a better footing professionally and financially. A consultant's report in 1994 recommended prompt disciplinary action internally to clear up an issue which the father denied, but which was costing the firm financially and causing a degree of frustration and concern for the son. The board of directors was effectively a rubber-stamp board and so the son had no allies on this and other matters. The son also wanted to go into some form of diversification to balance the high risk of exposure to another cash flow crisis posed by the family business.

The son had made approaches to his father about other business opportunities the firm could go into, but his father had not agreed to any of them. The father regarded the business as his pension; after the financial crisis in 1984, he and the other director-shareholders took as much money as they could out of the business and did not want the risk of extra borrowing.

The son described how he missed his professional accountancy career, his peers and the Friday afternoons after work in the pub. As the son came to realise that his Dream of running a growing business, 'hands-on', would not be achieved in the family firm, he also saw how trapped he was literally and developmentally. He and his wife resolved not to start a family until he left the business, but he felt unable to leave out of fear of the guilt that a relapse in his father's health would happen due to the strain of his leaving. The emotional process of differentiating himself from his family of origin was a long and painful one. He resolved to put his energies into getting the internal dimensions of the business 'fit enough' financially and structurally, rather than fight the growth strategy issue, so that he could leave with a clear conscience. He slashed overheads and implemented a marketing plan. He then left during late 1997 to return to the accountancy profession and he and his wife started a family straight away. In this case, personal, family and business developmental tasks were not aligned.

The father made no progress with the developmental task of entering late adulthood, while the son worked, almost frantically, to secure his life structure and get his Dream back in focus before the age of 30. These factors together led to the pressure to differentiate himself from his family of origin. This meant coming to terms with how he felt about being emotionally trapped as his parent's insurance policy, and reconciling what he thought about his situation with how he was going to act, especially how he would manage himself if he felt pressured to stay longer or change his mind.

As in Case A above, the business planning task at succession time brought about for Case B the need to attend to unfinished emotional and developmental business before a strategic outcome could be achieved. In Case A, where personal, family and business developmental tasks were reasonably well aligned, clear outcomes in the business task dimension were achieved. However, when they were misaligned as in Case B, there were conflictual emotional responses in the family that led to the business planning task not being attended to. As with the family sub-system tasks, in the business sub-system the firms ended up with different outcomes to the business planning task, but they went through the same emotional process of adult development and it was the outcome of this process which influenced the strategic direction of these businesses, and the extent to which the strategy could be implemented.

Emotional functioning in the ownership sub-system

Another consistent pattern of emotional functioning in the three cases was the extent of apparent emotional triangling of family and non-family members. This was present in all sub-systems but was most evident in the ownership sub-system task of ownership transfer. While the families' use of this emotional response led to different task outcomes, its functional effect in the family systems was consistent. That is, anxiety was shifted away from the developmental and succession tasks at hand and brought into focus in other areas of the family business system.

The two families' approaches to ownership and estate planning demonstrate this as follows. In reality, the transfer of business ownership will take place whether the family plans it or not, because transfer of ownership is a legal requirement on death. The families in this study did begin work on the planning of share and asset transfer. However, they struggled emotionally when it emerged that spouses or offspring in the families, occupying different constituent positions in the structure and therefore having different self-interests to defend, had different priorities and views on the matter. It became even more complex when the issues of tax avoidance and equal inheritance for their offspring were brought into it.

In Case A, attempts were made by the parents to resolve how and in what proportion the ownership of the business and the rest of their estate would be transferred. In Case B, this was presented to the spouse and daughter as a non-negotiable solution to the ownership transfer problem. The way in which each family embarked on the communication process for this task mobilised emotional triangling behaviour and led to entrenchment in both cases. The father in Case A triangled-in the company accountant (in a family and a business sense because the accountant was also his wife's brother), isolating the successor in the process, even during the handing over of the title of MD (see Table 5.1). All parties, and in effect the whole succession process, became 'stuck' as a result because there were disagreements about equality for the successor's brother and the family were unable to get the matter resolved. There was a preference in this family (present in previous generations) for conflict avoidance and the family–business triangles served to put off dealing with the matter. For this family, their family mission for the business was incongruent and this led to the inability to achieve mutual support in the implementation of the family mission. The father wanted to implement a sibling partnership solution to the ownership dilemma, but this lacked support. The G3 successor wanted a controlling ownership solution. Both were incompatible and the family had no other behaviours in their repertoire upon which to draw to work towards a mutually acceptable solution.

The father and successor in Case B decided on the ownership transfer process between themselves in 1990, triangling-out the successor's sister. This repeated a pattern from the previous generation causing an emotional cut-off between the father and his sister over perceived inequalities in the division of the founder's estate. For this father and son, their family mission for the business (to have a controlling ownership solution) was congruent and this led to mutual support in its implementation, even though arriving at the solution had not involved the father's spouse and daughter.

Once again, families in business with the same succession task at hand mobilised the same triangling patterns of emotional functioning and used it to a similar end in that they all became emotionally stuck. However, the nature of their problem was determined by each family's own constellation of family patterns, values and expectations. The patterns served to address the senior generations' emotional needs of status, security and continuity by keeping the successor engaged in the business and in the family.

Discussion

Both of the families in this study were entering the advanced stages of the succession process and therefore had a common set of relationship–task themes to attend to. Setting to work on these tasks often generated acute anxiety, which led to a consistent set of emotional functioning responses. Reducing the anxiety, often by triangling a third person into the relationship to shift or dilute the anxiety, became the highest priority for the individuals concerned, as opposed to whether or not the task was completed or whether or not the outcome was satisfactory. These results were consistent in another three cases studied conducted as part of the same doctoral research (Dunn, 1999c).

The case studies illustrate the flow of anxiety around these family systems during times of transition, and the inevitability of highly anxious situations faced by business families. A clear conclusion from this work is that families in business ,and the individuals therein, should expect to live under conditions of chronic, sometimes acute, anxiety especially during transition periods when the status quo is threatened by many uncontrollable factors. Family systems theory and adult development theory add the perspective that progress with succession tasks is to be expected to the extent that families and the individuals within them are able to reduce the anxiety they experience in situations rather than sustain it.

The results from both cases support a second conclusion that is in tune with the identical predictions offered in family systems theory, family life-cycle theory and adult development theory. It is harder to reduce the anxiety generated when working on adult developmental tasks through the adult life cycle if the task outcomes of *previous* developmental stages are not felt to be satisfactory by the individual or the family doing the work. The same applies if the family of origin's functioning and culture are inconsistent or impaired. Although the family business offers the potential for these tasks to be achieved, this depends upon the *quality* of family functioning and the *prevailing culture* of the owning family.

Implications for business-owning families

These findings have important implications for business-owning families, and for policy-makers. For business families, a first point is that some business-owning families appear to travel along two routes simultaneously in their journey through the succession process. One route involves the public version of the succession process, whereby other stakeholders in the system can observe and sometimes judge how well the succession process is going. Behind the scenes, a different route is taken involving the unfolding emotional dynamics that are triggered when the family system is challenged to change its leadership and transfer power, wealth and authority among its members. Based on these cases, a realistic time-scale of the generational transition process itself appears to be between 3 and 7 years. A second point is not to underestimate the emotional intensity placed on these systems as they work out who gets what in the succession solution, and to be familiar with the types of behavioural patterns triggered by this intensity.

From this, a third point follows that families in business should think about the key task of succession being *to identify and explore succession solution options that are feasible and acceptable to the key stakeholders in the system, rather than adopt an untested solution.* Both families had assumed at the outset that their working ownership and leadership solutions were feasible, only to discover at a key point in the transition that a major element of the solution was in fact untenable to certain parts of the system. This called into question the continuity of the businesses under their family ownership.

Implications for business development policy

The implications for policy-makers in the area of business and economic development stem from these conclusions. Throughout the 1980s and 1990s in the UK much of the emphasis of policy formulation for family business continuity centred around creating the fiscal conditions that would enable the continuity of ownership through long-term retention of the capital employed in the business. Consequently, the UK has for some time enjoyed the most favourable inheritance tax environment in the EU, and other countries are now following in these footsteps (GEEF, 2001). Having legislated for continuity in terms of the economics of succession, it is assumed (from the absence of family business growth and continuity policies) that these firms have the same business continuity requirements as non-family-owned firms.

The first implication for business development policy formulation is whether and how to take account of the intrinsic challenges that stem from the patterns of emotional dynamics at work in business families. These are the challenges that determine the family's ability to work on and reach succession solutions that are feasible for the next generation's leadership and ownership of the business. Such dynamics cannot be legislated for, but their effects are profound and carry a considerable risk of failure or sub-optimisation of the business after the succession.

The conclusions from this study support the conceptual ideas for policy formulation presented by Dunn (1996). The current study builds on these ideas and offers ideas for initiatives that should operate on several levels, starting with a policy for awareness raising and education of business-owning families and their advisers. The aim of this first-level initiative would be to highlight the time realistically required for the generational transition process itself, and to help business families recognise and appreciate the work involved and the emotional intensity to be expected as the transition unfolds. The next level of policy initiatives should include assistance in the form of facilitation of the family, the owners and the board, with the aim of encouraging exploration of feasible succession options. This, however, raises questions about the specialist nature of family business consultation and facilitation. Mainstream business approaches and the training undertaken by consultants and advisers who conduct mainstream intervention do not take account of the family factor: the family's influence on their decision and decision-making processes. For this reason, families are often mistakenly encouraged to 'leave the family out' of business decisions that have consequences for their investment and involvement in the business. If such an initiative were to be considered, a first step in its implementation would therefore need to be the education and training of facilitators and advisers to family business systems.

Conclusion

This study has taken forward earlier studies by Hollander (1983) and Handler (1989a) in order to highlight, through in-depth case analysis, how family emotional functioning was found to be a major driver for business decisions and during transitions. It has also built upon findings in other research studies exploring family life-cycle issues in family businesses (Davis, 1982; Crampton, 1993, 1994). This study used multiple case study analysis, and there is still a need for further case studies and other longitudinal qualitative work to develop the framework presented above. Hershon (1975), J.L. Ward (1987) and Gersick *et al.* (1997) integrated the life-cycle concepts of family, business and ownership sub-systems theoretically and this research has attempted to study in depth the transition of ownership as it was recycled from one owner-manager (the father) to another (the son). There are many permutations in the overlapping of life cycles, and detailed research into how families manage the tasks associated with more complex transitions (siblings to cousins, for example) is required.

The family business cannot be studied, advised upon nor managed without a thorough understanding being gained of the family factors at work that lead to the generation and management of anxiety by individuals within the family enterprise system. Business development policies that fail to take account of the family factor are likely to miss their target.

Note

1 An earlier version of this chapter was published in 1999 in the *Family Business Review* (vol. XII, no. 1, pp. 41–60).

6 The dynamics of family firms

An institutional perspective on corporate governance and strategic change

Mattias Nordqvist and Leif Melin

Introduction

This chapter investigates the intertwined nature of ownership and management in small family firms by linking corporate governance to strategic change. The concept 'corporate governance' did not exist in the English language twenty years ago (Zingales, 1997) but since the mid-1980s the field of corporate governance has been the subject of great interest from scholars, practitioners and public policy-makers alike. However, little attention has been shown to the particular governance problems faced by family firms with concentrated ownership and where the shareholders are directly involved in the executive management (Turnbull, 1997; Huse, 1998). The literature on corporate governance might thus be misleading for a serious analysis of family firms, where the control over both ownership and management rests in the hands of a given family.

In times of constantly changing environments and high competition, strategic change is important for all firms in order to secure competitive advantage and organisational development (Johnson, 1988; Pettigrew and Whipp, 1991; D'Aveni and Gunther, 1994). Family firms are no exception. However, due to the inherent nexus of three intertwined spheres – the family, the ownership and the business – family firms have important characteristics that distinguish them from other types of organisations. Even if an increasing number of scholars are now interested in processes of strategic change in different types of business firms, including family businesses (Pettigrew, 1992; Rajagopalan and Spreitzer, 1996; Melin and Nordqvist, 2000), studies that link corporate governance to the processes of strategic change in family firms are missing.

The aim of this chapter is twofold. The first is to understand how family firms are governed and what this means for strategy making, i.e. how the owners organise and exercise their interest in the family firm in order to influence the strategy process. The second and more general objective is to contribute to theorising on family firms by paying close attention to the particular governing dynamics that characterise them. We combine theories on corporate governance and strategic change with institutional theory in analyses of empirical results from in-depth case studies of strategic change and generation succession in two Swedish family firms.

Corporate governance and strategic change in family firms

The definition of what constitutes a family firm is crucial in empirical research. In this chapter, we follow the definition proposed by Westhead *et al.* (1996), meaning that one family group controls a company through a clear majority of the ordinary voting shares, this family is represented in the management team, and leading representatives of the family perceives the firm to be a family firm.

This definition fits our interest in family ownership and its influence on the strategy process. Knowledge about this particular ownership structure remains under-developed (Daily and Dollinger, 1992; Wortman, 1994). Most existing studies are based on the argument that agency costs are minimised in family (owner-managed) firms since the owners and the management are the same individuals (Jensen and Meckling, 1976; James, 1999b; Ang *et al.*, 2000). In such a situation there is no need for incentives to ensure that the agent acts for the best of the principal. The agency theory view of corporate governance is based on the assumption that the relationship between the principal (the owner), the intermediate (the board of directors) and the agent (the top management) functions as a distinct chain of command. However, the governance process in family firms does not easily fit into this description. The main reason is that the three levels of command – owners, board and top management – often are composed of the same individuals or at least individuals from the same family (Wortman, 1994; Gersick *et al.*, 1997). In the small family firm there is an overlap, or sometimes even a total amalgamation, of these three roles and functions while the dominant business logic and corporate legislation in most western countries tend to separate these roles. To further stress the special governance characteristics of small family firms, research has shown that an active board of directors with external non-executive directors is rare in those firms (Ward, 1991; Brunninge and Nordqvist, 2001).

Considering their special governance characteristics, it becomes important to study the particular relationships and interactions between owners, board of directors and top management in family firms in order to understand the specific corporate governance systems that these firms represent. The character of these relationships is likely to be dependent on traditions, norms, rules and objectives in each family firm (Melin and Nordqvist, 2000). It is also in the nature of small, family firms that the ownership is strongly concentrated in a limited number of people within a definable family, compared with the more dispersed ownership in public corporations. However, the way owner-families choose to exercise their control over the family firms varies. Family members may choose to act mainly as owners and leave the executive power to managers outside the family, or to act as both owners and top managers (Dyer, 1989; Neubauer and Lank, 1998). In small family firms, the way the owner-family chooses to participate in the governing structure thus directly indicates their governance intention for the firm.

Having said this, corporate governance in the family firm may be divided into *structural elements* and *processual elements* (Neubauer and Lank, 1998; Melin and

Nordqvist, 2000). As the structural elements of corporate governance in family firms we reckon the owners and their forums (family council, family meeting, etc.), the board of directors, and the top management team. The processual elements imply power relations, interactions between actors, institutional forces and cultural patterns, with impact on how the governance process actually unfolds in the family firm. The processual elements also include the dynamics that rise as a result of the interplay between the structural elements in action (Pettigrew, 1992; Huse, 1995).

Since we are guided by an actor-oriented view and interested in the meaning that actors assign to their actions, we use the language of *strategists* and *strategic arena*. The strategist refers to the human actor who plays a crucial role in the strategy process (Ericson *et al.*, 2001), i.e. someone who has a considerable impact on the strategy making in the family firm. The strategic arena is where the strategic actors meet and interact. This arena is defined 'through the dialogues around the issues that are strategic to the individual organisation' (Ericson *et al.*, 2001: 68). Based on the framework of strategists and strategic arena, we have elsewhere (Melin and Nordqvist, 2000) presented a model for understanding corporate governance and strategy processes in family firms. The model (in Figure 6.1) is a tentative tool for exploring the role of strategists and strategic arenas in the governance and strategy processes of family firms. It is based on the stance that strategic and governance processes are so intertwined in family firms, that they should be examined jointly.

In this chapter the model is used to describe *how* family firms change in the strategy processes we investigate. The model represents a first level of interpreta-

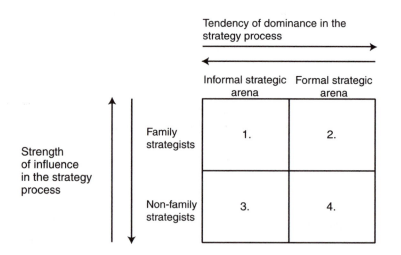

Figure 6.1   A model of governance and strategy processes in family firms

Source: Melin and Nordqvist, 2000.

tion of how family firms are governed and what that means for strategy making. In other words, the model is used to make sense of the empirical accounts we present. To further interpret *why* certain changes in corporate governance systems occur (or not) in the case studies, we turn to institutional theory. By doing this we move beyond the descriptive character of the model and enhance our understanding through further levels of interpretation.

In accordance with Cadbury (1992) and Neubauer and Lank (1998), we define corporate governance as a *system of structures and processes that arise as a result of the interaction between the owners, the board of directors and the top management team in directing and controlling the firm*. In using this definition, we explicitly link corporate governance to the strategy process. The framework of strategists and strategic arenas allows the investigation of structures and processes of corporate governance and their link to the strategy process. It also allows us to distinguish between formal arenas and appointed strategists, and more informal arenas with other strategic actors who do not readily appear in formal arenas (such as board meetings and executive team meetings). Moreover, it allows us to address the inherent duality of the family firm as an institution in which it both arises from and constrains social action (cf. Giddens, 1984; Barley and Tolbert, 1997). In the next section an institutional perspective is outlined in order to further elaborate on the important link between corporate governance and strategic change.

Linking institutional theory to corporate governance of family firms

Broadly, the institutional perspective addresses the issue of how and why organisational structures and processes come to be taken for granted and also the consequences of such institutionalisation processes (Judge and Zeithaml, 1992). This means: 'much organizational action reflects a pattern of doing things that evolves over time and becomes legitimated within an organization and an environment' (ibid.: 769). Furthermore institutional theory suggests that 'institutionalised activities are the result of interrelated processes at the individual, organisational, and interorganisational levels of analysis' (Oliver, 1997: 700). At the individual level, institutional activities refer to managers' norms, habits and unconscious conformity to traditions, at the firm level, to corporate culture, shared belief systems, and political processes supporting given ways of managing, perpetuating institutionalised structures and behaviours and at the interorganisational level 'pressures emerging from government, industry alliances, and societal expectations define socially acceptable firm conduct and those social pressures common to all firms in the same sector cause firms to exhibit similar structures and activities' (ibid.).

This is close to DiMaggio and Powell's (1983) theory of institutional isomorphism, which suggests that three general institutional mechanisms, *mimetic, coercive* and *normative*, lead organisations in a particular field to conformity and homogenisation. Mimetic processes refer to the situation when organisations imitate, or model themselves on other organisations. Whereas coercive processes result from formal and informal pressures exerted by other organisations upon which they are dependent and by cultural expectations in the society (DiMaggio and Powell, 1983). Finally normative processes refer to pressures of professionalisation, or the collective struggle to define conditions and methods of a particular occupation. In the same vein, Pettigrew (1992) argues that structures and processes of corporate governance are shaped not just by the activities of actors at different levels inside and outside the firm, but also by a much broader range of contextual forces and processes emanating from economic, political and industry sector conditions. In other words, institutional forces at different levels provide pressures that shape the corporate governance system. Similarly, Ingram and Simons (1995) observe that firms are constrained by social rules and follow taken-for-granted conventions that shape their form and practice. Institutional rules establish the parameters by which the political game is played, through both enabling and constraining decision-making (Ocasio, 1999).

Related to the controlling dimension of corporate governance, Meyer and Rowan (1977) note that the use of formal control systems in organisations is mostly for symbolic purposes. Rather, the exercise of control over organisational members is done by more social and idiosyncratic measures (ibid.). Hence, even though the board of directors has the formal role of controlling and monitoring the performance of top management on behalf of the owner, this may in reality be done in more informal ways through socialisation, habit, norms, and taken-for-granted-procedures (cf. Florin Samuelsson, 1999). Taken-for-granted and shared rules, norms and beliefs systems govern social life (Berger and Luckmann, 1967; Aldrich, 1999). This supports our view that corporate governance is not limited to its three structural elements, owners, board of directors and top management team. As we have argued (above) attention should also be given to the processes of corporate governance where cognitive and cultural aspects such as norms and rules are important.

Our perspective on corporate governance, rooted in theories on strategy process and institutional theory, focuses on the interplay between structures and processes, as well as on their creation and recreation. In terms of Berger and Luckmann (1967), the structures of corporate governance that we have identified can be seen as highly objectified and externalised features (cf. Hung, 1998). In fact, the establishment of a new formal arena in a family firm such as a management team can be seen as the result of a process of formalisation through socialisation, externalisation and objectification (Barley and Tolbert, 1997). Therefore, the institutional perspective pays more attention to the social contexts in which actors are embedded than most other theories applied in corporate governance research.

Methodology

Applying an interpretive approach we carried out in-depth, longitudinal case studies of two family firms. An actor-oriented view guided the fieldwork (interviews, observations, and documentary studies), which focused on tracking where, when and by whom key strategic decisions and actions were made. In order to ensure the relevance in terms of corporate governance, succession of generations was chosen as the strategic process for investigation. This type of change is a governance issue for most family firms since it typically involves alterations in either (or both) ownership and management and can be tracked over longer periods of time. The studied cases, ValveTech Ltd and Agricult Ltd, are relatively small, manufacturing family firms. The reason for selecting these two cases as a matched pair was their different ways of approaching the succession between two generations. In ValveTech Ltd a third-generation son took over after his father as CEO. This family firm underwent a major change in their corporate governance system during and after the generation succession. In Agricult Ltd the oldest son in the second generation took over as CEO after his founding father. This family firm, on the other hand, did not experience any significant change in their corporate governance system. Our methodological approach is consistent with the research strategy suggested by Barley and Tolbert (1997) who argue that studies that aim to investigate the dynamics of institutionalisation should choose a setting where change can be expected, visible and possible to follow over time.

A comparative analysis between the two family firms is made in order to interpret and understand the processes in relation to theory. The comparison between the firms provides rich empirical insights and the opportunity to theorise how small family firms are governed and what this means for their strategy making. We use an institutional perspective combined with the model of strategists and strategic arenas to reach understanding. The case studies produce empirical texts that represent our first level of interpretation. The second level of interpretation is to summarise and conceptualise our empirical findings, using chosen theoretical perspectives. The two levels of interpretation represent different levels of theoretical abstraction. The institutional perspective means that we treat family firms as a set of organisations with the particular ownership structure as a common denominator (Greenwood and Hinings, 1996). Hence, family firms are viewed, in aggregate, as constituting a recognised area of institutional life (DiMaggio and Powell, 1983), and while they are not homogeneous, thereby we expect them to be exposed to similar institutional pressures.

Two stories from the empirical field

Agricult Ltd

When Rowan got tired of the low-quality equipment he found at the local dealer, he decided to start producing his own machinery for the small-scale farm he was running together with his wife in the southeast of Sweden. It did not, however, take long until the other farmers in the neighbourhood asked him to produce machinery for them as well. As Rowan and his wife were poor and enjoyed producing the machinery, Rowan soon found himself with a small workshop in the barn where he earlier had kept wheat and rye. Since those early days back in 1962, the company has grown into a well-established second-generation family firm, serving the European market with high-quality agriculture equipment. From the humble start in 1962 until the mid-1980s, Rowan ran his firm together with his wife and four children. Rowan was the single owner, the CEO and the chairman of the board, even though the board of directors only existed on paper. Apart from advice from his wife, Rowan was the single person involved in most strategic decisions. A top management team did not exist, occasional meetings with key managers, such as the production manager, was the substitute. Sometimes, when the company faced larger strategic decisions, Rowan gathered the family over a dinner in order to hear the children's views.

In the mid-1980s, Rowan decided to pass on the management to the second generation and to his oldest son, Chris. Sometime after the generation succession, the family attempted to formalise the board work and included an external member. However, as Chris points out: 'I cannot say whether it was good or bad, but at the time we did not think it gave us that much. Perhaps we weren't ready for it.' Hence, after a few months the external member was excluded.

Instead, the family continued to work as they had done during Rowan's tenure. Of course, Chris regularly consulted his father on matters that were important for the company's long-term direction. The family also continued to meet under informal circumstances to discuss and evaluate various strategic options. The board of directors returned to be a 'family affair' and the top managers did not have a formal arena for several more years. As time passed by, more and more of Chris's siblings advanced in the family firm and currently all family members are involved in the management in one way or another. Besides the CEO, the marketing manager, production manager and the international sales coordinator are all second-generation family members. Moreover, the CEO's wife is in charge of human resources, whereas Rowan's wife, Angela, is the engine of the financial office. At an age of 75, Rowan is still a common sight at the head office. He would never miss the 10 a.m. coffee.

During the past five years (1995–2000) Agricult Ltd has grown rapidly both in terms of employees and turnover. In 1999 a top management team was formed and became the only more formal arena in the company. Besides the top management team, the family continues to meet occasionally; either at the company, or in the house of Rowan and Angela, in order to address important decisions. The board of directors is hardly active.

> *No, the board of directors has meetings a few times a year in order to discuss the financial reports. The members of the board are same people from the family as you see here at the office plus two representatives from the union. We have talked about changing the board of directors but nothing has still been decided.*

(Chris)

Bill, the marketing manager and a younger brother of Chris, agrees and adds that most issues that in many companies are dealt with in the board of directors in Agricult Ltd are treated 'as they unfold. Since we all work here it is so easy to get together, or go away for a lunch.'

The respondents comment on how easily and quickly the CEO gathers the family members when they need to discuss a strategic issue. This is most often done in addition to the more regular top management team meetings that Chris recently has initiated. One non-family manager and member of the top management team describes the 'feeling' that the issues to be discussed seem to be, in one way or another, already settled before the meetings.

Admitting the dominance of informal family meetings, Chris's younger sister, Carla, still fears that many ownership issues are discussed in the top management team, since all of her brothers are members there. Carla would therefore like to formalise the board work as an arena for 'ownership-related questions' since 'these become more and more important'.

Apart from the three brothers, the top management consists of several other non-family managers. Despite the weekly meetings, one of these non-family managers asserts that most important decisions seem to be made on other arenas by the family members.

> *With this background I think it would be good for Agricult Ltd to formalise the board and include a few external members. However, since the company has grown successfully six, seven years in a row, I suppose the family think that they better continue to govern the firm as they always have done. In this situation it is difficult for the family to see the need for a more 'professional' governance and strategic management. Involving external influences in this situation can in the worst case lead to a severe clash, since they want to keep control.*
>
> (Andrew, administrative manager, non-family member)

Similarly, the CEO and his siblings admit that they still make most strategic decisions within the family without much influence from external actors and that they have 'always done that'. Nevertheless, in the absence of a formal board of directors, several respondents assign significance to the top management team, since it is the only formal arena in Agricult Ltd. It is interpreted as a first step towards more formalisation with influences from people outside the family. One non-family manager says that it takes time to find the right procedures to work with top management teams in family firms and that he therefore expects a learning process to take place in Agricult Ltd, which can eventually lead to the creation of other formal structures, such as a board of directors. Several family members also confirm this.

In conclusion, it can be said that in Agricult Ltd the succession from the first to the second generation did not result in any major impact on how this family firm is governed. Not even recent years of rapid growth seem to have had more impact than the creation of a top management team. Although the top management team meetings have increased the presence of non-family actors, the interpretation of most respondents is that strategic decisions are made within the family, with little external influence and treatment in formal meetings, as has always been done. A smooth generation succession and years of high performance seem to have provided little reason to revise the corporate governance system in Agricult Ltd in any major sense. Instead, the family members' roles as both owners and managers have been taken for granted and supported by traditions, norms and implicit rules throughout the company.

ValveTech Ltd

In 1999 ValveTech Ltd proudly celebrated its 60th anniversary. The founder started his small-scale manufacturing firm in early 1939 and managed it for almost thirty years before his son, Martin, took over when his father died in 1968. During Martin's tenure ValveTech Ltd has developed into an international company with around 130 employees and bright future prospects. Successively, Martin's three sons have entered the family firm both as owners and employees. In 1999, shortly after the 60th anniversary the oldest son, Jeff, replaced his father as the CEO.

Respondents describe how Martin's concrete dominance as both the owner and the CEO, together with his personal beliefs and values, came to characterise the management of the family firm. And even though Martin is very people-oriented, he made most strategic decisions himself. Shortly, before the generation succession, one manager describes the situation:

> *Martin has an extremely strong position, but I do not think he planned it that way. Now this has come to the point where his co-workers are his cloned copies. They have become like him and they uncritically support his ideas. Of course, this is nothing positive but still very true. It is also rather strange since he is a very quiet and shy person.*
>
> (Ned, R&D manager)

In the view of others, Martin operated ValveTech Ltd as a 'one man's show':

> *I don't think he ever had a natural partner for conversations and influences external to the firm. Instead I reckon that the now retired production manager was his closest 'ally'. He has, of course, called me many times so I guess I have been of some importance. But that has, undoubtedly, to do with my role as the firm's accountant for so many years.*
>
> (Tom, CPA)

As time went by, the number of family members working in the company increased and at the time of generation succession five family members worked in the firm, which made the family rather visible at several levels of the firm. However, besides Martin and the oldest son, no other family members held managerial positions. The picture of Martin's dominance in the company is further enhanced when related to the role of the third generation.

> *It is very rare that I have met with the boys and talked about the future. I actually don't think it has ever happened that we have discussed issues related to our role as owners.*

*Well, in fact, the first time was at the inaugural board meeting half a year ago. I commu-
nicate, of course, with my son who is replacing me, but that is more about the daily
management.*

(Martin)

During Martin's time as CEO, ValveTech Ltd had no active board of directors
and no formal top management team. On the few occasions when the family
needed to gather in order to talk about their company it happened around the
kitchen table in the home of Martin and his wife. However, when the time came
for Martin to step down, ValveTech Ltd needed change. A first step in this
change was to initiate an advisory board. The succession of CEO from Martin
to his son Jeff was the most extensive strategic change in the firm's history and
Martin realised that the family would not be able to manage this change by
themselves. He contacted a consultant, initially for the recruitment of managers
to the top management team that would be created as a part of the succession
process. However, the consultant saw a need for a wider change in ValveTech
Ltd, apart from the creation of a top management team, if the son was to be
able to take over the family firm after the strong dominance of his father. An
advisory board was formed with the consultant, the former CPA and a
marketing expert as members. One aim of the advisory board was to teach the
owner-family to work in a more structured way and to take in influences from
outside the family:

*The advisory board has been very important. My father always avoids difficulties and
problems, but the members of the advisory board force us to deal with everything, also what
is perceived as troublesome. Thus, their influence has made us realise many aspects that we
did not pay attention to before. The reorganisation of the firm, and me taking over after
dad, have been both initiated and supported by the external members of the advisory board*

(Jeff)

The advisory board suggested the need to activate and formalise the work of the
board of directors. The aim was to create an arena where the owner-family
could have a dialogue about the future of their firm. Moreover, in dialogue with
Martin and Jeff, the advisory board proposed changing the board and take in
directors that were neither family members nor working in ValveTech Ltd.
Hence, in a rather short time and during the succession process, ValveTech Ltd
moved from being a family firm dominated by one person and with no formal
arenas for strategy-making, to a family firm with a new CEO (still from the
family), a completely new management team, and a new board of directors, with
two family members (Martin and Jeff) and three external members (the consultant and two directors with no earlier contact with the firm).

As indicated, the succession of CEO also resulted in a new top management
team. The new members are highly qualified managers recruited from outside
the firm and the family. Together with the new CEO they work regularly on
strategic issues, which they in turn report to the board of directors. The idea is to

have different agendas for the board meetings and the management team meetings in order to underline their distinctive roles in the strategy process and the governance of the firm.

Some time after Jeff took over from his father he realised, in dialogue with the consultant and a recruited R&D manager, that it was not enough to simply establish formal structures in order to accomplish a real change in the corporate governance system. Rather, a deeper cultural change in norms, beliefs, power relations and implicit rules was needed if ValveTech Ltd really were to move out of Martin's historical dominance. Thus, they launched educational programmes (internal seminars, leaflets, etc.) in order to inform their customers better about the changes that had taken place related to the succession of CEO, and the rationales behind these changes.

In conclusion, the generation succession in ValveTech Ltd has had a major impact on how this family firm is governed. The creation of formal structures such as board of directors, advisory board and top management team leads to a radical change in the corporate governance system. Most respondents also state that this change has had a major effect on the strategy making in ValveTech Ltd, in the sense that external influences and formal meetings are much more important now than under Martin.

Discussion

The following discussion is structured around the model (Figure 6.1, see above) as a means of understanding corporate governance and strategy processes in family firms. When analysed in the light of *strategists* and *strategic arenas* the two family firms exhibit different patterns.

Under Rowan's tenure, he and other family strategists in Agricult Ltd met and interacted in informal arenas, either in the context of the firm, or within the family. During this period family members shaped strategic decisions mainly at occasional, quickly organised meetings. Hence, in the matrix model (Figure 6.1) Agricult Ltd was situated in square 1. The only external influence during this time was Rowan's sporadic talks with a long-serving manager. The same pattern is found during the succession, when Chris took over. The succession went smoothly without the need of external assistance. Shortly after the succession, Agricult Ltd made an attempt towards formalisation. More influences from non-family strategists and the use of a more formal strategic arena were to be secured by the board of directors. However, this attempt to change the corporate governance system did not succeed. Instead, we observe how the dominance of family strategists and informal strategic arenas continued over time. The second attempt to formalise the strategic arena and attract influences from non-family strategists, this time through changing the top management team, was more extensive than the earlier attempt. However, as illustrated by the case study, it did not change the corporate governance system in any deeper way. The most important strategic arena is still neither the top management team nor the board of directors. The visible dominance of the family, both in the top management team and in the family firm in general, and the view of non-family managers about decisions being already made before meetings confirm this. Hence, an implemented change in corporate governance structure has not led to a change in the corporate governance processes. There seems to exist a wish in Agricult Ltd, at least from a majority of the family members, to increase the influence of non-family strategists and the use of formal strategic arenas. However, a smooth generation succession, growth and good performance have put little pressure on *actually* changing the corporate governance system, which instead continues being family-dominated and characterised by little external influences.

ValveTech Ltd was for a very long time internally dominated by the majority owner and CEO, Martin, which made him the sole strategist. As a result of his strong influence, the strategic arena was informal and often presided over by Martin himself, or at the most with family members, leading to the conclusion that the governance process occurred within the boundaries of the family. The only non-family strategists with some influence were the production manager and the CPA. In ValveTech Ltd no attempts were made to formalise the strategic arena, or to consciously attract external influences, before the succession process started. Hence, during Martin's tenure, this family firm had a corporate governance system that was similar to the one in Agricult Ltd. In terms of the matrix model, ValveTech Ltd was also situated in square 1. However, major differences surface along with the generation succession in ValveTech Ltd. The change in governance leading to the use of formal strategic arenas and external influence from non-family strategists, started before the actual succession, and intensified during and after the son had taken over. The case study shows that a real change actually occurred in ValveTech Ltd's corporate governance system. In other words, the structural changes carried out were accompanied by processual changes. Indeed, ValveTech Ltd moved from a position in square 1, through square 3 (the consultant's and the CPA's increased influence) via square 2 (initiation of family-dominated board meetings) to finally reach square 4 with first the advisory board, succeeded by the externally dominated board of directors and a new top management team with just one family member. Due to more structured board work and an active top management team, formal strategic arenas now dominate in ValveTech Ltd with strong influence from non-family strategists. Compared with Agricult Ltd, that tried to move towards square 4 but did not accomplish it, the reason for the change in ValveTech Ltd seems to be connected to two factors. First, the changes that occurred were necessary in order to secure that the son would be able to take over and run the family firm after the strong dominance of the father (i.e. to neutralise his power position still being the majority owner). Second, the institutional pressure to change (on which we will discuss in the next section) became much clearer in ValveTech Ltd. This pressure was to a large degree transferred by the consultant, a strong believer in active boards in small family firms.

The case studies show that there is a limited core of key actors that initiate, shape and take strategic decisions. The composition of this *strategic core* differs both between family firms and over time in the same family firm. This is clearly indicated in the case studies, where for instance family strategists are much more dominant in Agricult Ltd than in ValveTech Ltd after the succession to a younger generation. However, a common denominator of these cases is that *specific* family members dominate the strategic core. In other words, even if non-family strategists secure external influences, the family members keep their ultimate dominance. Thus, family involvement is considerable, especially when a family member is CEO and several family members are active in the top management team.

In summary, the empirical observations confirm the assumption that processual elements play an important role in the governance of family firms. Indeed, the interaction between strategists in different types of strategic arenas influences and shapes both structures and processes, which eventually give rise to a particular institutionalised corporate governance system in each family firm. The corporate governance process is closely related to a strategic core, which is dominant also outside the formal structures. The governance process is, however, constrained and supported by the particular corporate governance structure, and vice versa. The model used in this chapter can be used to describe the corporate governance system in each family firm and how this changes over time. It is seen here that both companies begin in square 1 but end up in different positions. Next, we will analyse the observed changes from an institutional perspective, in order to address *why* the changes occurred, or not, in the two family firms.

Analysis: an institutional perspective of corporate governance

In ValveTech Ltd the strategic change led to an increased domination of formal strategic arenas where non-family strategists exerted greater external influences. Agricult Ltd did not undergo the same change in the corporate governance system as ValveTech Ltd. But why is this the case? In this section we will argue that this is partly because of the different ways the two family firms responded to the same institutional pressures.

We regard institutional factors as a primary force that guide firms through the processes of strategic change (Bloodgood and Morrow, 2000). Currently, most Swedish family firms experience a time of strong institutional pressure to change arising from changes in corporate law, increasingly active organised networks of family businesses (e.g. the Family Business Network, FBN), of specialised family business consultants (e.g. the Family Firm Institute, FFI), and of 'professional' board members, together with governmental support bodies, loan-giving banks and more academic research (cf. Tricker, 1996). If we relate this discussion to DiMaggio and Powell (1983), we observe that there are coercive and mimetic, as well as normative institutional factors, pushing towards homogenisation and conformity of family firms in the hunt for legitimisation. Regarding the *mimetic mechanism*, the contemporary debate on corporate governance is creating a particular discourse on how family firms should be governed (Karlsson-Stider,

2000). A common theme is that family firms must become more similar to publicly traded firms (Melin and Nordqvist, 2000). Hence, family firms increasingly imitate and model themselves on their publicly traded counterparts. This mimetic behaviour is further spurred by so-called professional board members, often with many years of experience in other types of firms, who are campaigning for more active boards with external board members in family firms. Moreover, family firms are often viewed as inert, closed and unprofessionally managed organisations (Kets de Vries, 1993; Dyer, 1994a; Gersick *et al.*, 1997). In order to attract interest from potential employees, capital providers and media, they must make an effort to look more professional and 'business-minded' (DiMaggio and Powell, 1983).

However, the conformity driven by the mimetic mechanism does not necessarily mean that changes will occur in every firm (DiMaggio and Powell, 1983). And even if the mimetic force seems to be the strongest, there are other mechanisms of isomorphism in play. The normative mechanism refers to how collectives of a particular profession attempt to define conditions and methods for that profession. Recent research into family firms has shown that family firm owners and managers often define themselves as belonging to a particular group and that they build networks with similar people in order to establish some kind of professional belonging (Karlsson-Stider, 2000). This development is further enhanced by organisations such as FBN and FFI that regularly provide forums where this professionalisation can take place. Through the activities in these forums family firms are exposed to the same pressures, which eventually lead to conformity. Examples of these pressures are the reproduction of certain values, norms and other characteristics that family firms share, as well as recipes for how to govern and manage the family business. The same educational institutions that exercise this normative mechanism tend to act as carriers of mimetic pressures. The messages of how important it is to attract external influences and be similar to publicly traded firms are communicated in the same forums. Moreover, as globalisation and technological change put strong demands on family firms, the importance of attracting well-educated people increases. In order for family firms to stay competitive it is necessary to secure competence from outside the family. Employing more highly educated special staff and managers, such as in ValveTech Ltd with the new top management team, means that new professional norms and traditions are brought into the family firms. Often, these new, highly skilled people arrive with a university degree, experience from other types of firms and industries and with extensive personal networks. These factors are important normative mechanisms for homogenisation (DiMaggio and Powell, 1983; Greenwood and Hinings, 1996).

Finally, we can also identify some carriers of coercive forces towards isomorphism. As pointed out by DiMaggio and Powell (1983), the coercive mechanism is not simply legal pressures, but also related to more social and cultural expectations and norms experienced as highly coercive by the family firms. For instance, many family firms need capital and since they often prefer not to sell out equity to external owners, bank loans are a common way of financing expansion of family firms (Bruns, 2001). In order to issue larger loans, banks often demand some kind of monitoring of their investment. Family firms are increasingly facing the precondition that they should include an independent member of the board in order to get a loan. Over time such demands from banks merge into a coercive mechanism causing family firms to conform. Another coercive force in the Swedish context is the new corporate law for limited companies that was carried through in 1999. The new law applies to all limited companies, and stipulates much clearer roles and defined areas of responsibility for the owners, the board of directors and the top management respectively. Since the law does not take into consideration special ownership structures that lead to the amalgamation of ownership and management, such as in family firms, the law forces all firms to homogenise. Finally, the myth of being professional can put coercive pressure on family firms since it can be perceived as a socio-cultural expectation that all firms should be governed in a specific way. This seems to be further enhanced by the general corporate governance discourse.

Conclusion

The institutional framework facilitates understanding of 'why some organizations adopt to radical change whereas others do not, despite experiencing the same institutional pressure' (Greenwood and Hinings, 1996: 1023). In these authors' terms we can conceive the change of corporate governance system during a strategic change process as moving from one template to another. As shown above, family firms can change position in terms of the matrix (Figure 6.1) towards a new corporate governance system in times of substantial strategic change. In ValveTech Ltd, the strategic decision to start formalising the strategic arena and to increase external influence from non-family actors was clearly triggered by the succession of generations. This eventually resulted in a major change in the corporate governance system. When family firms change corporate governance system, it can be a question of *institutional change* as a result of both external and internal institutional pressures. The external institutional pressures equals, in this case, the coercive, mimetic and normative forces discussed above whereas internal institutional pressures are more related to internal organisational dynamics such as changes in ideas, power relations, shared belief systems and unconscious conformity to traditions (Meyer and Rowan, 1977; Greenwood and Hinings, 1996; Oliver, 1997).

For an institutional change to take place, it is not enough to merely change the structural features of corporate governance in the family firm. Change must also occur in the processes of governance (Greenwood and Hinings, 1996; Barley and Tolbert, 1997). Meyer and Rowan (1977) observe that the use of a formal structure, such as the board of directors, may simply reflect a myth and be adopted ceremonially rather than represent a real change in actual work activities. In our cases, the myth can, for example, be that 'all family firms should have external board members', which is currently advocated by several institutions in Sweden with interest in family firm governance. However, the initiation of formal board work does not necessarily mean that strategic decisions are shaped and actually made in this arena. Instead, as pointed out by Ocasio (1999), informal rules can continue to prevail over new more formal rules and procedures, and thereby dominate the decision-making even after a structural change. In Agricult Ltd the creation of a top management team did not lead to any considerable change in the set of dominant strategists and strategic arenas. In ValveTech Ltd, on the other hand, we have seen how this family firm underwent an institutional change since changes in both structures and processes led to a move to a totally new corporate governance system as a result of both external institutional pressure and deliberate actions to change internal institutionalised patterns. In Agricult Ltd, no similar actions to change were taken, and consequently the institutionalised governance system did not change despite experiencing similar external institutional pressures.

Following Greenwood and Hinings (1996), this could be understood with reference to intraorganisational dynamics. Internal institutional factors such as shared belief systems, traditions, and family norms, trust relations and routines (Oliver, 1997) were so robust in Agricult Ltd that a change in corporate governance system did not occur. Compared to ValveTech Ltd, the internal institutional forces in Agricult Ltd were stronger in driving behaviour than the external institutional forces. In particular, the owning family's wish to remain in control reinforced the traditional taken-for-granted way of governing the firm and created resistance to change. As observed by Greenwood and Hinings (1996), change will only occur if the dominant coalition recognises the weakness of existing template arrangements and is aware of potential alternatives. Evidently, the dominant coalition (or strategic core to use our terminology) in Agricult Ltd did not experience the same weakness in their corporate governance system, as did ValveTech Ltd. Nor was the need of the owner-family to remain in total control and dominance as strong in ValveTech Ltd as in Agricult Ltd, explaining the greater openness, change orientation and readiness to welcome new actors in the strategic core in ValveTech Ltd. This observation highlights the importance of internal political dynamics and the strength of family values as crucial forces in the institutionalisation of governance in organisations (Greenwood and Hinings, 1996). Coupled with positive performance records and a smooth generation succession, the intraorganisational dynamics in Agricult Ltd provide an explanation why this family firm did not change in the same way as ValveTech Ltd.

Bloodgood and Morrow (2000) argue that managers who understand the effect that institutional factors have on themselves, their firms and their competitors will be in a position to outperform rival firms when faced with the need for strategic change. Hence, if owners and managers of family firms are aware of the internal and external institutional forces that affect them, they can choose whether to change their corporate governance system or not (cf. Giddens, 1984). The conceptual model and framework used in this chapter can help to visualise the corporate governance system in each family firm. By explaining this system, and the institutional forces affecting it, an understanding can be reached of how family firms are governed and what this means for strategy making. Moreover, the model and framework help us to understand how intimately linked corporate governance and strategic processes are in family firms. In particular, the model defines the strategists as well as the type of strategic arena on which they tend to meet. In constituting both structural and processual features of corporate governance in different constellations, the framework also highlights the need for members of family firms to work towards creating active ownership in order to manage corporate governance and strategic change.

7 The financial affairs of smaller family companies

Panikkos Zata Poutziouris

Despite the fact that the small family firm is the predominant form of business organisation, the small family business sector has received sporadic attention from academics and policy-makers. This chapter aims to highlight the financial agenda underlying the development of smaller family companies. Following a brief introduction concerning the definition and role of the family business, the debate on the finance gap restraining the survival and long-term growth and prosperity of smaller privately held companies (including the prolific family business) is briefly reviewed. Evidence is drawn from a database of 150 smaller family business owner-managing directors (OMDs), in order to establish their views and experiences about venture capital (VC) financing and other capital options (such as employee share ownership schemes – ESOPS and flotation). In conclusion, some tentative policy implications from the perspective of owner-managers, service providers (financiers and advisors) and policy-makers, are discussed.

Introduction

The small family business is the most prolific form of business organisation. Despite this historical prevalence, the family enterprise theme is relatively new on the UK research academic agenda. Early investigations have focused on more sizeable family firms (Stoy Hayward, 1989, 1992). In recent years, more empirical studies have investigated the structure, conduct and performance of the privately held owner-managed family business economy (Dunn, 1995a, 1995b; 1996; Cromie *et al.*, 1995; Poutziouris and Chittenden, 1996; Birley, 1997; 2000; Westhead and Cowling, 1997; 1998; Birley *et al.*, 1999; Reid *et al.*, 1999; Poutziouris, 2000). Westhead and Cowling (1997, 1998) compared the structure and performance of independent unquoted companies and revealed, among other issues, that the adoption of certain family business definitions have a profound impact on the scale and performance of the family business activity . In an investigation into the management succession and performance of family businesses, compared to that of their mainstream counterparts, Cromie *et al.* (1995) found that owner-managers play a more dominant role in family businesses, are reluctant to delegate managerial responsibilities, are less likely to take external advice, to use formal recruitment methods and to invest in employee training. These factors result in lower efficiency levels and lower growth rates in family businesses. Empirical work generally shows that family businesses are smaller than non-family businesses (Poutziouris *et al.*, 1998; Westhead and Cowling, 1998). Also, given their higher need for control, family firms are less growth-oriented and this influences their short-term attitude to financing.

This chapter examines the financial development of smaller family companies and draws evidence from a recent empirical investigation into the financial development of UK private and family companies. This chapter builds on the research of Poutziouris (2000) and Poutziouris *et al.* (2000) who investigated the financial structure of family versus non-family companies and reported that the behavioural side of financing is stronger in family firms as the business tends to be an extension of the ethos of owner-managers. Following this brief introduction, the first section explores the definition and role of the small family business sector in the UK. The next section reviews the literature on small family business finance and highlights the 'pecking order' principle. The statistical analysis of family companies is reviewed and how they finance their development is examined. Finally, the chapter concludes with a brief discussion on certain policy initiatives that can stimulate the flow of long-term finance to owner-managed family enterprises and can contribute, therefore, to the entrepreneurial development of the family business economy.

Family business: definition and characteristics

Broadly speaking, any company, irrespective of size, business operations and organisational structure, when owned or controlled by one family (or family units), may be described as a family firm. However, such general descriptions are perceived as too imprecise for the purposes of rigorous study. The discussion on the definition of the family is ceaseless, and beyond the scope of this chapter (see Chapter 1 in this volume). In general, a business (irrespective of size, legal form) can be (openly) defined as a family enterprise when family members are predominantly involved in its operations, management and ownership regime, and thus can determine its destiny. In the case of the incorporated limited company, the family business is characterised by (active or passive) family members exercising majority ownership control. Since the family business sector is a heterogeneous group, in some sense any academic attempt to develop a universally acceptable definition may be doomed to fail. However, as Westhead and Cowling (1998) demonstrate, the adoption of different definitions as to what really constitutes a family business has a profound impact on the scale and performance of the family business economy.

Family businesses are often cited as the seedbed for social entrepreneurship because of their ability to nurture a business culture characterised by a sense of loyalty, long-term commitment and pride in the 'family' tradition (see Wheelock, 1991; Ram and Holliday, 1993a, 1993b and Fletcher, 1997 for ethnographic studies exploring family business entrepreneurship). The 'family' can foster high ethical standards, positive commercial values, and a sense of responsibility which may contribute to the transfer of entrepreneurial skills from one generation to the next. Other advantages of family businesses include concern and respect for the individual and operational flexibility in terms of sourcing human and financial capital from the family network. Moreover, owner-managers of family firms are credited for their financial prudence and business acumen that often enable family ventures to outperform (in terms of certain financial variables) and outlive their commercial counterparts.

However, family firms may also suffer from disadvantages such as lack of professionalism, nepotism rather than meritocracy in promotion practices, rigidity, informal channels of communication and family feuding. Conflicting family and business politics can 'derail' the development of family firms, as the process of business growth may be incompatible with the objective of perpetuating family control. The less proactive and rather sporadic attention to strategic succession planning remains the key destabilising factor in family business continuity. Only 30 per cent of family firms reach the second generation of owner-managers and 10 per cent reach the third generation, and beyond.

Stakeholders with an interest in the survival, long-term growth and sustainable corporate prosperity of the prolific small and medium-sized family enterprises have been concerned about the financial affairs of owner-managed smaller companies. Strong financial health and a wide capital base are paramount not only for survival across the swinging macro-economic business cycle, but also to finance investment in R&D-led technological innovations as they are central for market and/or product diversification and other growth strategies. Moreover, financial planning is an integral part of the strategic succession plan when founders and/or owner-managers transfer management and ownership to insiders (family OMDs or loyal non-family management) or outsiders. Sourcing supplementary outside capital (such as private equity/venture capital) to finance liquidity and other capital requirements that might result from generational management or ownership transitions will increasingly be central to sustainable business growth and to family harmony.

Financing the development of small family companies

Numerous comparative studies into the financial affairs of small and medium-sized enterprises (SMEs) and large companies have reported that small companies adopt different financial practices from their large counterparts. Smaller companies in particular suffer from a disadvantage in obtaining long-term debt and external equity. This disadvantage may be triggered by the overlapping owner-managerial dynamics, business characteristics and financial market imperfections (Ang, 1991; Cosh and Hughes, 1994; Chittenden *et al.*, 1996; Michaelas *et al.*, 1998; Lopez-Gracia and Aybar-Arias, 2000). Also, in private SMEs, control for ownership and management is associated with the person who owns the majority shareholding. The marriage of ownership and management allows personal and behavioural issues to influence capital structure decision-making (Myers, 1984; Barton and Matthews, 1989; Matthews *et al.*, 1994; Poutziouris *et al.*, 1998). Moreover, evidence has shown that family business owner-managers juggle a range of objectives, personal, familial and commercial aspirations.

In the small business venture, where concentration of ownership in the founder, owner-manager and the family often plays a central role in the provision of talent, labour and capital, a number of social, familial, behavioural and economic motives are interwoven. While the most important factor impacting on business growth is the overall market demand for its products/services, management capacity and attitudes towards change, succession and growth do play an equally significant role in determining business success and continuity. Not surprisingly, small business owners often jeopardise their growth potential because they do not address evolving growth barriers on the financial, managerial, technological and marketing side (Poutziouris and Chittenden, 1996) or they may even eschew growth in favour of other objectives.

The *finance gap*, hampering the strategic financial development of all private SMEs has been under the microscope of economists and policy-makers for decades (Bank of England, 2000). This finance gap is a multi-dimensional barrier and involves the following:

1   *The debt gap*: this represents the problematic flow of development debt, mainly bank loans which are rated as too costly, insufficient and rather too short-termist.
2   *The equity gap*: this represents the shortage of equity capital which is due to asymmetrical objectives of owner-managers who are antithetical to relinquishing control and investors who wish to invest in more open, growth-inspired companies requiring more sizeable equity investment. The equity gap exists as early stage, younger and smaller (relatively more risky, e.g. high-tech activities) companies experience problems in accessing smaller amounts of financing, i.e. between £50K to £200K (Bank of England, 2000).
3   The persistence of the equity gap exacerbates the aforementioned debt gap.
4   *Short-termist cultures*: it has been documented on many occasions that owner-managing directors (OMDs) of closely held SMEs – especially family firms – do have a more short-termist approach to strategic financial management and development planning, They are often sceptical about the deployment of externally generated long-term funding – this is symptomatic of the under-capitalisation of private SMEs as a result of the over-reliance on short-term financial options (Poutziouris *et al.*, 1998). On the supply side, evidence reveals that the majority of the SME-venture capital funds are being channelled towards restructuring ownership (MBO/MBI deals, of which, according to anecdotal evidence, about a third involve family companies) rather than enabling entrepreneurs to start up and grow their businesses (Joseph, 1999). Private equity providers and venture capitalists do not have the time and expertise to evaluate and monitor large numbers of small deals.

Although there has been considerable policy effort (through the promotion of the business angel network (individual small venture capitalists); the Enterprise Investment Scheme (a tax-efficient vehicle to encourage equity investment in unquoted companies and certain smaller PLCs); the establishment of the Alternative Investment Market (a secondary market regulated by the London Stock Exchange, but with less demanding rules than the official list, designed primarily for smaller companies); and the promotion of tax-efficient share ownership schemes to broaden equity share ownership), the equity gap still prevails. To be addressed more rigorously, it is paramount that we better understand the factors (financial and behavioural) that govern the financing of privately held, family and non-family small and medium-sized business economy.

Given the overlap of ownership and management control in the majority of smaller privately held and family companies, in terms of accessing external finance they tend to experience relatively more restrictive transactional and behavioural costs (Pettit and Singer, 1985), have lower marginal corporate tax rates for tax saving on debt repayment, higher bankruptcy costs, and greater costs of resolving the larger information asymmetries. The main conclusion from this discussion about agency costs (the empathy gap between owner-manager and their minority stakeholders, including financiers) and information asymmetries is the *pecking order hypothesis*, which suggests that privately held companies tend to finance their needs in a hierarchical fashion. First, using personal savings and internally generated funds, followed by short- and long-term debt, and then finally external equity that dilutes control (Myers, 1984; Myers and Majluf, 1984).

The problem of information asymmetries is more serious in small businesses for a number of reasons, including: fewer instruments to send a signal to outside investors of the information held by insiders (e.g. dividends, business valuation and growth potential, etc.); the high cost of gathering and monitoring information; and the low value of such information to analysts (Ang, 1991) and the variability of the quality of their financial statements (Pettit and Singer, 1985). Moreover, smaller company owner-managing directors do not try to optimise their capital structure, and show a clear preference for those financing forms that minimise intrusion into their business (Chittenden *et al.*, 1996; Lopez-Gracia and Aybar-Arias, 2000). This is particularly relevant to family companies where owner-managers can flexibly and freely (free from any transaction condition and costs) formulate reward and dividend policy, share ownership distribution and internal equity capital tactics based on family plans. Furthermore, inter-generational and other business transfers could deepen such information asymmetries since outsiders have limited understanding of the co-evolutionary development of the family and business and the operationalisation of certain family-tuned reward systems and succession plans.

According to the pecking order hypothesis the preference for using internally available funds, followed by debt, and finally external equity, reflects the relative costs of various financing options, which are due to the existence of information asymmetries and family-induced agency costs, i.e. the empathy gap between active (board member) and passive shareholders. Arguably, the pecking order hypothesis is particularly relevant to family firms characterised by an aversion to outside capital infusions (Gallo and Vilaseca, 1996; Romano *et al.*, 1997; Poutziouris *et al.*, 1998; Poutziouris, 2001a). Furthermore, a stock market flotation and exit option (to family and non-family) minority shareholders would widen the share ownership of the firm, and could lead to loss of control by the original owner-managers or even a hostile take-over. As such, the rational response of owner managers of smaller private (family and non-family) companies is to avoid the use of external equity finance, and to rely more heavily on retained profits and short-term bank loan finance as they minimise external interference (Lopez-Gracia and Aybar-Arias, 2000).

In a recent empirical investigation Poutziouris *et al.* (1998) established that the financial development of private companies is influenced by the state of the economy, conditions in the capital markets, internal business characteristics, and the owner/directors' attitudes towards financial independence, business risk and (family)-business control. As a result, it appears that family companies, where their OMDs' antithesis to relinquish control is stronger, do not necessarily 'optimise' their capital structure when deploying external sources of finance. However, evidence from practice reveals that certain growth-inspired family companies do employ outside equity capital to finance strategic transitions (e.g. market-oriented business development strategies; family business transfer in the form of generational and management succession; MBO/MBI, and other exit options). Therefore, it is important to establish what the attitude of family OMDs is towards externally generated equity capital as they confront the 'growth versus control' dilemma.

In taking account of this literature and other studies focusing on the financial affairs of family firms, the following sections of this chapter will draw evidence from a database of smaller family companies in order to examine the following questions:

- Do family firms tend to use more internally generated funds for their development?
- Do family firms have a stronger antipathy towards external private venture capital deals? If so, why?
- To what extent do family firms operationalise or consider Employee Share Ownership Schemes?
- To what extent do family firms envisage flotation?

Research design

In a recent survey into the financial development of smaller companies, commissioned by Tilney Investment (Poutziouris *et al.*, 1999) and supported by BDO Stoy Hayward–Stoy Centre for Family Business, the MBS research team established a database of private companies, both family and non-family firms. The survey questionnaire invited participating owner-managers to self-classify their ventures as family controlled or not. Interestingly, 62.5 per cent of sample private companies perceived their business as a family firm.

Table 7.1 presents the profile of the database of sample companies, whose main characteristics can be summarised as follows:

- *Age distribution*: the majority of family companies (60.4 per cent) are in excess of twenty years old, giving an age median of 28 years.
- *Size distribution*: about 45 per cent of family companies have sales turnover in excess of £5m, while 22.1 per cent employ more than 100 employees; the median in terms of sales turnover is £4 million and that of employees stands at forty-five staff.
- *Sectoral activities*: it appears that family companies are more prolific in manufacturing, construction and distribution and less prolific in services.
- *High technology activities:* interestingly, 18.8 per cent of family companies classify their business activities as high technology, which compares very unfavourably to the high tech-intensity of the non-family business sector.
- *Business transfers*: only 12.6 per cent of family companies have been through ownership change, e.g. MBO/MBIs, acquisition, family sale/acquisition, etc., which is just one quarter of the level for non-family companies.
- *The strategic orientation of OMDs*: applying cluster analysis to the responses of owner-managing directors on a large portfolio of personal and business objectives, sample firms were categorised into four generic groups, namely: *controllers, survivors, exiteers and growth stars*. Based on this classification, Poutziouris (2000) concludes that family firms are not in business to actively pursue orthodox growth and financial performance objectives. Certainly, the strategic orientation of a family company will be influential on capital investment plans and subsequently financial sourcing.
- The *distribution* of sample family companies by generation in control highlights the deteriorating survival rate of family companies across the generational spectrum. It demonstrates that 25.4 per cent of family firms survive to the second generation, 7.7 per cent progress to the third generation of family owner-managers, and 6.3 per cent are 'generational firms' in the hands of the fourth generation and beyond. These results are broadly in agreement with other research that has reported on the transfer and survival rates of family businesses across generations (Dunn, 1995a; Cromie *et al.*, 1995; Westhead, 1997; Reid *et al.*, 1999).
- Generally, family firms are regarded as more traditional ventures whose OMDs' propensity to *keep in the family* results in a profound antithesis to outside investors and equity partners. The distribution of family companies by shareholding revealed that the majority of family firms – in fact 65.3 per cent – do adopt a *totalitarian* regime of ownership control, where the family controls 100 per cent of voting shares.

Table 7.1   Profile of database of private companies

Number of responding companies	Family firms 150 (%)	Non-family firms 90 (%)
Age distribution (median: years trading)	(28)	(18.5)
<10 years	15.6	27.1
11–20 years	24.0	23.9
20+ years	60.4	49.0
Size distribution	*1999*	*1999*
(Mean: sales turnover)	(£4.0m)	(£4.0m)
< £1m	10.9	10.4
£1m–5m	45.5	30.3
Size distribution (employment)	*1999*	*1999*
Median: number of employees	(45)	(50)
< 10	9.6	6.1
10–50	43.3	45.4
50–100	25.0	21.2
100+ employees	22.1	27.3
Sectoral distribution		
Agricultural, Forestry, Fishing	2.7	–
Manufacturing	27.0	23.2
Construction	19.8	7.2
Transport/Distribution	7.2	1.4
Trade (Retail and Wholesale)	9.9	10.1
Services	20.7	36.2
Other activities	12.6	21.7
Transfer of ownership in recent years		
Yes	12.6	49.3
No	87.4	51.7
Technology intensity		
High-tech	18.8	32.7
Medium-tech	44.3	47.7
Low-tech	36.9	19.3
Strategic orientation		
Controllers-traditionalists	61.1	35.7
Growth stars	21.4	38.7
Survivor–strugglers	14.5	19.0
Exiteers	3.1	7.1

The financial structure of smaller family companies

In previous investigations into the financial affairs of private companies, it was established that owner-managers of family and non-family companies have a hierarchical preference for sourcing capital to finance business operations and development, known as the pecking order (Poutziouris *et al.*, 1998, 1999).

Table 7.2 presents a comparative account of the funding structure of private companies. It demonstrates the importance of retained profits as the overriding source of capital, which is a very prudent practice. Moreover, it reveals that the external financing of private companies is heavily biased towards short-term

Table 7.2   Funding structure of private SMEs

Source of finance	Family companies		Non-family companies	
	of all funding	*of external funding*	*of all funding*	*of external funding*
Retained profits	51.5	–	42.8	–
Bank overdraft	17.9	52.4	15.5	37.5
Owners' equity	14.4	–	15.7	–
External loans	6.2	18.2	8.5	20.4
HP/finance leasing	4.7	13.8	10.9	26.3
Factoring	2.6	7.6	3.8	9.2
External equity	0.8	2.3	1.3	3.1
Other	1.9	5.6	1.5	3.5

Source: Poutziouris *et al.* (1999).

funds. It is evident that there is an aversion towards institutional finance and in particular an antipathy towards external equity. This antipathy to outside long-term finance (both debt and risk equity capital) is particularly strong in family companies.

Table 7.3 summarises the responses of OMDs about the perceived sources of finance they use and demonstrates that there are only a couple of statistically significant differences in the funding approach of family and non-family businesses. These are as follows: *Family firms tend to draw more social capital from the family network and are less enthusiastic about venture capital.*

Table 7.4 further extends the analysis of the financial structure of private companies and compares the balance sheet structures[1] of (353) family and (225) non-family companies (where variables are the average in the 1997–9 period and are expressed as a percentage of total assets) and reveals a number of statistically significant differences in their funding approach. For example, family companies – when compared to non-family counterparts – tend to invest relatively more in tangible and less in intangible assets; they have lower long-term liabilities (i.e. long-term bank debt, directors' loans, etc.) and retain more

Table 7.3   Sources of development finance for private SMEs

Source of finance	Family companies	Non-family companies	Anova F-statistic	Level of sig.
Retained profits	92.8	90.1	0.40	0.53
Bank overdraft/loans	72.1	81.7	2.19	0.14
HP financing/leasing	42.3	43.7	0.03	0.86
Owners' equity	22.5	31	1.62	0.21
Capital from directors	20.7	28.2	1.33	0.25
Capital from family	15.3	2.8	7.45	0.01*
Factoring	9.9	7	0.08	0.77
Business angels/private investors	2.7	7.0	1.94	0.17
Other sources	2.7	2.8	0.01	0.96
Venture capital	0.9	25.4	32.3	0.00*

Note: * t-statistic techniques: * statistically different at 5 per cent level of significance.

Table 7.4   The balance sheet structure of private companies (%, averages, 1997–9)

Variables	Family companies	Non-family companies	t-statistic	Sig. levels
Fixed assets				
Tangible assets	30.70	26.87	2.205	0.028*
Intangible asset	0.03	0.09	−3.315	0.001*
Total fixed asset	32.56	29.41	1.738	0.083
Current assets				
Stock and work in progress	20.55	17.35	2.321	0.021*
Trade debtors	32.76	36.48	−2.456	0.014*
Bank deposit	10.0	10.77	−0.930	0.353
Total current asset	67.63	70.97	−1.845	0.066
Current liabilities				
Trade creditors	23.07	27.63	−3.136	0.002*
Short-term loan	14.69	14.13	0.476	0.634
Current liabilities	52.60	60.78	−4.073	0.000*
Long-term liabilities				
Long-term loan	10.00	13.37	−1.507	0.133
Other long-term liabilities	1.53	1.79	0.73	0.47
Total long-term liabilities	11.53	15.16	−2.184	0.029*
Capital and reserves				
Issued capital	6.0	7.0	−0.950	0.342
Share premium	1.0	3.0	−2.183	0.029*
Retained profits	26.77	15.20	3.876	0.000*
Revaluation reserves	0.04	0.02	2.434	0.015*
Shareholders' funds	37.49	25.63	4.652	0.000*

Note: * t-statistic techniques: * statistically different at 5 per cent level of significance.

profits that enables them (over time) to build a stronger equity base (i.e. share-holders' funds).

The results have to be treated cautiously because they may have been influenced by the demographic characteristics of family companies: family companies tend to be older, proliferate in certain sectors with low capital intensity (where investment could be financed via leasing) and are smaller (with lower growth aspirations coupled with the a desire to retain control by insiders). However, Poutziouris *et al.* (1999), employing Analysis of Covariance (ANCOVA) models, re-examined the association of family business control and balance sheet structure after controlling for the impact of demographic variables. The ANCOVA results demonstrated that family-controlled firms (in contrast to non-family companies) tend to invest less in intangible assets; they borrow less long-term funds and re-invest more profits (see Table 7.5). This is partly explained by the family business culture but also by demographic variables (covariates: age, size and sector). Interestingly, given the adherence of family firms to the retention of profits (pecking order principles), certain traditional family companies (i.e. in production and distribution activities) have stronger corporate equity (share-holders' funds: total assets) than their private counterparts.

Table 7.5 Performance of family and non-family companies

Measurements	Family companies	Non-family companies	t-statistic	Sig. levels
Growth rates				
Sales growth	8.34	14.90	−2.964	0.003*
Employment growth	6.14	14.64	−2.889	0.004*
Asset growth	9.07	14.59	−3.120	0.002*
Profitability ratios				
Return on total asset	0.09	0.09	−0.419	0.675
Return on total equity (shareholders' funds)	29.10	70.13	−3.476	0.001*
Return on capital employed	23.55	24.49	−0.195	0.845
Adjusted ROTA (includes directors' pay)	17.92	21.91	−2.224	0.027*
Adjusted ROTE (includes directors' pay)	76.66	146	−2.041	0.042*
Adjusted ROCE (includes directors' pay)	64.02	62.98	0.048	0.961
Profit margin	4.33	2.99	2.058	0.04*
Gearing ratios				
Short-term debt	30.80	34.88	−2.187	0.029*
Long-term debt	11.53	15.16	−2.184	0.029*
Total debt	41.32	49.41	−2.904	0.004*

Note: * t-statistic techniques: * statistically different at 5 per cent level of significance.

This suggests that certain groups of family companies – especially growth-oriented ventures, with a more open culture – appear to be bankable and could benefit from the advantages of venture capital when they embark on growth agendas, provided the deal addresses certain restrictive aspects which are not compatible with their ethos, e.g. dilution of control, exit options, etc.

In summary, the analysis of the financial structure of family companies *vis-à-vis* that of mainstream private companies demonstrates that the majority of family business owner-managers have a relatively short-termist attitude to financing which may lead to capital deficiencies, especially during a downturn in the economy. Arguably, the sustainable development of the family company necessitates the steady flow of long-term capital, particularly when there is a need to finance certain strategic transitions (such as accelerated growth; internationalisation; transfer of ownership to successive generations, etc.).

The remainder of this chapter will reflect on the views, expectations and experiences of OMDs of family companies with respect to external financing options: private equity – venture capital; ESOPs and flotation.

Rationale for venture capital: the views of OMDs of smaller family companies

A number of scholars (De Visscher *et al.*, 1995; Coleman and Carsky, 1999; Poutziouris, 2001a) argue that the majority of private companies including traditional family businesses, where ownership is sustained in family hands for longer, have a profound antithesis to venture capital relationships (including both dealing with small private investors/business angels and institutional venture capitalists). Moreover, since a segment of the family business economy does not adhere to a totalitarian ownership control regime and has growth aspirations, such ventures will be open to long-term external capital in order to invest in new technologies and marketing strategies that can help them sustain and develop their competitiveness in the new economy.

Table 7.6 considers the rationale of private companies in using /considering external venture capital. Participating OMDs were asked to rate (on a Likert scale) in term of importance certain factors that would induce them to seek venture capital. The most important reason for raising external equity finance is to finance organic growth. Notably, family companies are *not* very enthusiastic about considering venture capital to finance acquisitive growth strategies nor investment in research and development (in order to enhance growth potential and the development of new products). Nor are family companies keen to strengthen the company's financial base in order to become more attractive to bankers (or to perhaps pursue flotation on SME secondary markets) and to realise capital wealth by selling shares. OMDs of family private companies have an idiosyncratic business culture – *remaining as an independent company.*

Table 7.6   Rationale of OMDs of smaller family companies for venture capital deals

Rationales	Average factor ratings	Important factors (%)	Not applicable factors (%)
To finance growth	3.18	45.6	12.9
To finance acquisition programme	2.45	29.2	22.8
To pass on company and retire	2.30	25.5	20.8
To develop new products/markets	2.45	24.8	22.8
To expand/move into new premises	2.21	24.2	24.8
To repay borrowings	2.20	19.0	28.4
To finance shaping up of balance sheet	1.83	16.1	32.9
To realise capital	1.93	15.4	24.8
To diversify wealth	1.82	11.0	26.0
To buy out existing shareholders	1.50	10.1	48.3
To finance research and development	1.74	6.0	27.5

Note: Sample: 150 family companies; 1 = not important and 5 = very important.

Opposition to venture capital: the view of OMDs of smaller family companies

According to Table 7.7, the major concerns about venture capital perceived by OMDs of private companies relate to the dilution/loss of financial and owner-ship control and the loss of management freedom of action. Other important considerations are pressure from third parties such as venture capital analysts to meet profit/dividend targets and the costs associated with external equity finance.

Table 7.7   Perceived problems, issues involved in venture capital dealings

Problematic issues	Average problem ratings	Important factors (%)	Not applicable (%)
Dilution/loss of control	3.78	71.6	9.2
Loss of management freedom	3.62	63.0	9.0
Pressure from 3rd parties to meet profit targets	3.46	60.0	10.0
Pressure to change the management team	3.09	40.5	9.0
Lack of knowledge about rules of the game	3.11	43.2	8.1
Financing costs	3.23	49.5	8.1

Note: Sample: 150 family companies; 1 = not important and 5 = very important.

OMDs of family firms (compared to the responses of non-family OMDs) more emphatically voiced their concern about probable displacement of family managers with outsiders as a result of VC-instituted reshuffling of board of directors. Moreover, OMDs of family ventures appear to feel less comfortable and knowledgeable about the rules of venture capital dealings.

In reality, the majority of mainstream private and family-controlled SMEs do not and will never reach a stage of business development where they will have to reconsider their financial strategies and practices with respect to private and public equity options. The majority of privately and closely held owner-managed ventures simply are not in pursuit of growth strategies, and consequently avoid adventurous financial options (Poutziouris, 2000, 2001). However, my argument (supported by anecdotal evidence and research noted above) is that, due to the prevalence among smaller company directors of the general antipathy (and myopia) about venture capital, there is an information gap about the mechanics of this problematic, but equally challenging (and promising) capital option.

ESOPs and the PLC route: the financial experience and attitudes of family companies

As Figure 7.1 demonstrates, proportionately fewer family companies opera-tionalise an Employee Share Ownership Plan (ESOP) including schemes for managers/directors. Nevertheless, of the 93.6 per cent of family companies (41.0 per cent equivalent for non-family companies) that do not currently operate a scheme, 41.3 per cent (62.2 per cent equivalent for non-family compa-nies) said that they will consider the introduction of one in the future.

Also, turning to the attitude of private companies towards flotation on SME equity markets, again, family company owner-directors are less enthusiastic about public equity financial development strategies. Only 18.2 per cent of family companies state that they have considered flotation, while the proportion of non-family companies considering flotation was 32.4 per cent. It follows then that a minority of family companies will, at some stage of their business develop-ment, open up ownership to embrace insiders (extended to relatives but also

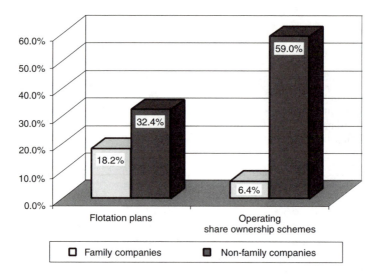

Figure 7.1   Experience and attitudes of family companies towards ESOPs and PLC options

loyal managers serving family owner-managers) or outsiders in order to strengthen both their human and financial capital base.

Policy issues

Proposed policy issues for the following actors are now discussed:

*   *Family business owner-manager directors* are in business for several reasons other than just the maximisation of profits. It is important that they manage to balance the market-imposed business growth with the desire to keep in the family control. In the context of enhanced capital requirements to finance fast growth activities and other concurrent business transitions (e.g. succession), external equity could prove to be indispensable to the sustainable growth of the business.
*   *Financiers* ought to receive more training about the critical issues (market-based and familial) confronting the survival and growth of the family company. Understanding the socio-cultural, financial, economic and legal aspects relating to the parallel development of the family and the business sub-systems would help them better understand the idiosyncratic family business dynamics. This will enable them to better segment and serve the *transitional family firms* (experiencing fast growth and/or business transfer across generations) with equity investment options that respect the family business ethos. It has emerged that family companies are not enthusiastic about venture capital deals due to mainly asymmetries relating not just to growth objectives, but also due to exit routes. New flexible approaches – like

SandAire's Equity Harvest – are central to the financial development of family firms with the growth potential. In the words of Hudson (2001): '*Equity Harvest* enables the family to diversify its wealth while retaining a controlling shareholding, introduces strong incentives for the existing or new operational management, and protects the family company name and heritage.'

- *Policy-makers*: the fiscal regime ought to recognise the importance of familial and social capital in terms of widening the financial (and human) capital base of closely held family firms. There is concrete evidence to suggest that private companies have an aversion towards external equity investments. Their favourite source of capital is internally generated funds mainly through the retention of profits *(sweat-capital)*. The operationalisation of the *pecking order* calls for more tax-based schemes seeking to offer an allowance for corporate equity (ACE). This will ensure that re-investment of profits receives the same tax treatment as interest paid to lenders (Poutziouris and Chittenden, 2001) and also incentivises the issue of new share capital. Moreover, although transfer taxes with tax planning can be rolled over where the business continues to trade (capital gains tax) or postponed (inheritance tax), they do mount a double taxation on business success and adversely affect investment in the long-term growth and prosperity of all private companies. They should be rationalised in order to promote family business entrepreneurship and also to facilitate early business transfers across generations.

Finally, in order to remedy the antipathy (and information gap) of family business owner-managers towards venture capital, there is scope for more case study-based research which will feature success stories where growing family businesses have benefited from venture capital support (both in terms of finance, management expertise and access to a network of corporate associates). Lessons can be drawn from the successful equity financial development of family companies across the globe as they master their transition in the context of multi-generational business transfers and/or corporate strategies. This is of particular importance to stakeholders with an interest in the survival, growth and long-term prosperity family businesses operating in countries where the development of private and public equity markets is still under way.

Conclusion

Smaller family firms are one of the engines of the market economy. They are often credited for their long-term strategic vision and financial prudence, but are criticised for their 'conservative' financial philosophy, which in some cases could hamper their business growth potential. It emerges from this empirical investigation that the financial development of family companies is governed by the 'keep it in the family' tradition. Conclusive evidence shows that smaller family companies are systematically more dependent on internally generated funds (i.e.

retained profits) for their survival and development. This is also consistent with the fact that they are not enthusiastic about parting with venture capital at the cost of family business control.

Moreover, family companies are more sceptical about fast growth as this entails relinquishing control and a dependence on external investors (long-term debt or private equity providers). Empirical evidence reveals that closely held family firms adhere strongly to the pecking order philosophy. As a result, family firms tend to depend more on internally generated equity (i.e. share capital plus retained profits). Despite their symbolic level of issued capital, family firms tend to build a stronger equity base over time through the retention of profits. This combination of monolithic ownership and management control, coupled with an idiosyncratic funding approach, enables family-owned firms to embark on business strategies and transitions (i.e. succession) with a minimum influence from outsiders.

Some family companies have survived many recessions and outlived many conglomerate-owned business competitors because they enjoy a pool of internally generated equity capital and strong support from the family and loyal associates (who exhibit an idiosyncratic knowledge about future strategic plans). Therefore, certain growth-inspired and well-established family companies could represent a less risky investment for private equity providers.

Note

1   Source of data: Fame Database which is provided on CD-ROM is based on the audited accounts of UK companies submitted to Companies House. The Fame database contains data for more than half a million companies trading in the UK.

8 Training and HRM strategies in small family-owned businesses

An empirical overview

Harry Matlay

Introduction

Small businesses make an important contribution to the development of the socio-economic and political infrastructure of industrially advanced nations (Matlay, 2000a). Significantly, both in Britain and in the USA, family firms operating in traditional manufacturing and service sectors constitute a large proportion of the small business population as a whole (Church, 1993; Hoy and Verser, 1994; Cromie *et al.*, 1995). Following the surge in academic, practitioner and policy-oriented interest in entrepreneurship and business development in Britain, there now exists an extensive body of general and specific knowledge that outlines and analyses the factors that are most likely to influence economic activity in both family and non-family small businesses (Carter and Jones-Evans, 2000). The current position contrasts sharply with the relative neglect that characterised the small business sector in general and family firms in particular prior to the publication of the findings of the *Committee of Inquiry on Small Firms* (Bolton Report, 1971). Unfortunately, however, the contemporary body of knowledge appears to focus mainly upon those issues that classical economic and business theory considers important for small firm growth and development: management, marketing, finance, production, and research & development (Goss, 1991; Storey, 1994; Matlay, 1996).

Importantly, the mainstream approach has left significant gaps in the specialist literature, a shortcoming that requires a more discerning and focused approach to understanding the full impact that small family businesses have upon a nation's socio-economic and political development (Ram and Holliday, 1993a, 1993b; Fletcher, 2000; Westhead and Wright, 2000). In this context, a great deal is now known about the age, location, managerial structure and marketing orientation of small family firms operating in this important sector of the British economy. Much less has been written in relation to the training and human resource management (HRM) needs of owner-managers and their workforce (Matlay, 1999). This chapter aims to redress the current imbalance in small business knowledge. It outlines and analyses the preliminary results of a longitudinal research study on training and HRM undertaken in a random sample of 6,000 small businesses. The results show that there are considerable differences in owner-manager attitude and approach towards the training and HRM needs of family members employed in the business as compared to non-family employees. The results would suggest that such differences could significantly influence employee development in, and the competitive strategies of, family-owned small businesses.

Training in small family businesses

The noticeable paucity of research that focuses specifically upon the training and HRM needs of small family businesses leaves a significant gap in the specialist literature (Matlay, 1996; Dunkley, 1997). Until recently, human resource issues in smaller firms have been largely neglected by academics, researchers and human resource professionals who assumed that the training solutions that benefited larger firms could also be successfully adapted to the specific needs of smaller businesses (Matlay, 1999). Holme (1992) argues that in practice, large-scale training and HRM solutions proved to be of little use in small family businesses. Dunkley (1997:82) reinforces this view and further claims that 'conceptual and empirical studies on Human Resource Management (HRM) to date have primarily concentrated on the largest firms and it is rare for SMEs and family businesses to receive a mention within the mainstream HRM literature'. The size, complexity and sectoral diversity that characterise the family business population appear to have hindered efforts to develop an empirical basis for specific training and HRM strategies (Welsch, 1993). Even though the importance of training and skill formation in small family businesses has belatedly been recognised by some academics, a number of related theoretical and practical problems still persist. For example, there are considerable definitional problems relating to the size and distribution of small family businesses. Furthermore, there appears to be little agreement among interested parties in relation to the optimum type, quality and quantity of training needed in small family firms. The role of government in targeting and allocating training-related funds as well as the timing and size of related grants have recently been scrutinised and critically appraised by academics, trade unions and small business representatives (see, for example, Matlay, 2000b). As a result, concerted efforts are being made to improve the flow of relevant funding towards those owner-managers who would benefit most from training-related outcomes.

Matlay (1997) has identified the existence of a potential training paradox that applies to both family and non-family small businesses. It appears that although owner-managers' attitudes to training were largely positive, actual provision rates failed to keep pace with the skill needs of their workforce. A number of tentative policy recommendations emerged from this study (Matlay, 1998). First, it was suggested that the overall quantity, quality and availability of training should be improved to at least a level commensurate with that provided by Britain's main competitors. Second, a programme of selective financial support should be initiated and adequate funds be made available through a more efficient and equitable infrastructure. Third, both higher education and the training industry should offer a wider range of customised and economically priced training, narrowly focused upon the specific needs of small businesses. To date, however, none of these recommendations have been implemented and the skill shortages affecting the small business sector of the British economy remain critically high (Matlay, 2000a).

In a recent study, Westhead and Cowling (1997) found that the specialist literature is characterised by a notable lack of consensus on the theoretical and operational definition of what constitutes a family business. Typically, researchers who focus on this topic tend to use their own definitions of family businesses, some of which rely upon ownership share, kinship relations or managerial composition (Daily and Dollinger, 1992; Ram and Holliday, 1993a, 1993b; Cromie *et al.*, 1995; Birley, 1997). In an effort to improve research in this area, Westhead and Cowling (1998) have suggested the widening of the relevant definition to include the interaction of complex conditions that influence the operation and competitiveness of family firms. In their study, Chua *et al.* (1999) have further asserted that perceptions and behaviour in relation to family businesses can significantly undermine stereotypical definitions and render them useless for research or evaluation purposes.

Research sample and methodology

The research study upon which this chapter is based was designed to combine, over a three-year period (1998–2000), three analytical approaches. First, it involved an exploratory telephone survey of 6,000 respondents who were randomly selected from the Yellow Pages Business Database of Great Britain. The telephone survey, which aimed to collect quantitative data on the personal and organisational characteristic of owner-managers and their businesses, achieved a response rate of 88 per cent. Second, a focused sub-sample of 600 small businesses was identified for a closely matched comparison of respondents from a wide variety of personal backgrounds, such as age, gender, ethnic origin, educational achievements as well as organisational characteristics that included size, location, market orientation and type of economic activity. These in-depth interviews elicited qualitative data that allowed a comparative analysis of both family and non-family small businesses. Third, 120 case studies were conducted in order to gather longitudinal data on annual changes in the training and HRM needs of family owned small businesses. The quantitative data relating to medium-sized and large organisations in the sample was retained for comparative purposes (see Matlay, 2001). A rigorous approach to data collection and analysis has facilitated the triangulation of the overall results that emerged from this research study and the postulation of a number of pertinent recommendations.

Size distribution and composition of the research sample

The exploratory telephone survey, which was carried out between January and September 1998, involved a research sample of 6,000 respondents randomly selected from the Yellow Pages Business Database of Great Britain (Table 8.1). The quantitative survey achieved an overall response rate of 88 per cent. Those respondents who declined to be interviewed (12 per cent) cited time constraints (7.2 per cent), too many requests from researchers (4.1 per cent) and other factors (0.7 per cent) as reasons for their unwillingness to participate in the study. The quantitative sample of 6,000 participating organisations comprised 2,129 respondents operating in the manufacturing sector and 3,871 in services. In order to provide a rigorous basis for longitudinal analysis and comparison, the official European Commission (1996) size definition was adopted and strictly observed throughout the study.

Numerically, service businesses (64.52 per cent) outnumbered manufacturing units (35.48 per cent), a trend that seems to be characteristic of the British economy as a whole. Furthermore, micro-businesses (89.17 per cent) and small businesses (7.93 per cent) dominated the research sample (97.10 per cent). In the case of micro-businesses, 1,872 were operating in manufacturing (31.2 per cent) and 3,478 in services (57.97 per cent). A similar distribution was observed in small businesses, among which 193 were manufacturing (3.22 per cent) firms and 283 were providing services (4.72 per cent).

Table 8.1 Size distribution and composition of the research sample

Size band	Size definition	Number of employees	Manufacturing (N = 2,129)	Services (N = 3,871)
A	Micro-business	1–10	1,872	3,478
B	Small business	11–49	193	283
C	Medium-sized	50–250	51	89
D	Large business	251+	13	21

Note: N = 6,000.

Small, family businesses in the British economy

The working definition employed in this research study has been widened to take into consideration Westhead and Cowling's (1998) model of 'multiple conditions' as well as the broader social context suggested by Fletcher (2000) and Chua *et al.* (1999), which incorporate 'softer' characteristics such as kinship, affiliation and personal relations. Accordingly, and in order to be defined as such, members of a family (or families) must be able and willing to exercise control of, and involvement in, the management, decision-making and operational aspects of a family business. Actual and/or perceived share- or stake-holdings in a family business are implied in this working definition only if the above conditions have been fulfilled (Barry, 1989; Matlay, 1996). For example, businesses where family members hold majority shares as 'absentee shareholders' and which are controlled and operated by unrelated managers or management teams have been excluded from the 'family' business category. In cases of multi-family ownership where at least one member was directly involved in the management, decision-making and operational

Table 8.2 Family business representation in the research sample

Size band	Size definition	Number of employees	Family businesses (%)	
			Manufacturing	Services
A	Micro-business	0–10	83.33	85.85
B	Small business	11–49	71.50	73.85
C	Medium-sized	50–250	50.98	51.69
D	Large business	251+	15.38	19.05

Note: $N = 6,000$.

aspects of the respective firm, these were classified as family businesses. A large proportion of micro- and small businesses in the sample were included in the family business category (see Table 8.2). Among the organisations that operated in the manufacturing sector, 83.33 per cent of micro- and 71.50 per cent of small businesses were in this category. In the service sector, the proportion of family businesses rose to 85.85 per cent in micro-business and 73.85 per cent in small business size band.

The telephone survey sought to establish the locus of training and HRM decision-making processes within the research sample (Table 8.3). Interestingly, the locus of control upon training and related decision-making processes showed marked similarities across both the manufacturing and the service sectors. In micro- and small businesses, the locus of organisational control and training-related decisions were retained by owner-managers. There were no distinctions made between general control of firms and the locus of human resource decisions in micro-businesses. This was also the case in the vast majority of small businesses, with the exception of a small proportion of firms positioned towards the upper limit of this particular size band. The consistency of owner-manager influence and control upon the daily activities of their micro- and small businesses applied equally to both family and non-family firms. Thus, in the vast majority of cases (100 per cent of micro-businesses and 92.71 per cent of small businesses), the owner-manager was identified as the main decision-maker, inclusive of issues related to training and human resource development. Only in a fraction of small businesses (7.29 per cent) were personnel managers responsible

Table 8.3 The locus of training and HRM decision-making processes

			Who makes training decisions?			
Band code	Number of employees	All firms (N = 6,000) (%)	Owner/Manager (%)	Personnel Manager (%)	Key personnel (%)	Other employees (%)
A	1–10	89.17	100.00	0.00	0.00	0.00
B	11–49	7.93	92.71	7.29	0.00	0.00
C	50–250	2.33	68.46	25.97	5.57	0.00
D	251+	0.57	0.00	11.39	88.61	0.00

for the human resource function. Even in these firms, owner-manager involvement was considerable and the final decision regarding the financing of training and release of trainees for that purpose appeared to depend on them. Training plans and related budgets were only encountered in 5.62 per cent of micro- and 8.84 per cent of small businesses. In each case, these were part of, and positioned within, an overall business plan.

A great deal has been written in recent years on the influence and crucial role of owner-managers in the day-to-day running of family businesses (Matlay, 1999). The preliminary results of the telephone survey have confirmed these findings and shown that in only a minority of family-owned small businesses were responsibility and control for training or any other managerial function delegated to other managers or key personnel. The acute need for control over their businesses was particularly evident in smaller family businesses and this was reflected in the owner-managers' choice of management style (see Table 8.4). Importantly, most of the respondents were acutely aware of the fact that they treated their businesses as an extension of their families and viewed them as safe and creative working environments for their kin. In total, 92.86 per cent of micro- and 70.05 per cent of small business respondents preferred informal management styles. In 5.46 per cent of micro-businesses and 19.67 per cent of small firms owner-managers claimed to prefer a mixed formal/informal management style. Interestingly, 1.68 per cent of micro-businesses were managed externally to the firm, by either consultants or specialist agencies. Formal management styles were reported by 10.29 per cent of small business respondents.

Owner-manager styles were reflected considerably in all the important managerial activities of a firm, including recruitment, training, HRM and employee relations. Typically, the vast majority of owner-managers in micro- and small family-owned businesses resorted to informal means of recruitment and tended to prefer a similar approach to training and HRM issues. Family ties and related informal networks appear to play an important role in these activities. Informal methods were used to induct, train and retrain employees in the vast majority of family-owned micro- and small businesses in the sample. Those owner-managers who indicated a preference for formal styles of management also used formal methods of recruitment, induction, training and retraining of employees. Their use of family-based networks was significantly reduced. All

Table 8.4   Management styles of owner-managers

Management style	Micro-business (%)	Small business (%)	Medium-sized (%)	Large business (%)
Formal	0.00	10.29	26.16	0.00
Informal	92.86	70.04	13.87	0.00
Mixed formal/informal	5.46	19.67	5.31	0.00
Professional	0.00	0.00	59.97	100.00
External/agency	1.68	0.00	0.00	0.00

Note: $N = 6,000$.

employees in these firms were treated with the same degree of formality, regardless of their position or length of service. Significantly, the formal management approach did not appear to differentiate between family members, friends and other employees. Interestingly, mixed formal/informal management structures were much less rigid than formal styles and allowed for a greater degree of flexibility in all aspects of training and HRM processes. Formal and informal approaches were used interchangeably to suit an owner-manager's general and specific needs and also depended largely upon their personality and temperament. These approaches were considered less flexible than informal management styles but much more effective in growth-oriented micro- and small family businesses. Typically, however, formal means of recruitment, training and HRM procedures were applied to non-family supervisory, management and other employees. In contrast, informal approaches were adopted in relation to all family members, as they appeared to prefer and respond more positively to this management style.

The qualitative data that were collected from 600 semi-structured, face-to-face interviews and 120 matched case studies have highlighted a number of subtle attitudinal, perceptional and motivational differences that appear to impact upon training and HRM strategies in small family businesses. The subtleties of family relationships in the workplace and the influence of kinship involvement in business strategy were both complex and intricate. Furthermore, only a minority of owner-managers in family businesses found it desirable or actually achieved a distinct dichotomy between business and family relationships, even though they admitted that occasionally such interactions resulted in conflicting and/or negative outcomes.

Attitudinal, perceptional and motivational influences

The importance of owner-manager attitudes towards training and HRM in small businesses has been discussed extensively elsewhere (Matlay, 1997, 1998, 1999). The 'paradox of training' that applies to the small business sector in general, still holds, to a significant extent, in the context of family-owned firms. This is not surprising, considering that a large proportion of small businesses in Britain can be included in this category (see, for example, Fletcher, 1997; Westhead and Cowling, 1998). Thus, it appears that although the vast majority of owner-managers in the sample held a positive or very positive attitude to training there were a number of subtle but important differences in their approach to its purpose as well the expected outcomes.

The data that were collected during face-to-face interviews have shown that, typically, owner-managers in family businesses perceived training and related issues in two distinct ways. First, and most importantly, the training needs of family members were viewed as investments, with potential medium- and long-term returns to the business as well as the family member. Furthermore, many of the training interventions that involved family members were approached in terms of individual career development and treated accordingly by both the owner-manager and the individual. Similarly, training options were usually considered within an overall medium- and/or long-term business strategy, adapted to suit not only the firm but also the perceived career needs, expectations and ambitions of family members. In general, non-family employees were not considered for succession to top positions in family-owned small firms. Second, the training of non-family members in this type of business was viewed strictly in terms of firm-specific, HRM needs. Thus, training requirements, choices and related feedback were approached in accordance with actual or perceived short-term organisational needs and related pressures. Similarly, the training of non-family employees was not perceived as a crucial element of medium- and/or long-term organisational strategy. Earmarked as an expense to the business, all needs and resources-related training and HRM were evaluated and distributed competitively within an overall business strategy. In contrast, short-term organisational needs were not deemed to be important to the overall career development aspirations of family members working in small businesses.

Owner-managers in non-family firms perceived training as an organisational expense. They viewed all related tasks, including evaluation, training identification and feedback, exclusively in terms of firm-specific HRM issues. The motivation to train was narrowly connected to existing (both actual and perceived) short-term training and HRM needs of the workforce. Importantly, owner-managers did not perceive the training function as a crucial element of the overall business strategy. Furthermore, designated resources, both human and financial, were considered and allocated in competition with other operational functions and within the conflicting demands of an overall organisational goal. In the vast majority of cases, training interventions were of a reactive rather than proactive nature. Succession issues, although present in some non-family small businesses, were perceived as 'political struggles' that would eventually be resolved under internal competitive conditions. Similarly, management buy-ins or buy-outs were viewed as feasible solutions to succession challenges in this type of small business.

Human and financial resource considerations

The data that emerged from matched case studies have highlighted further training and HRM dissimilarities between family and non-family small businesses. Such differential factors were related mainly to human and financial resources and, in particular, to their availability, provision and allocation. Individually and cumulatively, human and financial resources were identified as most likely to influence the provision of training in small family businesses. The directly relevant factors identified by respondents involved the market positioning of a business, prevailing economic conditions and the availability and cost of relevant training. The indirectly relevant category included time constraints, the lack of in-house trainers and a number of factors appertaining to trainee interest, motivation and cover. The market positioning of a small family firm and the economic conditions prevailing at the time that HRM-related decisions were made emerged as the main determinants of training in this type of business. Furthermore, it emerged that there existed a positive link between the management progression and the career development of owner-manager relatives involved in small family businesses. The respondents claimed that employing relatives in their businesses would generally have a mitigating effect upon both current and future managerial and supervisory skill shortages. This link was evident in most cases, including those small businesses in which owner-managers relied exclusively upon short-term, reactive rather than proactive HRM strategies, sometimes known as 'just-in-time' training.

Interestingly, in small family businesses, issues relating to succession, trust and job delegation seemed to over-ride some deep-rooted owner-manager beliefs and/or long-standing managerial practices. For example, family members were considered 'trustworthy' and expected to remain loyal and 'stand their ground' even under the most difficult circumstances. Thus, at least in theory, their commitment, motivation and propensity for hard work were taken for granted, trusted and guaranteed by virtue of family links and long-standing interpersonal relationships. In practice, however, owner-managers' expectations of productive, trust-based, family relationships often proved difficult to sustain both within and outside the workplace. In contrast, non-family employees were mostly perceived as 'assets on legs' and considered liable to 'walk away' or be 'poached' by external agents, including ex-employees who had set up in competition.

The availability of relevant training seems to have a direct effect upon the HRM strategies of small family businesses. Most respondents confirmed the strong link between firm-specific training needs and sustainable competitive advantage. Accordingly, a whole spectrum of skill shortages could not be overcome due to their failure to locate training relevant to organisational goals. Some respondents claim to have undertaken searches at local, regional and national level in an attempt to locate potential sources of economically priced training programmes relevant to the specific HRM needs. Apparently, few of them were successful in their procurement efforts. Thus, the lack of relevant, firm-specific and customised training appears to have handicapped some owner-managers' HRM strategies to the extent that new marketing drives had to be postponed or abandoned. Even when useful training programmes were occasionally located, the prohibitive cost of customised, low unit delivery tended to inhibit the uptake propensity of some of these owner-managers. Furthermore, some respondents claimed to have had difficulties in costing the training programmes on offer or to estimate related marginal or incidental expenditure. As a result, they tended to favour 'off-the-shelf' training packages that sometimes included additional after-sale support. In most cases, however, these proved too general in scope and focus and rarely match the full extent of their firm-specific training needs.

Time constraints, so prevalent in smaller economic units, were perceived to further handicap training provision in this type of organisation. The training function in small family firms was an integral part of a wider business strategy and in competition for scarce organisational resources. Nevertheless, an owner-manager often felt compelled, by successionary motives, to carve out the necessary time and continue a search until a suitable training programme was located. Where no relevant training could be found, owner-managers undertook intense and lengthy 'mentoring programmes' or 'bottom-up' job rotation in order to facilitate a family member's progression through 'the ranks'. Similarly, family members benefited from additional financial support, which on occasions, originated from sources external to the firm (including personal, institutional and developmental funding as well as debt equity guaranteed by family members). Usually, marginal and incidental costs attributable to family members' personal or career development programmes were absorbed by the firm. Typically, small business owner-managers and key personnel undertook most of the internally provided training in their firms. None of these firms could support a dedicated internal trainer and often had to rely upon external provision of specialised training programmes. Apart from the obvious direct financial considerations, external training also incurred short-term displacement costs for individuals who were trained 'off premises' or in 'non-productive' environments. In micro or small family businesses, even one employee away from his/her usual workplace could accrue a significant loss in productivity. Issues relating to trainee motivation and interest caused additional difficulties in this type of firm. Family members were mostly expected to comply with an owner-manager's choice of training or to find suitable alternative programmes. In the case of non-family employees, most such difficulties could be overcome by the use of various incentives, including modest financial inducements or productivity-related bonuses.

Conclusion

In Britain, government representatives, policy-makers and academic observers view a healthy small businesses sector as a crucial prerequisite to the development of a stable socio-economic and political infrastructure. According to a fast expanding volume of empirical research, a large proportion of the domestic small business sector in this country can be defined as family-owned firms. Within the growing body of knowledge appertaining to small family businesses there exists a paucity of empirically rigorous research on issues relating to the training and HRM strategies of this type of firm. The research study upon which this chapter is based sought to redress the imbalance by adopting a narrow focus upon this important aspect of small business development. The telephone survey established that the locus of control on training and HRM decision-making processes in small family businesses was retained by owner-managers regardless of size, location or type of economic activity. Furthermore, in family businesses, no distinction was made between organisational control and the locus of the human resource decision-making process. Even when other employees were involved in this important managerial function, the final decision on the financing of training invariably rested with the owner-manager. Their preferences in relation to management styles reflected considerably upon HRM strategies and their choice of recruitment, training and retraining.

The semi-structured interviews documented a number of subtle attitudinal, perceptional and motivational influences and highlighted their impact upon training and HRM strategies in small family businesses. The motivation to train appeared to be dependent upon the actual and/or perceived HRM needs of a workforce. In family businesses, training and related issues were perceived in two distinct ways: the requirements of family members were approached mostly in terms of individual career development while the needs of non-family employees were viewed strictly as firm-specific HRM issues. Succession issues in small family businesses represented an important consideration for owner-managers and affected their overall training and HRM strategies. In most cases, training decisions relating to family members were resolved proactively, usually as part of medium- and/or long-term HRM and succession strategies.

The in-depth data that emerged from the matched case studies have highlighted two types of human and financial factor relevant to the training and HRM strategies of small family businesses. Directly relevant factors included the market positioning of a business, prevailing economic conditions and the availability of relevant training. The indirectly relevant category involved time constraints, the lack of in-house trainers and various factors related to trainee interest, motivation and cover. In financial terms, family members tended to benefit from additional and/or continuous support that included personal, institutional and developmental funding as well as debt equity guaranteed by family members. Typically, owner-managers and key personnel undertook most of the internally provided training. Family members, however, were coached and mentored more extensively than other employee categories. This exploratory research study has identified a number of pertinent issues relating to the training needs and strategies of small family businesses. Further research is needed, however, to explore the long-term trends and variations in owner-manager attitudes, expectations and training provision, as affected by rapid socio-economic, organisational or technological changes.

9 The emergence of leaders in family business

Jill Thomas

Introduction

Research into leadership has been prolific since the inception of scientific management in the 1920s (Bass, 1981). Few researchers, however, agree on what constitutes effective leadership and few discuss specifics of leadership in family business. Given the variety of circumstances that family businesses find themselves in, it is recognised that there may not be one best way to manage a family business and more research may 'prove fruitful in helping to understand what leadership approaches make sense in the context of a family firm' (Dyer, 1994a: 111). Of particular interest in the family business context is the potential for the family members to be exposed to the business from an early age, perhaps during school vacations. Leadership development, therefore, can take on a different meaning with the development and training of family members sometimes being taken for granted, or left to chance.

An overview of existing research literature on leadership development in family businesses is presented in the first section of this chapter. Leadership is operationally defined as a process of influencing others towards a defined goal (Hughes *et al.*, 1996: 6), rather than attributes of an individual in a position of authority. This processual approach to leadership recognises the importance of individual leaders as well as the context in which those leaders are operating. This approach is suitable for exploring leadership in the family business environment where there are considerable challenges from the overlap of the family system and the business system. The second section presents an outline of the research strategy for this study. The third section draws upon qualitative data to explore influences on the emergence of leadership in the family business. While it is not possible to generalise from the small number of cases in this study, there are several influences on leadership development that may be of interest to those involved in the wider family business sector. The key implications of this research are summarised in the final section.

Leadership development in family business succession processes

Much of the research about leadership development in family businesses is undertaken in the context of succession. This is not surprising as, according to the stereotypical view of family business, a parent establishes the business, then controls and directs it until advancing years enforce a decision about succession or sale. Failure to survive beyond one generation is frequently attributed to some aberrant dynamic of family relationships or some problem with both ownership and management succession. The issues of selection, training and development of successors are integral parts of the management succession when succession is seen as a process which occurs over a period of time rather than a one-off discrete event (Longenecker and Schoen, 1978; Handler, 1989b).

However, unlike succession, the issue of leadership development has not received much attention in the family business literature (Dyer, 1994a; Wortman, 1994). The way in which family businesses approach the appointment of leadership successors may well shape subsequent career and personal development paths. J.L. Ward (1987: 62) referred to successor selection as a watershed event with some businesses becoming 'increasingly leaderless unless one successor takes control through a revolution of some sort'. In his view, families should pay attention to planning for the succession of the new leader and he identified several options, for example, creating a fixed rule that 'the oldest child will be president', selecting the best candidate from the group, or developing an interim, non-family leader (ibid.: 62). More recently, research on the attributes of successors found that integrity and commitment to the business were considered the most important attributes of successors, with gender and birth order being rated the least important (Chrisman *et al.*, 1998: 28). However, what is of interest is the particular influences (such as integrity, commitment, degree of choice, prior work experience) that shape leadership development. These aspects of leadership development have not received much explicit attention.

The main emphasis in studies of leadership development has been on barriers to effective leadership development. Barnes (1988) investigated difficulties that sons or daughters in the business may have in integrating their own identities with roles expected of the family system. For example, a new CEO may be considered senior in terms of the business hierarchy but may be still relatively junior in the family hierarchy; the existence of such an incongruity may hinder the effectiveness of leadership development in the family business. The need for development opportunities to be matched to the individual was recognised by Handler (1992) in her identification of three kinds of needs of next generation family members: to have a satisfactory career in the family business, to be personally accountable, and to have their own identity. Dyer (1994b) discussed several aspects of the development of successors, such as the use of mentors, the specific period of time required for successor development and whether informal or formal training is more appropriate.

Furthermore, in terms of education and training, Davis and Harveston (1998: 34) have noted that there has been only limited research which examines the specific needs of leaders in family business. Also, Kets de Vries (1996: 18) noted that training prior to joining the family business often leads to accelerated management development for family members. While Seymour (1993) investigated the role of training in the family business in relation to planning successors' development, he did not include education level in his study. However, Neubauer and Lank (1998: 252) argue that basic business education results in better informed family discussions on family business matters and, where applicable, a better balance of influence among shareholders: 'The MBAs and those experienced in management have new discussion partners "who speak their language", thereby increasing the probability of quality decision-making by the owners' (ibid.: 252–3).

Just as Brown (1993) concluded that resistance to dealing proactively with succession in family firms is often a strategy used to avoid thinking about the concomitant loss (possibly death of the CEO), so too has the development of leaders perhaps been avoided. The willingness of the CEO to relinquish the senior role in a timely fashion has been discussed frequently in the literature (for example, Danco, 1980; Churchill and Lewis, 1983; Kets de Vries, 1985). In particular, the extent to which the former CEO is able to let go and allow the next generation family member to develop their *own* leadership style is a significant factor. Davis and Stern's (1980) view was that the older generation members may have difficulty re-defining their relationship with the company on retirement and that this may present special problems for the children. Aronoff and Ward (1992) recommend that once the decision on the leadership successor is made, the family member CEO needs to resist the temptation to control the successor with advice, criticism and problem-solving. As part of their ongoing development, successors need to be given the opportunities to make their own mark and not be stalled behind ageing parents who are disinterested in relinquishing control (Aronoff and Ward, 1992). Harvey and Evans (1995: 8) showed that the level of involvement by members of the older generation after retirement influences the amount of change that is possible by the next generation.

Other studies, however, have focused on factors aiding the development of successors. From her experiences with non-family businesses, Foster (1995) proposed that leadership development in the family business should be treated as an ongoing process and should include practices such as giving successors challenging assignments, providing ongoing feedback, learning from others, participating in coursework and reading, and other self-directed learning opportunities. From their comparative research, Fiegener *et al.* (1994) found that family firms used network-building tasks for development purposes more often than did non-family firms. They speculated on the reasons for this:

Family firm leaders walk a fine line between wanting to develop their heirs to be effective leaders but not wanting them to develop too well, too quickly. Perhaps network building experiences are a preferred form of development experience for family leaders because they are somehow less threatening than other development alternatives by virtue of being perceived externally oriented and peripheral to the core operations of the business.

(1994: 326)

The behaviour of CEOs, the relationships they build with potential and actual successors, and family dynamics generally, affect leadership development (Stempler, 1988). He found that in focusing on the relationships between successor, successee, families and non-family employees, five major factors emerged which are necessary for successful leadership succession: complementary management behaviour; respect; self-insight; understanding the needs of others; and understanding the structure of the organisation, lines of authority, and the delegation processes. The extent to which these emerge is worthy of further exploration.

In view of the lack of studies about how to develop leaders in the family business context, this chapter explores the influences of leadership development in family business. This research draws upon Thomas's (2000) earlier study which examined the exercise of leadership and the identification of key leadership responsibilities in a small sample of Australian small to medium-sized family businesses. As noted by many researchers (for example, Shanker and Astrachan, 1996), the family business sector is not homogeneous and care must be taken to define those family businesses which are the target of the research. The particular cases discussed in this chapter (see also Table 9.2) are small to medium-sized businesses with between 12 and 110 employees, have family members involved in day-to-day management, have progressed to the second generation and beyond, and are more than 95 per cent owned by related family members. The research strategy shaping the collection, analysis and presentation of fieldwork data is now discussed.

Research strategy

The emergence of leaders in family businesses was explored through a research design which combined elements of grounded theory, ethnography, single case study and cross-case analysis (see, for example, Yin, 1984; Eisenhardt, 1989; Stake, 1995). It was a qualitative study achieved through inductive reasoning rather than by logical deduction from *a priori* assumptions as is the focus of quantitative research (Patton, 1990: 66). Accordingly, no hypotheses were put forward. Rather, initial exploratory discussions with members of family businesses in the preparation of this study identified several recurring themes relating to leadership. Family business members talked of their businesses being special, of family relationships influencing business operations, and of generation gaps between

Table 9.1   The emergence of leaders in family businesses

Interview questions related to	Findings related to
Selection and recruitment practices	1 The degree of choice on entering the family business
Entry points into business	2 The approach to prior work experience
	3 The attitude to formal education
Performance management	4 The nature of career development opportunities
Retirement provisions	5 Timely departure of older generation

the older and younger members of the business. They felt that their business leadership requirements were closely related to the nature of their businesses, even unique, but were unable to define them. These recurring themes pointed to a recognition that family businesses carry out the same tasks as other businesses, but that there was something qualitatively different about their experiences. These exploratory questions, together with the existing literature, informed an open-ended interview guide so that the questions asked included the topics detailed in the left-hand column of Table 9.1. Following analysis of the responses, key influences on the leadership development emerged as detailed in the right-hand column. The study was therefore largely inductive.

The research sample

Consistent with studies from the USA and Europe, studies have found that Australian family-owned businesses are estimated to make up approximately 80 per cent of private companies, employ about 50 per cent of the workforce and represent a wealth of approximately $A1.2 trillion (see Smyrnios and Romano, 1994; Smyrnios *et al.*, 1997). These studies have also profiled Australian family business through broad-ranging surveys and questionnaires examining character-istics such as ownership, employee numbers, sales and revenues, key objectives, and the presence of some key human resource management practices. Thomas (2000) aimed to build up a picture of how leadership is exercised in the family business by pursuing a more detailed examination of a small number of cases.

Data were collected through in-depth one-to-one interviews, participant observation, and through the review of documentation and field notes in six small to medium-sized family business cases (see Table 9.2) ranging from the second to the fifth generation of ownership and management, as follows (for details of ownership classifications, see J.L. Ward (1987) and (1991); Gersick *et al.*, 1997):

- Andersons, a fifth-generation family business owned and managed by a cousin consortium.
- Bensons, a fourth-generation family business owned and managed by a controlling owner.
- Carlsons, a third-generation family business owned by a sibling partnership and employing a non-family CEO.

Table 9.2   Summary characteristics of cases

Case	Generations[a]	Approx number of employees[b]	Gross annual sales 96/97	Industry sector	Interviewees[c]		
					O[d]	Y[d]	Non-family
Andersons	4 and 5	110	$70m	Manufacturing	2	3	1
Bensons	3 and 4	70	$12m	Manufacturing	1	2	2
Carlsons	2[e] 3	80	$11m	Manufacturing	–[f]	2	2
Dawsons	3 and 4	70	$5m	Manufacturing	1	2	1
Emersons	1 and 2	30	$12m	Construction	2[g]	2	2
Fletchers	4 and 5	12	$4m	Property and investment	1	1	2
				TOTAL	7	12	10

Notes:

[a] Indicates which generation(s) are actively involved in the business either in executive roles or non-executive board roles.

[b] As at 30 June 1998 and reported by the family business; approximate full-time equivalent numbers.

[c] The number of individual participants in the study; some were interviewed more than once.

[d] 'O' is the number of interviewees who were members of the older generation of the family business; 'Y' is the number of interviewees who were members of the younger generation of the business.

[e] The second generation CEO is deceased but a director of his choosing, and of the same age, remained on the board.

[f] Former CEO deceased but the legacy of his policies and practices being contended with.

[g] One of these was a member of the extended family with no ownership.

- Dawsons, a fourth-generation family business owned by a controlling owner and managed by a sibling partnership.
- Emersons, a second-generation family business owned and managed by a controlling owner.
- Fletchers, a fifth-generation family business owned by a cousin consortium and employing a non-family CEO.

The 29 interviewees across the 6 cases included 19 family members: 4 family member CEOs, 9 family member managers, 4 family member board chairmen, 2 non-executive family directors. Non-family members interviewed included 2 non-executive directors, 2 CEOs, 5 managers and 1 member of support staff. The 'older' generation interviewees' ages ranged from 52 to 75 years, the younger generation's from 29 to 52 years, and the non-family member's from 28 to 56 years. Interviewees were asked how they perceived that leaders emerged in their own family business and how they may have been more appropriately developed for leadership roles.

Data analysis

The nature of the data analysis was not tightly structured before data collection began, consistent with the qualitative researcher's aim to develop categories from the data through constant comparative analysis throughout the study (Janesick, 1998). Data analysis evolved and took place in a number of phases.

The first phase involved the ongoing recording of thoughts and impressions gained during the company visits and interview sessions. A second phase of analysis took place when the field notes and interview transcripts were prepared in a suitable form for NUD_IST (1997), a computer-based qualitative data analysis package that was used to organise the data. The third phase of analysis and interpretation was more structured, involving coding and retrieval processes developed with the aid of the NUD_IST software. This enabled the data to be reduced because, as noted by Janesick (1998: 46): 'The process of reduction of the data into a manageable model constitutes an end goal of the qualitative research design.' Thus, the research process was an iterative one with interpretation and analysis ongoing during the collection and transcription of interviews.

Qualitative data were presented in the form of Case Ordered displays (see example in Table 9.3 on p. 145) to facilitate meaningful and structured presentation of that qualitative data and to look for reasons for similarities and differences between cases (Miles and Huberman, 1994).

Research findings

Four factors (see Table 9.1) which were found to have influenced the emergence of leaders in these family business cases are now summarised. The fifth factor, the timely departure of the retiring CEO, is not addressed here as the findings were consistent with the literature in that family businesses recognised the need for the CEO to leave the business in a timely fashion to enable the younger generation to establish their own leadership approach in the business (see, for example, Davis and Stern, 1980; Danco, 1992; Harvey and Evans, 1995).

Choice on entering the family business

While no cases had formally written procedures or policies about who would enter the family business and how this process would be managed, views were expressed as to how the older generation considered whether the younger generation 'should' or 'might' join the family business. Table 9.3 presents a case-ordered display categorising the cases into three prevailing views and relating them to the extent to which the younger generation interviewees were satisfied with being members of the business and also an estimate of their current leadership ability (Thomas, 2000). Cases were categorised as follows:

- *High expectation*, that the younger generation will join the family business: e.g., 'There is a business for them to join so why not?'
- *Moderate expectation*, providing some element of choice for the children when deciding whether or not they wish to join the business: e.g., 'The family business is there if the younger generation wish to take the opportunity to join.'
- *Low expectation*, encouraging the younger generation to pursue their own careers: e.g., 'They may then be invited to join the business if, and when, an opportunity arises.'

Table 9.3 Case-ordered display: relationships between the older generation's expectations for younger generation to join family business, younger generation's level of satisfaction in business, and their subsequent leadership ability

Cases	Younger generation's level of satisfaction in family business[a]	Prior outside experience	Performance rated as	Prime factors culled from field data contributing to leadership ability
High expectation to join family business[b]				
Dawsons	#16 Moderate	Nil	Fair	Performance adequate with outside support from mentors. Resigned to being part of family business, no overt level of pleasure with the role.
	#18 Moderate	Nil	Poor	Reasonably satisfied as may not have developed skills for another workplace. Has a technical niche which he is following; moved from joint CEO role.
Emersons	#21 High	Nil	Excellent	Would have 'chosen' different career but now resigned to family business opportunity. Undertaken tertiary study to complement practical skills development. Highly respected in the industry.
	#25 Moderate	Nil	Poor	Moved in and out of family business several times. Not focused on work; very interested in money. Moved to administrative side because of a back problem.
Moderate expectation to join family businesss[b]				
Bensons	#11 High	Moderate	Good	Sufficient optimism that things can be turned around. Medium level of frustration with lack of information. Modelling some of his father's negative characteristics.
	#8 Moderate	Moderate	Good	Frustrated with current CEO's style. Uncertain about future. Practising own style (empowerment and consultative) in his business unit. Seeking outside networks to widen experience and to provide external stimulus.
Carlsons	#14 Moderate	Substantial	Fair	Apparent expectation for son to go into the business, but no encouragement to develop organisational skills. Did not get on with father. Query whether suited to business.
	#12 Low	Substantial	Good	As daughter definitely not expected to enter business but on father's death needed to take responsibility as a director.

Table 9.3   Continued

Cases	Younger generation's level of satisfaction in family business[a]	Prior outside experience	Performance rated as	Prime factors culled from field data contributing to leadership ability
Low expectation to join family business[b]				
Andersons #5 High		Substantial	Excellent	Told that job may not be available – go out and do your own thing. Developed in unrelated profession. Then retrained to be attracted to family business – since undertaken management training. Likely successor.
				Very proud and committed to be part of family business.
#3 High		Substantial	Excellent	Understood precedent that no expectation that he would be invited in. Developed successfully in own profession and own business. Assessed as having skills 'adding value' to family business so invited to join.
Fletchers #29[c] High		Substantial	Fair	The roles are in theory non-executive board roles but the exception is the Chair/MD which bridges executive/non-executive.

Notes:
[a] For each younger generation interviewee in management positions.
[b] Assessment from interview data and case scene reports.
[c] Reporting of the former CEO's expectation.
# Denotes interviewee transcript.

There was an overwhelming view from the interviewees that ideally a choice should be available to individuals to join or not to join the family business and that being coerced into the business will often lead to an unsatisfactory outcome in terms of the development of leadership ability. However, in practice the data demonstrated two extreme outcomes of high expectation to join the business, represented by the probable successor at Emersons and the current CEO at Dawsons.

The likely successor at Emersons, Elliot, admitted he had no choice when he left secondary school other than to join his father's firm, commenting that he would have disappointed his father if he had not gone into the family business. The trigger which he identified that turned his attitude and commitment to the family business around, was the suggestion from a member of the support staff that he do part-time study as this helped him to see the opportunities the business could offer him. He began to recognise the practical advice available from his father, whose technical abilities he had always respected but, by his own admission, had not fully appreciated.

At Dawsons, the current CEO had also been expected to go into the family business soon after leaving school. His comments about his own leadership abilities suggested that he was not altogether comfortable with the role of CEO and that his development for the role had not been altogether satisfactory. He demonstrated considerable unease with the responsibilities required of him as CEO and commented that he sought outside independent advice on a regular basis.

In those businesses where there was an element of choice in the decision whether or not to join the family business, there were no formal strategies to assess appropriate talent for the family business. At Bensons, having outside experience was almost enough; there was no conscious attempt to assess the performance in the former place of work although there were comments such as 'he was promoted in that company very quickly' (family member CEO interview transcript) which implied a measure of good performance. At Andersons there were informal assessments of the gaps that family members' skills and experience might fill.

The cases demonstrate a negative impact on the younger generation's leadership effectiveness (as perceived by interviewees) when they were 'expected' to join the business rather than choosing to do so. Genuine choice of entry was considered to be a valuable indicator of subsequent leadership potential. However, the lack of choice did not mean that leadership talent would not emerge. While it is generally acknowledged in organisations that companies 'buy talent when they need an immediate infusion of new skills, knowledge, and ideas' (Tobin, 1996: 144), the process may prove to be more complicated for the family business. The selection of family members for the family business should ideally be aligned to real job opportunities in the business, rather than creating a job for a family member.

The approach to work experience before joining the family business

The nature and extent of work experience prior to joining the family business were identified as a key factor influencing the subsequent development of leadership skills. Interviewees identified such experience on two levels: first, the nature of opportunities available to family members through work in the family business during their school and university holidays; second, whether or not family members had real work experience outside the family business prior to joining it.

In four cases, interviewees commented on their long-term association with the family business, including dinner-table discussion and school holiday work experience. The younger generation interviewees at Emersons and Dawsons commented that they in fact missed some of their own childhood by always being in the business during holidays. At Fletchers and Andersons, where this early experience was not evident, interviewees specifically commented that they were not exposed at home to their fathers' comments about the business. When one younger generation member subsequently joined the family business in his thirties, he considered that he was disadvantaged by this lack of 'history' about the business. He commented that family members were treated as 'out of sight, out of mind' if they had no formal contact with the day-to-day operations of the business.

However, working in the family business at an early age was not considered by the younger generation as being a replacement for outside experience as an adult. There was clearly an inverse relationship between the amount of outside experience and the expectation or assumption by the older generation that younger generation members would join the family business. While the majority of younger generation members considered work experience outside the organisation to be an essential prerequisite to joining the family business, only two older generation members agreed that it was important. The board chairmen at Dawsons and Emersons considered that their family businesses were unique and experience elsewhere would not necessarily be helpful. The younger generation members thought that outside experience would provide exposure to alternative points of view, alternative structures and alternative ways of operating. It also gave them time to contemplate whether or not they wished to join the family business; they 'learned about themselves' and 'got away from the family', supporting Handler's (1992) finding that the need for that sense of identity is strong.

In Andersons, while there was no written policy, there was a strong precedent for prior experience as a deliberate leadership development strategy. The family business relied on family members building their management experience outside the company prior to being invited to fill positions in the company. Family members were then informally assessed on their competency in their chosen fields and their ability to add value to the family business.

The experiences of the majority of interviewees concerning their informal associations with the family business as children, either around the dining-room table or working in the family business during holidays, are consistent with Longenecker and Schoen's (1978) view that successors were usually aware of the facets of the organisation, and exposed to the jargon and the organisational environment prior to employment in the family business. However, the link between subsequent leadership abilities and these early experiences was less obvious in this study than the link between work experience outside the family business. Some who had work experience in the family business while at school or during holidays talked of this work as a chore.

Attitude to formal education

Attaining formal education qualifications was perceived as being complementary to other forms of leadership development. In all except one case, at least one of the younger generation members of the family had undertaken formal tertiary education, whereas while none of the older generation CEOs had done so, most were supportive of it for their children. Most members of the younger generation took it for granted that some type of formal education beyond secondary level was crucial in order to cope with the complexities of the contemporary family business, an attitude that is consistent with the literature previously discussed (Davis and Harveston, 1998; Neubauer and Lank, 1998). However, only 20 per cent of the younger generation had postgraduate management education.

At Dawsons, where no younger generation members had formal education qualifications, a number of non-award training courses were accessed in an attempt to bridge the gap (perceived by the younger generation members) in the formal education. Not surprisingly, Dawsons was identified earlier as one of the two cases where the older generation had a 'high expectation' that the younger generation would enter the business. The Chairman expressed the view that his sons had no need to go elsewhere, and particularly not to university, because they had a family business to go into.

At Carlsons, while all interviewees thought it most probable that the former (deceased) CEO wished the business to remain in the family, he had not given the children any opportunities to be involved on their own terms, nor had he encouraged them to study an appropriate area of expertise. Both children went to university and followed professional interests unrelated to the family business. The father made no attempts to acquaint them with the operations of the family business or to equip them for a role he 'assumed' they would take on following his death. As they found their father difficult to work with, they avoided contact with the family business. In response to this somewhat negative experience, the current younger generation managers were purposefully familiarising their children with many aspects of the family business: two of the children were currently university students who had worked in the family business during holidays.

The nature of career development opportunities in the family business

Another factor seen to influence the emergence of leaders was the way in which development opportunities were provided to family members once in the family business, and whether or not those opportunities took account of prior experience. While several interviewees discussed various leadership development practices that they might wish to introduce, there was only one case in which clear guidelines for subsequent development opportunities had been established. These guidelines were not formalised in a written policy statement as recommended by Neubauer and Lank (1998: 91). However, as Neubauer and Lank's interest focused on the larger family conglomerates, the lack of formalisation found in this study for cases within the SME sector may not be unexpected nor undesirable.

Table 9.4 is a case-ordered display demonstrating the three different approaches to the way in which family members approached the teaching and learning of leadership skills and competencies (Thomas, 2000):

- *Development approach aligned with experience on entry*, giving them appropriate work commensurate with their background and experience;
- *Development approach not aligned with experience on entry*, where young family members were apprenticed from the 'shop floor', irrespective of their experience;
- *No specific development approach*, having a *laissez-faire* approach to leadership development and hoping things worked out for the best.

Table 9.4   Case-ordered display: relationship between family business approaches to developing leadership and younger generation's acceptance of that approach

Case	Prior experience	Satisfaction with development opportunities	Factors contributing to degree of satisfaction with the development opportunities
Development approach aligned with experience on entry			
Andersons	Substantial	High	Abilities assessed prior to joining family business.
			Mentored by non-family managers where possible, on entering the business.
			Family manager 'observes' board meetings.
			Managerial roles given were commensurate with ability and experience.
Bensons	Moderate	Medium	Given time to develop in outside employment.
			Perceived degree of choice as to whether or not they join the family business.
			Managerial roles established for family members to come into the business as a result of expansion and acquisition.
			Responsibilities considerable but only as far as CEO would 'let go'.
Development approach not aligned with experience on entry			
Dawsons	Nil	Low	Required to learn trade from the bottom and develop interest in the industry. 'Right way' was father's way.
			Family managers now access a number of external management development opportunities to address deficit.
			Always 'sons' of CEO and not confident in their own abilities.
			Positions into which they are 'promoted' are created positions for family members.
Emersons	Nil	Moderate	Would have liked the opportunity to work elsewhere but accepted father's offer. Shop floor experience. Shadowing in specific areas.
			Learning aspects of leadership in the business has been complemented by formal education.
No specific development approach			
Carlsons	Substantial	Low	Older generation's desire for the younger generation male to join the business was strong but no meaningful development opportunities were given to him. Father 'assumed' the son would 'come along'.
			Female director not informed about progress. She was not regarded as being an active member of the business. Chauvinistic attitude to women learning the business.
Fletchers	Substantial	Low	Previous chairman ruled with very authoritarian attitude and son (now chairman) got 'no airtime with discussions around dinner table'. 'Dad assumed he was immortal' – no conscious consideration of what would happen after his death.

Also shown in Table 9.4 are the relationships between the learning approaches and the level of satisfaction of the younger generation to that approach.

At Andersons and Bensons, the four younger generation members believed that their experience was taken into account in allocating their initial duties in the family business. However, in neither of these cases was any explicit developmental plan revealed, and the subsequent development of the younger generation members once in the businesses differed. At Andersons, the two contenders for the CEO role judged themselves to have had ample opportunity to train for that role in the family business, with development opportunities readily available and time spent with non-family mentors. The current family member CEO and chairman realised that their time in the active positions in the family business was limited and they were keen to ensure the younger generation was equipped to take over the business. One younger generation member, not yet a director, was invited to observe all board meetings to ensure he was kept aware of all activities. However, in the view of one younger generation manager, family members were treated more harshly than their non-family colleagues, as they were considered to be 'in training' for more senior roles.

At Bensons, while the positions to which the younger generation members were appointed were commensurate with their previous outside experience, their development was seen to be halted by their father's hesitancy to expose them to increased responsibility in the organisation. The family member CEO made no appointment of an acting CEO to cover his absence when he was overseas. He said that he was in touch with 'home' (home and the business spoken of as one) regularly and expected each manager to cover his (in this case) own areas.

At Dawsons and Emersons, where the learning approaches were not perceived to be aligned with the younger generation's level of experience, there were differences of opinion between the older and younger generations. At Dawsons, while the younger generation members understood they had to learn how the business operated, they did not agree with the length of time they spent on the shop floor to do so. At Emersons, the younger generation members relished the opportunity to shadow their father in the factory as they did not have the technical background they so respected in him. At Carlsons and Fletchers there was no specific approach by the older generation members to the development of leaders. The younger generation was expected to pick up what they could when they could and they were thrust into positions of responsibility without the necessary experience.

Career development for family members was not supported by any formal performance management programmes. Three cases reported using performance management for shop floor and other support staff to varying degrees. Bonuses were used for senior non-family managers in two cases, with the family member CEO in each of these cases being the main decision-maker. The criteria for the bonuses were unknown to recipients. A low number of performance management programmes is consistent with the finding by Smyrnios *et al.* (1997: 15), that only approximately 30 per cent of third- and fourth-generation Australian family businesses indicated having performance appraisal in place for family members. They also found that family business owners appeared to have a low regard for management incentives and where these were offered, they were at the owner's discretion (ibid.: 16).

While there was no evidence of career development, including 'focused learning plans', nor of the formalisation of matching successor skill gaps with development opportunities, as suggested as being beneficial by Foster (1995: 208), some informal strategies for leadership development were evident (see Table 9.4). Overall, where career development opportunities were available, albeit informally, they were found to have a positive outcome on subsequent leadership performance. This confirms Malone's (1989: 351) finding that family business participants identify with 'acts of selecting, developing, and communicating with successors [as] the actions that continue a business' rather than with more formal plans for the future which are considered too distant to be meaningful.

Conclusion

The field data from these cases revealed a variety of policies and precedents about entry of individuals into the family business and their subsequent development in the business. Even if older generation members had built the business up with the hope that younger generation members would maintain it, the need to allow them some time for reflection and outside experience was the strong message that emerged in these cases. As a minimum this would mean the individuals would not resent later in life that they knew nothing else, were good for nothing else, or wished they had at least worked in a work environment other than under their fathers or uncles or other family members. However, more tangible outcomes were perceived for this opportunity for choice and exposure: it facilitated the learning of alternative work approaches; it enabled a wider working life experience on which they could draw as their responsibilities grew; and they could judge more realistically whether or not the older generation's traditional way of doing things in the family business was the best approach available.

A challenge for some leaders in family business is to recognise the value of formal education and integrate it into the business rather than be threatened by it. A tendency to 'assume' that leadership development would occur because an individual is a member of the family should be avoided. Even if there are no formalised written development plans, some processes to address development needs, which are specific to the individual, should be set up.

Implications for theory, policy and practice

While there were no formally presented rules in these cases as proposed by Drucker (1995: 45), there was some agreement about what should be done to facilitate the emergence of leaders in the family business. This agreement can be expressed as guidelines for leadership development in the family business:

1   Where possible, ensure younger generation members want to join the family business, rather than assuming they will join; that is, provide the younger generation with a realistic choice.
2   Where possible, ensure that family members gain outside experience before joining the family business.
3   Encourage family members to gain some additional educational qualifications after secondary school before joining the family business.
4   Identify career development once in the family business which is commensurate with the individual's background and qualifications.
5   Establish a process to encourage the older generation to retire in a timely way.

The lack of homogeneity of family businesses as a sector is evident from this study. Those designing education and training programmes, as well as advisors and consultants to family businesses, should be made aware that each family business, and indeed generations within those businesses, has its own emphases for leadership development which arise from the dynamics and context of that business.

While the focus in these cases was on developing 'family' talent as potential leaders, the integration of non-family managers into the businesses is an important area for future research. Strategies are also required to ensure that future needs of those family businesses wishing to have professional, non-family managers in CEO roles, are met.

Part III

A critical discourse in studies of the small family business

10 Exploring the connection
Ethnic minority businesses and the family enterprise

Monder Ram and Trevor Jones

Introduction

The portrayal of the family as a vital support mechanism is a notable feature of the literature on ethnic minority enterprise. Indeed, the family is seen as a veritable generator of entrepreneurial activity among immigrant-origin communities. By implication the family is a provider of crucial business resources not available to 'ethnic majority' enterprise. As such, it confers a competitive advantage over mainstream businesses, which in most other respects might be assumed to have the upper hand. One of the most emphatic statements of this relationship is proffered by Sanders and Nee (1996), who portray immigrant-origin business in the USA as rooted in the social capital derived from the kind of traditional close-knit family solidarity which, it might be thought, no longer plays a central part in mainstream modern urban society. At first sight, this seems a plausible explanation. In contemporary Britain as in the USA, ethnic minority entrepreneurs display a remarkably high profile among the ranks of the business-owning class, with self-employment rates among the South Asian (Indian, Pakistani, Bangladeshi) population, for example, standing at least 60 per cent higher than that of the white population (Barrett *et al.*, 2001).

Given that these communities were initially founded by migrants recruited to the very bottom layers of the British labour market, their subsequent entrepreneurial prowess is at the very least thought-provoking, all the more so in view of the racist exclusionary processes to which they have been subject (Miles, 1982; Brah, 1996). Even taking account of the many East-African Asian refugees who arrived with previous business track records, the general impression is of a significant socio-economic role reversal in which the disabilities of racialisation, migrancy, lack of human capital and low economic status have, on the face of things, been transformed into entrepreneurial enrichment and upward class mobility (Srinavasan, 1995).

British Asians are of course simply one representative of that near-universal phenomenon, the entrepreneurial minority, the immigrant group usually from a Third World place of origin seeking salvation in modern urban society through independent business ownership. Historically the phenomenon has been most marked – and most remarked upon – in the USA, where immigrants have been over-represented among the self-employed since the nineteenth century (Light,

1984) but more recently it has been noted in various West European countries (Rath, 2000), Australia (Collins *et al.*, 1995) and Canada (Razin and Langlois, 1996). Among the various explanations offered – labour market exclusion, 'hungry fighter syndrome', cultural value systems placing a premium on independence, industriousness and thrift – the family as entrepreneurial support mechanism looms large (Ram *et al.*, 2000).

In this chapter, it is argued that ethnic minority business is indeed often deeply embedded in family processes, but that this relationship needs to be qualified in several ways. First, it cannot be assumed that the influence of the family is necessarily positive in all circumstances. Nor is it sufficient to say that the influence of the family in business is exclusively confined to migrant groups from pre-modern societies, for whom the 'traditional' family is part of their tradition. There are also question marks over the standard depiction of the typical ethnic minority business family as a non-conflictual unified whole, devoid of internal tensions between generations and sexes. Prior to amplifying these points by reference to recent research on African-Caribbean and South Asian enterprise in Britain, relevant literature in this field is reviewed to identify salient theoretical issues.

Ethnic minority businesses: the discourse

Much of the essential thrust of the burgeoning literature on this issue (Bonacich and Modell, 1980; Werbner, 1984; Kim and Huhr, 1985; Nee and Wong, 1985; Wilson and Stanworth, 1988; Light and Bonacich, 1988; Fernandez-Kelly and Garcia, 1990; Waldinger *et al.*, 1990; Zhou, 1992; Srinavasan, 1995; Ram *et al.*, 2000) is encapsulated in Sanders and Nee's (1996) recent analysis of the family as social capital which, though almost entirely confined to American empirical evidence, contains much that is universally applicable. Controlling for a range of non-family variables, these authors find that self-employment among members of the Chinese and other migrant-origin communities is positively correlated with marriage, number of children in the household and other family variables. According to Sanders and Nee, the logic behind this is that the family represents an invaluable source of social capital, both tangible and intangible. Here we would stress that, given the inherently insecure, precarious, vulnerable, isolated and self-motivated nature of self-employment (see Granger *et al.*, 1995, on the contrasts between employed and self-employed individuals' relationship to work), any form of collective material and moral support can make the difference between success and failure; and even determine the business entry decision itself.

At the material level, the ethnic minority family typically offers an informal (non-market) source of vital businesses resources (capital and labour in particular) which would be far more costly and unreliable if obtained via the market. More intangibly but equally importantly the family fosters an ethos of 'mutual dependence' (Sanders and Nee, 1996: 233), 'mutual obligation and trust' (ibid.: 237) and 'common self-interests' (ibid.: 246), with the family seen as a collective entity for the common good.

In the matter of raising capital, it is clear that the capacity to draw upon interest-free loans, pooled savings and other forms of subsidy from family members (Werbner, 1984; Sanders and Nee, 1996) confers substantial cost advantages over competitors who are obliged to rely on the financial market. For British ethnic minority business people, the question of access to alternative informal finance becomes even more urgent in the light of the realisation that British 'banks are not equal opportunity providers of credit' (Jones *et al.*, 1994b: 164; Barrett, 1999). In such circumstances, the ability to mobilise family finance takes on yet greater significance still. Thus the ultimate contribution of family finance is its function as a fall-back, plugging the gaps and compensating for the inadequacies of an external financial environment which is often hostile to ethnic minority business owners. As Sanders and Nee (1996: 233) observe, family financing takes a variety of forms, including loans between members and free accommodation arrangements, which 'reduce living costs and promote the accumulation of financial capital'. Perhaps the most significant practice is 'the pooling of financial resources' (ibid.), a practice well described by Werbner (1984) in her portrayal of British Pakistani business families, where the earnings of individual members of the household are treated as part of the collective family fund. This is the 'family business' in its purest and most literal sense, an institution in which the boundaries between work and personal relations are completely blurred, so that the family *is* the business and vice versa. Indeed, the forms of capital-raising taking place within such an institution derive their strength from the very fact that they are based on 'interpersonal bonds' (Sanders and Nee, 1996: 246), relationships of trust (Werbner, 1984) which eliminate the insecurity and risk inherent in the impersonal marketplace.

In addition to funding, the ethnic minority family is also seen as an invaluable source of labour power, enabling the family firm to make reductions in operating and transaction costs. For immigrant-origin firms, this enables competitive niches to be carved out; immigrant entrepreneurs have tended to gravitate towards various labour-intensive sectors of the economy which have been gradually abandoned by indigenous entrepreneurs (Light, 1984; Light and Bonacich, 1988; Jones *et al.*, 1999). As documented by writers such as Waldinger *et al.* (1990) in the USA and Phizacklea (1990) and Ram (1994a, 1994b) for the UK, one version of this is for ethnic minority firms to arise in sectors like the clothing industry, for whom a First World location has become progressively uncompetitive in world markets. Hence, over the past few decades, the survival of clothing manufacture in Western Europe and North America has been largely dependent on the presence of Third World-origin entrepreneurs. For example, Turks in the Netherlands (Rath, 2002), South Asians in Britain (Ram, 1994a, 1994b), Chinese and Koreans in the USA (Waldinger *et al.*, 1990) are seen as having the capacity to mobilise ample supplies of low-cost labour from kinship and ethnic networks.

A second form of labour-intensive niche is low-order retailing where, in societies like Britain, fewer and fewer indigenous corner shopkeepers have been willing and able to work the kind of burdensome hours necessary to stay afloat in face of the lethal threat posed by supermarket retailing in a society of mobile and demanding consumers (Barrett *et al.*, 2001). In Britain, South Asian and African-Caribbean entrepreneurs are especially prominent in branches like food retailing and (especially in the Asian case) confectionery-tobacco-news (CTN), where they have progressively displaced the previous incumbents in many areas (Aldrich *et al.*, 1989). Since these retail branches impose particularly heavy demands on labour through long and unsocial opening hours, family labour comes into its own in the fullest possible sense, often working in circumstances unacceptable to hired workers beyond the family circle. Yet, given the diminutive scale typical of these micro-businesses, it is usually possible to operate entirely within the confines of family labour power, much of which is uncosted (Jones *et al.*, 1994a). Significantly here, one early British research study found Asian small retailers as both having larger families and sustaining longer opening hours than their white counterparts (Aldrich *et al.*, 1981).

While clothing manufacture and low-order retailing might be regarded as abandoned niches, other more positive markets have also opened up for ethnic minority suppliers. Outstanding here is the restaurant trade where, throughout much of the advanced Western world, demographic and cultural change has created a growing demand for 'ethnic' eating-out (Ram *et al.*, 2002). Yet despite enjoying the double advantage of buoyant demand for their product and an ethnic monopoly of supply, ethnic minority restaurateurs and take-away opera-tors are by no means guaranteed a lucrative easy ride. Recent British research on South Asian restaurants confirms that, as well as being subject to ferocious competition, the inherent nature of the business imposes long and unsocial hours, once again placing a heavy premium on family labour (Ram *et al.*, 2002). Equally this applies to the take-away trade, where the Chinese are heavily involved and heavily reliant on family members, who account for the vast bulk of the work performed (Parker, 1994). By contrast, in the restaurant trade, the scale of the operation is often too great for the immediate family to sustain, necessi-tating wider labour recruitment from extended kin and from the ethnic community. Even so, the immediate family tends to be located at the core of the operation, usually in management roles (Ram *et al.*, 2000). In this respect, it closely resembles the typical overseas Chinese family business where, even in fairly large-scale operations, immediate family members continue to predomi-nate in top management roles, while 'other strategic posts are usually reserved for close relatives' (Weidenbaum, 1996: 142).

A 'family ethos'?

In order to account properly for the kind of family work input described here, we need to go beyond immediate material considerations and consider once again the question of *ethos*. Materially, of course, family workers tend to be cheaper and more productive than outsiders (Sanders and Nee, 1996), but this is only part of the story. In the highly competitive labour-intensive sectors charac-teristic of ethnic minority enterprise, they are often required to deliver this self-sacrificing industriousness in circumstances that would probably not be tolerated by any worker bound only by rational contractual obligations. Moreover, they are also subject to a high degree of time- and job-flexibility and have been seen by some as veritable exemplars of the flexible production that drives the new post-Fordist economy (J.L. Ward, 1987). Partly their motivation stems from their direct financial stake in the enterprise but essentially the relationship is cemented by non-monetary values such as emotional commitment, bonds of loyalty and traditionalist moral authority.

For Pakistanis in Britain, various authors have described a system of family obligations, in which it is virtually automatically assumed that members will contribute work to the family business from quite a young age (Dahya, 1973; Werbner, 1984). Essentially this is a classic patriarchal regime, whose working arrangements stem from the moral authority of the male 'head of household'. A similar picture of benevolent authoritarianism emerges of overseas Chinese enterprise, predominantly family firms headed by a 'paterfamilias, all-powerful in both social and economic spheres ... within the family, confidence in his judgement borders on the absolute' (Weidenbaum, 1996: 141). Interestingly both Chinese and Pakistani family business values are argued to be underpinned by religious traditions, though in the one case these are Confucian, while in the other they are Islamic. Elsewhere these values have been pinned to Sikhism (Helweg, 1986) and Hinduism (Lyon, 1973), a somewhat sweeping picture of Eastern religions as the key to family business success. As we shall see, this particularistic tendency to attach certain entrepreneurial attitudes and behaviour to specific ethno-cultural groups is problematic (Ram *et al.*, 2000).

Whatever the origin of these values, what is unarguable is that they promote a very high degree of trust within the family workforce and indeed this trust element might be held to be the decisive advantage of family labour for the ethnic minority entrepreneur. Furthermore, if Weidenbaum's (1996: 143) assertion that 'within traditional Chinese culture, you can only trust close relatives' is applicable to other migrant communities from traditional societies, then this would go far in explaining the widespread preference for family labour within ethnic minority enterprise (Ram, 1994a). Trust is clearly important in working relationships. At the extreme, trust may even allow the family firm to breach normal limitations on business activity since, for example, 'family labour can be trusted in under-the-counter cash transactions aimed at evading taxes and other state regulations' (Sanders and Nee, 1996: 233; see Ram *et al.*, 2001, for discussion of responses by Asian firms to the National Minimum Wage).

It is important to note that, while the above reasoning seems to have wide application especially to Asian origin communities, it cannot be applied in a blanket fashion to ethnic minority entrepreneurs *per se*. On the contrary, the literature notes sharp inter-group differences in propensity for self-employment, with the role of the family once more invoked as a possible explanation. Both in Britain and the USA, African-origin people have been singled out as singularly lacking in family resources and other forms of social capital, and as entrepreneurial 'under-achievers' in consequence (Blaschke *et al.*, 1990; J.L. Ward, 1991; see also Cashmore, 1991 for a critical review of the argument). Because of their slave history, it is argued, African-Caribbean and African-American people have suffered something tantamount to cultural genocide, one of the chief casualties of which has been any kind of stable family life. Certainly it is observably true that in Britain African-Caribbeans display almost a polar opposite profile to that of South Asians, being not only sharply under-represented in self-employment but also with an over-large share of single-person and lone-parent households (ONS, 1996). One interpretation would be that they palpably lack the collective resources necessary to support them in self-employed business. Less obviously, there are other probably more potent forces at work here, a matter to be discussed in the final section of this chapter.

Exploring the connection: theoretical issues

During the early phase of ethnic business studies, the kind of reasoning outlined above rested heavily (if often implicitly) upon that tried and trusted classical model, the supposed dichotomy between pre-modern and modern society. In this view, immigrant groups like Chinese Americans or British Bangladeshis are essentially represented as islands of traditionalism in a sea of modernity, stubbornly retaining their heritage cultures within close-knit communities, socially (and often spatially) isolated from contact with the mainstream (Bonacich and Modell, 1980; Robinson, 1986). Frequently this exclusiveness is reinforced by chain migration 'whereby the immigration process itself selects immigrants who are integrated into these networks' (Metcalf *et al.*, 1996: 7). Essentially the model is one of 'acculturation lag' as Light and Bonacich (1988) put it, with various traditional institutions continuing to thrive as part of the heritage culture within ethnic minority communities even as they wither away among the general population. Thus the family, often embedded in extended kinship networks, is retained as a highly valued and practically useful organisation within ethnic minority culture at the same time as it is replaced in mainstream society by single-person households, pared-down nuclear units and various other manifestations of the rampant 'narcissistic' individualism which is taken to be one of the hallmarks of late capitalist culture.

Though at first sight this ethnic minority cultural retentionism might appear as a social and economic disability, their high profile in self-employed business activity immediately belies this impression, suggesting that actually it may represent a crucial source of collective strength. This is well put by Metcalf *et al.* (1996: 7) who argue that ethnic minorities 'can create resources which offset the harshness of the environment they encounter', and can succeed entrepreneurially where 'social structures exist through which members of an ethnic group are attached to one another and if these structures can be utilised for economic purposes'. Implicitly this statement is consistent with the 'new economic sociology' (Flap *et al.*, 1999: 146), an increasingly influential perspective which recognises that economic activity, for all its inherent calculative rationality, is also based on warm-blooded human social relationships. Hence the importance attached by writers like Sanders and Nee to the concept of *social capital*, defined by Flap *et al.* (ibid.: 147) as 'the resources that are available to a person through his or her social relations with others'. Such resources are likely to be richest for individuals who are members of a social network of people collectively bonded by powerful reciprocal ties of interdependence. Social networks, according to Flap *et al.* (ibid.: 147), 'are a capital good that helps to produce goals that would otherwise be difficult to achieve' and, in the light of all that has been argued so far in this chapter, it becomes clear that the ethnic minority business family is the social network *par excellence*. Except of course in the case of groups like African-Caribbeans, for whom this logic still applies but in the inverse manner; i.e. a lack of social capital and networks acts to retard their entrepreneurialism.

Evidently, then, the recognition of social capital has added a new and distinctly more progressive twist to theories of ethnic business resources. No longer are ethnic community institutions to be seen as aberrations that, despite their archaism, may nevertheless be translated into commercial advantage within the context of modern society. Now they are reconstructed as cutting edge weapons of competitive success in that society, so that what was once construed as 'pre-modern' is now effectively translated into 'post-modern'. This intellectual development is to be welcomed for its rejection of the previous rather condescending depiction of 'traditional' cultural institutions and its substitution of a perspective more consistent with contemporary multiculturalism. At the same time, however, this does not necessarily eliminate all possible flaws. As we shall see in the following sections there remains a range of issues to be resolved concerning the hidden complexities of the ethnic business family; and the question of how far the ethnic minority business family should be seen as an exotic special case (Ram and Jones, 1998).

The ethnic business family – accelerator or brake?

For all his stress on the positive qualities of the overseas Chinese business family, Weidenbaum is also prepared to acknowledge its limitations, which may be quite acute in some respects: 'There are serious disadvantages associated with the family-run business. Keeping control within the family almost inevitably restricts the size and especially the complexity to which it can grow' (1996: 143). Independently of Weidenbaum, this view has also been expressed in respect of South Asian entrepreneurs in Britain. For example, Basu (1998) finds that family contributions to capital investment are only very weakly related to business success. Ram and Holliday (1993b) argue that the family orientation of British Asian firms can, in certain circumstances, stand in the way of economically rational notions of business practice, which ought to rest upon management and labour skills and adequate funding rather than nepotistic blood ties.

Placing this in a broader context, Ram and Hillin (1994) reason that future development in the Asian enterprise economy needs to 'break out' from the labour-intensive, low-profit corner shop markets in which they are concentrated. Yet reorientation towards new markets in such sectors as high-order retailing, manufacturing, producer services and high-technology production cannot be sustained without parallel changes in organisation and operating methods. Informal social capital may well be an ideal resource base for operating in localised abandoned niches of the economy, such as inner city corner shop retailing, where many firms can depend on a virtually captive clientele and where there is a high premium on labour-intensiveness to sustain long opening hours.

Moving into the mainstream, however, means competing in highly desirable markets against well-established and well-equipped indigenous rivals, a situation which requires 'working smart' rather than merely working hard (Jones *et al.*, 1994a). Here social capital tends to be replaced as a key resource by human capital, in the form of management and labour skills, qualifications and credentials; and financial capital through access to market sources of finance. In this much more professional environment, the seamless intertwining of family and work spheres (Finch and Mason, 1993) starts to become unpicked, as commercial imperatives become ever more powerful and the need for efficiency must eventually take precedence over 'incompetent and untrained relatives' (Weidenbaum, 1996: 143). At some point, the entrepreneur is faced with difficult choices about how far to prioritise profit-seeking efficiency over such typical family firm practices as job creation and business training for relatives (Riordan and Riordan, 1993).

Hence, over-dependence on the family can pose an actual barrier to development. It is at the level of management that this contradiction is perhaps most acute, as demonstrated by studies of South Asians in the West Midlands clothing sector where, as Ram (1994a) discovers, many firms tend to under-perform because of inefficient and unsystematic organisational practices. Significantly here, Ram documents many cases of family resistance to the hiring of qualified outsiders, even where recommended by business consultants. In a similar vein, Flap *et al.* (2000) refer to the problem of having too much social capital, so that non-economic influences interfere in the design and implementation of entrepreneurial strategies.

Exploring the connection: harmony or conflict?

In itself this tension between 'familial' and economic goals raises further questions about the idealistic stereotype of the ethnic minority business family as a unified collective working for common ends. Essentially, this idealistic tendency has been part of a liberal multiculturalist agenda (Kundnani, 2000) celebrating minority cultures as sources of enrichment for their adopted society and centrally concerned with promoting minority rights within that society. More recently, however, there is increasing acknowledgement that minority rights may in some circumstances clash head-on with individual rights (Deveaux, 2000) and that within ethnic minority communities and families there may well be conflicts of interest along gender and generational lines. In the case of gender, there is now an accumulated body of research which argues that the notion of the family as functioning for the common good is an artificial construction which masks its potential to serve as an arena of exploitation in which the role of women is often subordinated (Ram *et al.*, forthcoming; see also Hoel, 1984; Ram, 1994a). Particularly trenchant in their unmasking of this hitherto hidden patriarchal exploitation are writers like Mitter (1986) and Phizacklea (1990), who argue that family ideology acts as a means for reproducing a cheap and docile female labour force. This applies with special force to the Asian-owned clothing industry, whose viability largely rests on the availability of low-cost, loyal, female workers, both family and non-family.

It is not only as workers that women's role in the small enterprise is often unacknowledged. Reflecting a wider picture (Metcalf *et al.*, 1996; Basu, 1998), the direct involvement of wives in Ram *et al.*'s (forthcoming) study tended to be rare in the South Asian-owned restaurants. 'Religio-cultural' reasons for the absence of South Asian women's formal participation in the business were discernible in the responses of many of the Bangladeshi and Pakistanis owners:

> She [has been] a housewife all the time. Most of the restaurateurs' wives have never worked and are housewives. This is common in the Bangladeshi community ... We as a family and community-wise, we do not like our wives to work. That's how the family goes.
>
> (Ram *et al.*, forthcoming)

This finding seems to concur with Metcalf *et al.* (1996: 34) on the matter of women's involvement in the family business. They found that four-fifths of Indians compared to only two-fifths of Pakistanis agreed that wives should work in the family business if they wanted; indeed, most Pakistani respondents objected to married women performing any paid work. Although wives rarely played a direct role in Ram *et al.*'s study, it should be noted that they were often engaged in key 'enabling roles' (Wheelock and Baines, 1998). This involved primary responsibility for the domestic sphere, including looking after the children and maintaining the home.

Exploring the connection: universalism versus particularism

The tensions described above are not necessarily confined to Asians or indeed to any other specified ethno-cultural group (Riordan and Riordan, 1993). There are numerous grounds for arguing that the kinds of conflict described for Asian family firms are best seen as variants of a more generalised phenomenon rather than as specific ethno-cultural phenomena. First, the family firm itself is by no means a characteristically 'ethnic' institution. According to Beehr *et al.* (1997), family firms – defined as businesses worked by the owner and one or more relatives – comprise the overwhelming majority of the total organisational units in the modern economy. They estimate that family businesses comprise as much as 95 per cent in the USA (Beehr *et al.*, 1997). For Britain, Wheelock and Baines (1998) found a smaller though still significant proportion of small enterprises to be family businesses, typically husband–wife partnerships. To a great extent, this reflects the size-skewedness of the modern economy, in which a relative handful of giants account for the bulk of production but where the great majority of economic units are actually small and medium sized (Storey, 1994). Basic though this point may seem, it is easily overlooked and it is all too easy to infer from sources like Sanders and Nee (1996) that immigrant minorities enjoy some kind of monopoly of the family firm, whereas the evidence suggests there is little or no significant bias towards selected groups.

Shifting the focus now to more specific issues, it would seem that conflicts depicted as inherent to the ethnic minority firms are also part of a universal family business genre. Thus, the contradiction between management by family members and management by professionals (as discussed in two previous sections) is probably best seen as less an expression of Chinese or South Asian attributes and more an expression of a generalised contradiction between economic rationality and what Riordan and Riordan (1993) call 'noneconomic … personal family goals'. Here it should be pointed out that, while the family firm certainly is an integrated whole in which the spheres of work and life are inextricably bound together (Beehr *et al.*, 1997), the two spheres are at the same time contradictory in many vital respects, pulling against one in a state of constant tension. This clash of opposites is inherent in all family firms irrespective of the national origins, culture or religion of the actors involved. For example, in their study of micro-business households, Baines and Wheelock (1998b: 590) noted the 'very considerable turbulence in owner-managers' employing experiences'. They provide ample illustrations of how unfavourable the often-noted solution of employing family and friends actually is. Employers often struggled to create understandings and establish working relationships with newly recruited employees. Similarly non-specific are the role conflicts engendered by this opposition between work and personal spheres. As Beehr *et al.* (1997) point out, conflicting roles can afflict workers in any kind of organisation but are more likely within the family firm, where the individual's role within the household can clash with their work role, with different behaviour expected in the two differing situations.

Alongside these issues, it is also necessary to address the pervasive view of ethnic minority business as being unusually and specifically advantaged by family resources in a way denied to others. Recent comparative research in Britain, which analyses ethnic minority entrepreneurs alongside their white counterparts, suggests that this point is frequently over-argued, resulting in a misleading caricature of reality. For example, Jones *et al.*'s (1994a and b) nationwide survey of Asian, African-Caribbean and white firms found that the typical Asian organisation is a very small micro-business, in which the labour of the proprietor accounts for the overwhelming bulk of the firm's work; and which makes no more use of family labour than its white counterpart. Moreover, in the matter of capital-raising, it was found that Asians are actually less likely than whites to raise money from family and friends and that the most frequent users of this source were African-Caribbeans, supposedly devoid of such social capital

(Jones *et al.*, 1994b). Similarly, in the Ram *et al.* (2000) study of the Birmingham restaurant trade, it becomes evident that vital family work inputs are by no means confined to Asians, with white and African-Caribbean owners also the beneficiaries of decisive contributions from spouses and even from members of their extended families also. In the broadest sense, this chimes in with work by sociologists such as Wilson and Pahl (1988) and Scott (1998) suggesting that reports of the death of the family in modern 'ethnic majority' society have been much exaggerated.

Conclusion

This chapter has sought to reveal some of the complexities of an issue that appears relatively simple at first sight. The attractiveness of the classic model of the ethnic minority family business as a special form of social capital derives from its apparent explanatory power in addressing the paradox of the entrepreneurial achievements of disadvantaged migrant communities. As we have now seen, however, the pure version of this model rests upon questionable and sometimes untenable assumptions. At its most literal, it requires us to believe in a linear model of development, which presents traditionalism and modernity in a way that has been undermined by our better understanding of the workings of contemporary social and cultural change. Because of this it is very important that discussions of the ethnic business family – and indeed all other aspects of ethnic enterprise – are conducted with reference to broader academic discourse and not restricted to the narrow confines of cultural approaches to ethnic minority business activity. With this in mind, two broad external themes have been alluded to in this chapter: first, the economic sociology perspective, which insists that those activities generally classified as 'economic' or 'entrepreneurial' are essentially grounded in social relationships; second, the recent re-evaluation of the family, which rejects the thesis that 'modernity' has rendered this institution extinct for all practical purposes. The first of these reminds us that the business resources derived from social capital and social networks are not the exclusive preserve of any given national-origin or religious group. The second, more specifically, reminds us that the family, that most obvious of entrepreneurial social networks, is much more ethnically generalised than is sometimes portrayed.

11 A household-based approach to the small business family

Susan Baines, Jane Wheelock
and Elizabeth Oughton

Introduction

Our contribution to this book concerns the interaction of household and economic life for people who depend, in whole or in part, on micro-businesses for their livelihoods. It is increasingly recognised in accounts of the labour market that systems of production and reproduction do not operate autonomously but that labour markets and households interact continuously (Bruegel *et al.*, 1998). Moreover, there is now a growing volume of research suggesting that a micro-business is as likely to be a household as an individual undertaking. Yet small enterprise policy rhetoric for the most part remains rooted in a model of business behaviour based on *individual* rational choice. That is, a model borrowed from economics and applied to many areas of policy, as well as to other academic disciplines. The result is an asocial view of economic behaviour which conceptualises economic activity as carried out by isolated individuals. It is our argument in this chapter that the world of the micro-business should rather be understood in the context of changes in labour markets and household livelihoods. Moreover, if social scientists are to make sense of micro-business behaviour, analysis which takes account of the household is essential.

The first section of this chapter overviews changes in the institutions of work and the household in the post-war period and argues that the growth of self-employment and small businesses as forms of livelihood should be understood against that background. In the next section we expand upon our reasons for looking at micro-business behaviour through the lens of the household. We start from the household as the livelihood unit, recognising that a micro-business may be just one element in a 'jigsaw' of components which provide for individuals within a household. We outline a schematic representation of how the micro-business is embedded in the household and its wider economic and social context. There follows a summary of empirical evidence from research that starts at the level of the business household, rather than the individual businessperson (classically the entrepreneur). As we shall demonstrate, our studies of micro-business households in urban and rural settings have shown a distinctive pattern of a return to 'old ways of working', whether this be in the form of long hours for low rates of return or to traditionally gendered work roles. This raises questions about the direction of small business policy-making which we take up in the conclusion to the chapter.

Understanding businesses and households against a background of economic restructuring

Only a quarter of a century ago self-employment and micro-businesses were thought to be marginal and residual in developed economies. Marx described the 'petite bourgeoisie' as a legacy of an earlier type of production doomed to wither away. Steindl (1945) saw small businesses as characterised by low wages and insecurity. Their survival, he argued, was thus dependent on factors 'not very creditable to our economic system' (ibid.: 61). Bechhofer *et al.* (1974) argued that the apparent individualism and independence of the petite bourgeoisie often turned to a form of serfdom. Over the past two and a half decades, however, there has been a shift in the economic formation from a 'regime of security' during the long post-war boom, to one of insecurity (Wheelock, 1999a). This change has gone alongside trends towards more individualised forms of work, including small business and self-employment. An industry of enterprise promotion has been developed in many countries as governments look to small enterprises to create new jobs to replace old ones (Bridge *et al.*, 1998). The United Kingdom, which once pioneered the standardisation of work, now pioneers its individualisation in 'a precarious new culture of independence' (Beck, 2000: 54).

How has the shift to a regime of insecurity come about? On the labour demand side the hollowing out of large institutions, whether in the public or the private sector, through an increasing use of market mechanisms such as outsourcing has provided a means of offloading increased economic insecurity onto those in the least powerful position to avoid it: small contractors and the self-employed. On the labour supply side, household livelihoods are now rarely dependent upon the family wage of a male breadwinner supporting a home-making wife, the model under the post-war regime of security. That gendered model came under increasing strain from many causes including more insecure labour markets, the abandonment of Keynesian employment policies, more means-tested welfare benefits, a new wave of women's liberation and aspirations for higher living standards (O'Hara, 1995; Bruegel *et al.*, 1998). The result has been a shift in the predominant pattern of household provisioning from the family *wage* to family *employment*, with all adults earning (Wheelock, 1999b). Although the family employment model was the most common development after the long post-war boom, a further contrasting model became increasingly persistent: the long-term benefits-dependent household. Two different tendencies gave rise to this. First, there were increasing rates of family breakdown due to divorce and separation. Second, labour market and benefits changes meant that many men were unable to earn a family wage, while at the same time it did not make sense for the family to earn thanks to the constraints of an insecure labour market (Jordan *et al.*, 1992; Nelson and Smith, 1999).

Business start-up was encouraged as a direct alternative to benefit dependency under the Conservative administrations of the 1980s and 1990s in Britain (MacDonald, 1996), and this remains true under New Labour. Recently government publications on small business policy have associated it with action to reduce social exclusion, proposing that barriers to business start-up for disadvantaged groups (e.g. inner city dwellers) should be removed. (See, for example, DTI, 2000.) Enterprise culture policies rely on personal motivation, attitude shifts and behavioural change – basically psychological concepts – as both instruments and targets of economic policy (Gray, 1998). That approach overlooks the growing empirical evidence that self-employment and micro-enterprise should be seen as 'family self-employment', essentially a variant on the family employment model.

A few large-scale surveys conducted in the 1990s offered empirical evidence that family participation in small and micro-businesses in the UK is the norm rather than the exception (Rosa *et al.*, 1994; Dunn and Hughes, 1995; Poutziouris and Chittenden, 1996; Cromie *et al.*, 1999a). In studies of ethnic minority-owned businesses the central importance of familial and community resources has often been stressed. Although the picture accepted in popular imagination is that family labour is typical of Asian-owned micro-businesses, there is evidence that family labour is a traditional and important feature of small businesses which does not stem from ethnic origin so much as from the intrinsic disadvantage of small business enterprise (Jones *et al.*, 1994a). A qualitative study of a subgroup of micro-business owners, low-income self-employed parents, found that certain forms of self-employment nominally carried out by men are often in practice heavily dependent on the participation of their spouses (Corden and Eardley, 1999). Our empirical research on micro-businesses,[1] as we shall demonstrate below, has shown that their much cited flexibility characteristically involves a return to distinctly old ways of working. These ways of working include long hours, the use of the family home as a workplace, a gender-stereotypical division of labour and co-operative, reciprocal values operating at the level of the household. Such a precarious economic existence, with heavy reliance on household labour, never ceased to exist for many small-scale traders although it increasingly came to look anachronistic (Bechhofer *et al.*, 1974). That is why we have described new micro-businesses in the 1990s as a re-invented form of the traditional business family (Mariussen *et al.*, 1997; Baines and Wheelock, 2000).

Conceptualising the micro-business household

Let us briefly put the argument for using the household as a focus for research in general terms before going on to elaborate the specific case of the micro-business. The foundation for economic behaviour lies in provisioning people's needs. Needs are composed not just of material wants, but also comprise the ways in which women and men – in relating with others – create and achieve lives of 'human flourishing'. Focusing upon provisioning highlights the mediating role of the household, within which economic actors develop their beliefs and contextualise their behaviour (Wheelock and Oughton, 1996). In our analysis we follow Nancy Folbre's (1994) view of the economy as a set of structured constraints in which assets, rules, norms and preferences all form part of the determination of individual behaviour. For provisioning is a social process, where – since most people live in households – household-level analysis of behaviour provides the most appropriate starting point. Thus we approach the micro-business from an understanding that it is the household that is the economic provisioning unit for individuals. This provides an essential counterweight to ideas that the household (or the micro-business) can be modelled as though a single economically rational individual were acting as proxy for all.

We turn now to a further exploration of our conceptualisation which examines the way in which the micro-business is embedded in the household and its wider social and economic context. Since provisioning is a social process, we must consider the business within a set of household social relations. Household provisioning may be dependent on a complex set of activities of which the business is only one part. Figure 11.1 shows that households may provision themselves largely from one or more businesses (B), with additional elements from the state (S) and the household itself (H), but additionally from participation in the labour market (M) (Wheelock, 1996). We posit that business and household social relations overlap to a greater or lesser extent in the partial containment of the business (B) within the household (H). Both the business and the household are embedded within wider family (F) and local and community relations (C). The arrows depict movement between different elements of the models. Arrow 1a describes the contribution of household members to the business in terms of financial, human and social capital. This is one of the senses in

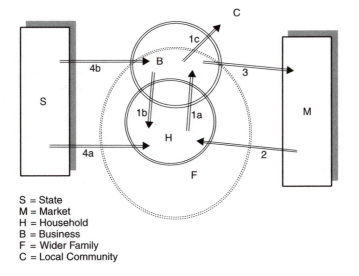

S = State
M = Market
H = Household
B = Business
F = Wider Family
C = Local Community

Figure 11.1   A schema of the micro-business as embedded in the household

which the business is embedded within the household. Arrows 1b and c describe the contribution of the business to the household and local community in terms of income and employment opportunities. Arrow 2 depicts the earning of income from the labour market by members of the household outside the business, while arrow 3 shows the flow of goods and services between the business and the market. Arrows 4a and b show the ways in which the state may support the household and the business via family income support schemes and business subsidies respectively. This simplified schema allows us better to understand the attitude and behaviour of the micro-business in relation to the wider economic environment.

Our next task is to apply this schema in the light of empirical evidence that arises from undertaking research at the level of the business household. We start by outlining general levels of household embeddedness from a review of recent studies of urban and rural micro-businesses, to provide support for the overall conceptualisation represented in Figure 11.1. In the following sections two aspects of this schema are considered in more detail: (1) the contribution of family members to the business in the form of human capital, highlighting interaction between the spheres of the business (B) and the household (H); and (2) the 'jigsaw' of livelihood elements assembled to provision the household, where business household (B, H) interaction with the market (M) and state (S) spheres are also considered.

The micro-business as embedded in the household

At the end of the 1980s, the 'decade of enterprise', Jane Wheelock conducted a pilot investigation of micro-businesses in Wearside in the North East of England.[2] She found that their survival often depended on a very specific form of flexibility based on self-exploitation within the business family (Wheelock, 1992). This was strikingly at odds with the model of business behaviour based on individual rational choice which dominated academic and policy oriented discussion of entrepreneurial behaviour and business performance. How typical was this resort to pre-modern practices of the new enterprises which had been founded in increasing numbers under the enterprise policies of the Thatcher administration? Wearside had historically depended on shipbuilding and suffered extreme disadvantage in the 1980s. Perhaps the presence of a 'familial economic unit' in the late twentieth century was a function of severe decline of traditional employing industries and lack of economic opportunities. Evidence from other research with which to make comparisons across different kinds of location was lacking. It was rare at that time for academic or policy-oriented enquiries into small businesses in industrialised urban settings to forefront, or even to notice, the household and family.

A larger study followed the Wearside research, using a combination of survey and in-depth methods to investigate the internal and external resources drawn upon by micro-businesses in two urban locations: the city of Newcastle upon Tyne in the North East of England and the new town Milton Keynes in the

South East.[3] In accordance with policy concerns this focused on survival and growth. The research was distinctive in small business studies in that it examined the links between market and non-market activities inside the business household and focused on a 'new' economic sector, business services. In contrast to longer-established sectors (e.g. shop-keeping, construction, farming, clothing manufacture) business services are not readily associated with tradition or with the family. Moreover, business services had experienced rapid expansion in the 1980s. It was therefore not surprising that the 200 businesses in the study proved to be relatively young, although that was not a criterion for selection.

The micro-businesses in Newcastle upon Tyne and Milton Keynes, then, were recently founded ventures in an expanding sector associated with a modern economy. Nevertheless only an exceptional minority bore any resemblance to dynamic and innovative models of business behaviour. The few owners who sought and achieved growth were the most energetic in seeking out information, support and ideas from people and organisations outside the business and the family. Owners in this minority were also the least likely to embed their economic behaviour in social relations with their immediate family.

Here our emphasis is not growth, but a subject of much more concern to most micro-business owners: the survival and flourishing of households dependent on micro-businesses and self-employment. The relationship between micro-business growth, family and wider network support which came out of this study has been written up in detail elsewhere (Baines and Wheelock, 1997; Baines *et al.*, 1997; Baines and Wheelock, 1998a; Chell and Baines, 2000). Pursuit of a business livelihood was closely integrated into the household, as in farming and other traditional sectors. This demonstrated that, with a handful of exceptions, the everyday experience of owners and their families resembled distinctly old ways of working described as anachronistic in the mid-twentieth century (Steindl, 1945; Bechhofer *et al.*, 1974). This was as true in a 'new' town in the south of England with a service-oriented economic base and relatively low unemployment, as in the North East where Wheelock's pilot study had been undertaken, and where others have noted the presence of precarious, survival self-employment (Storey and Strange, 1992; MacDonald, 1996).

In rural areas micro-businesses are much more significant providers of employment and services than their urban counterparts. Indeed, rural economies are overwhelmingly made up of small businesses (Lowe and Talbot, 2000). Nevertheless there is lack of information on the kinds of livelihoods they provide for the women and men who participate in them outside a literature on farming. Survey data from nearly 1,300 rural micro-businesses in the north east of England showed variations across sectors, but overall, nearly one-third had spouses and/or other family as partners (Raley and Moxey, 2000). Hours reported by owner-managers themselves were extremely long, although subject, in many sectors, to seasonal variation. There was considerable evidence of self-exploitation. For example, ninety-one owners worked more than eighty hours per week for an annual turnover of less than £20,000 (ibid.). The three authors undertook follow up qualitative research (1999–2001) across all sectors of non-farming businesses in remote, rural Northumberland, to investigate the provisioning of rural micro-business households in more detail.[4] Twenty-eight households, initially identified from the larger survey, were interviewed. This research confirmed that, as in urban micro-businesses, husbands and wives characteristically participate together whether or not they are co-owners or formally employed. Work from other family varied enormously in its nature and intensity but our analysis suggests that for rural business owners their contributions are more diverse than for their urban counterparts.

Overall, studies of rural and urban small businesses in a variety of economic sectors show micro-business activity to be embedded in the family household along a number of dimensions. This evidence suggests that at the heart of micro-business behaviour is a strategy of securing opportunities at the boundaries of the household and the market. Let us use the model outlined in Figure 11.1 to look at the specific nature of some elements of these boundaries, which often proves to be gendered, and where relations may or may not be monetised.

Sources of human capital in urban and rural micro-businesses

Figure 11.1 suggests that business and household social relations overlap in the context of who supplies labour to the micro-businesses. Arrow 1b indicates that the business may provide employment opportunities to household members, while arrow 1a describes the various contributions that household members may make to the business, where gender and generation may underpin unequal power relations. Under what circumstances and conditions do these exchanges of labour between household (H) and business (B) spheres take place? In both urban and rural contexts, difficult choices were faced by husbands and wives around who did what in the home, the business and the labour market. We have already established that spouses typically worked together in micro-businesses, but not usually under conditions of equality (Baines and Wheelock, 2000). Some women who participated in businesses alongside their husbands, especially in the urban sample, had given up paid work (in the market sphere, M) to do so. Sometimes they had left jobs they enjoyed and forgone their own career opportunities. As one urban woman co-owner reflected: 'these sorts of pressures [clients' unpredictable demands and childcare needs] I suppose make me having an independent career ultimately unviable.' In the rural study this direct conflict was less overt, perhaps because employment opportunities for women are more limited in the countryside (Hardill, 1998). In both urban and rural cases the business project was often acknowledged as a joint marital project, where an affective commitment as spouses became additionally an economic commitment (Baines and Wheelock, 1998b), affirming overlap between household (H) and business (B) spheres. One rural woman, for example, made the following comment about leaving her job to work with her husband in a micro-business (which they jointly owned but both partners referred to as his): 'The me bit really doesn't come into it, it's always been an us thing.' However, the work that spouses undertook in the business was frequently not monetised in that no formal wage was paid, so that financial independence for women may be even more constrained in the family self-employment model than is the case in family employment households. Women, to a larger degree than men, adjusted to the household's needs, especially children's need for care. Decisions were made according to the income-earning needs of the household in part, but socially structured norms about appropriate roles for each family member, and how children should be cared for, also determined business behaviour. Underpinning the overlap between work in the business (B) and the household (H) is what Folbre (1994) defines as an unfair structure of constraint based on a patriarchal division of domestic labour.

In the urban study involvement in micro-businesses by family members other than spouses (from sphere F) existed but was not the norm. In the rural cases members of the younger (H) and older (F) generation provided substantial amounts of labour so that effort and rewards were divided by age as well as gender. When money changed hands within business families it was almost invariably for the work of young people. Teenagers frequently participated in their parents' rural businesses. There were variations in the nature, extent and rewards of such work but the most typical arrangement was casual or occasional work, which was paid. It was in this respect in stark contrast to the non-monetised relations between spouses in business. Owners' daughters and sons assisted when the business workload was high on account of seasonal or other peaks of activity. They usually worked alongside other casual staff at these times. Rarely was work in the parents' business seen as likely to be long term. There were instances when older, non-resident, family members provided labour (from sphere F) but this was almost never paid for.

All this points to the conclusion that micro-businesses are reliant for their operation upon partially decommodified work relations taking place at the boundary between household and market. Owners often work punishingly long hours for precarious rewards and even so their businesses are often sustainable only because members of their families also adjust their daily lives around their unpredictable workloads. The contribution of household members to the business in terms of human capital, however, is only one important sense in which the business is embedded within the household.

Viable household livelihoods and micro-business provisioning

Another significant form of embedding relates to the fact that households (sphere H) may provision themselves from one or more businesses with additional elements from participation in the labour market (M) and contributions from the wider family (F) and the state (S). In the urban study a typical pattern was for a woman to supplement income from her husband's business in the start-up period and then, as discussed above, to leave her job to contribute to the business with her labour. This was not necessarily a case of linear progression towards a micro-business becoming viable enough to support two adults and (often) a young family. Sometimes women in business households moved several times between the labour market (sphere M) and the micro-business (sphere B), with periods of working in both, usually in response to peaks and troughs of business activity.

In rural economies a 'jigsaw' of household livelihood components from one or more business and from outside work, often low paid and seasonal, was a general pattern. Income from business sales of services or products relies on markets which may be highly seasonal and sometimes vulnerable to unpredictable weather conditions (e.g. hospitality, animal care, retail and other services in tourist areas).[5] It is not surprising then that for the rural business families there was often a more complex livelihood jigsaw. Members of the household contributed earnings from a variety of sources and tried, where possible, to balance precarious components with more reliable ones. Their success in achieving this varied enormously. For example, business households with high levels of financial, human or social capital were able to take risks without ultimately threatening the ability of the household to maintain itself. Secure professional employment for one member of the household could underpin temporary dips in business income. At the other extreme there were examples where people had tried and failed to establish an income package (combining H, B and M) capable of sustaining the household. This was particularly likely to be the case when businesses were set up post-redundancy by older men with limited or outdated skills. Another vulnerable group were women returning to economic activity following divorce and periods out of the labour market. In such cases livelihood jigsaws were characterised by over-dependency on the business and a lack of other reliable income sources.

The previous section touched on the interweaving of market and non-market relationships in the ways in which members of the household, as well as wider family from outside the household, support micro-businesses by providing labour. In addition, childcare on the part of grandparents (sphere F) could enable owners and their spouses to work long hours for the business and/or undertake wage-earning work outside. Moreover, gifts and transfers of money or property from within the wider family (from sphere F) could be vital resources for making a micro-business livelihood viable. Transfers from the state (sphere S), on the other hand, rarely made a significant contribution. Where support from the state did occur, it was in the form of moderate sums (usually loans or grants requiring a matched contribution from the owner) from small business support agencies or the Countryside Agency.

The livelihood jigsaw as a whole can be seen as structured by household responses to the insecurity of livelihood that, under a regime of insecurity, inevitably threatens the business-based element of income in particular.[6] For many rural micro-business households, in addition, intergenerational redistribution of time and sometimes other resources can do something to substitute for income and well-being gaps left between the labour market and the benefits system. Opportunities are indeed sought out at the boundaries between the household and the market as the model posited in Figure 11.1 suggests, rather than being based on individual entrepreneurial response to the market.

Conclusion

It is salutary to read the commentary that great political economists have made about the anachronistic characteristics of small business, and this should make us pause and take stock of whether the current ideological context might have blinded us to the disadvantages of small business. To Marx, small business was 'petty commodity production' lacking the dynamism and competitive advantages of capitalist business. Steindl, as we have seen, was scornful of the backwardness inherent in small business production. Recent small business research has too often remained within a specialist ghetto dominated by an economic model of behaviour based on individual rational choice. As a result, insights from other fields have not been sufficiently interrogated by either academics or policy-makers. We have argued in this chapter that it is useful to consider small business behaviour in the context of institutional models of the labour market, models which engage with the (gendered) interrelations between market, household and the state. This helps us to recognise that micro-business activity is a matter of securing opportunities at the boundary of the market and the household and that this is a process which is driven by a need to maintain livelihoods in conditions of economic insecurity, rather than being primarily driven by business returns in the context of economic risk.

The sheer hegemonic power that notions such as the entrepreneur, entrepreneurship and the entrepreneurial society have acquired since the late 1970s has discouraged serious assessment of policies promoting the small enterprise (Curran and Storey, 2000). In this chapter we have contributed a new assessment by taking a household, rather than an individual, approach. We have provided evidence of the ways in which all micro-businesses, whether urban or rural, are more or less embedded in the household and family, regardless of which sector they are in. We have presented a model of business behaviour which outlines the basic format of that embeddedness. The model recognises that businesses may be embedded in wider socio-economic networks, but emphasises that relations with family and household are a crucial element for understanding business activity. Paying attention to the household dimension lays bare the ways in which the 'new' forms of enterprise – promoted in policy agendas across North and South – involve a return to older, family-based, ways of organising work. The glamorous view of the individual entrepreneur alone heading up a dynamic and growing business is a far cry from the multitude of households dependent in whole or in part on micro-businesses. The reality for this majority is better understood as a self-exploitative version of the family employment model of ensuring the household livelihood.

The post-1970s' 'regime of insecurity' has undermined notions of a single income high enough to support a family and earned in a 40-hour working week. The long and unsocial hours that business owners are likely to work, and the low incomes that many receive in reward, have been acknowledged in the small business literature. This chapter indicates that immediate and even wider family members are also likely to be putting hours in to the business in a variety of different forms, making income per person even lower. There are pressures to return to more gendered divisions of labour in business, in paid work and unpaid work. Women in business families often do not take a wage from the business, severely limiting their financial independence. The family-embedded small business operating close to the economic margins can also find itself excluded from elements of support available to the employed household (such as the minimum wage, health and safety legislation or employment legislation limiting hours of work). This was recognised in a recent investigation into rural poverty and social exclusion which noted low pay, especially in the small workplaces which dominate rural economies, and the high incidence of poverty among self-employed people in rural areas (Shucksmith, 2000).

What are the implications of all this for policy? First, small business policy needs to be more closely linked to social policies of ensuring social inclusion. For the current Labour Government these consist of a set of labour market policies which focus on 'making work pay' while at the same time facilitating 'family–work balance'. Yet Working Family Tax Credit and Childcare Tax Credit (both of which aim to make work pay for households with children and which are payable to the self-employed) effectively provide a subsidy to employers and marginal small businesses. The second implication for policy concerns another key government objective, raising skill levels. It has been argued that the promotion of yet more small enterprises could actually be harmful to the national skill base (Curran, 2000). The reproduction of a skilled workforce has come to look uncertain in creative industries which rely heavily on self-employment and micro-enterprises after large-scale downsizing and outsourcing (Stanworth and Stanworth, 1995; Dex *et al.*, 2000; Baines and Robson, 2001). Family members involved in micro-businesses frequently report learning-on-the-job without the benefit of formal training. Small business households are older than the average for the workforce (the average age of farmers is as high as 58) and for new entrants skills have often been acquired in earlier formal employment settings. If policy continues to encourage younger members of the labour force to set up in business, an already low skills base is likely to be further eroded.

So long as policy-makers continue to adopt the over-simplified model of the enterprising individual that many of those researching small business espouse, the disadvantages of small business, both for the lives and well-being of small business households and for the vitality of the economy as a whole, are unlikely to be addressed.

Notes

1 Businesses employing 0– 9 people.
2 J. Wheelock, *Small Business, 'Flexibility' and Family Work Strategies*, ESRC Award no. R 000 23 2529.

3 J. Wheelock and E. Chell, *The Business Owner-managed Family Unit: An Inter-regional Comparison of Behavioural Dynamics*, ESRC Award no. R 000 23 4402.

4 *Enterprising Livelihoods in Rural Households: New and Old Ways of Working*, ESRC Award no. R000 23 8213

5 Rural micro-businesses can be vulnerable to other events, as the foot-and-mouth crisis has demonstrated. The fieldwork was undertaken before the outbreak of foot-and-mouth.

6 With only a few exceptions, respondents described a strong reluctance to enter into debt even if they could see ways in which doing so could expand the business and help to generate higher household income.

12 Emotions and the moral order of farm business families in Finland

Saija Katila

Introduction

Promoting family business and understanding its dynamics became a popular theme of research during the past decade. However, family business research has more often focused on the firm than on the family. The main interest has been success and management succession in family firms (Dyer, 1986; Cromie and Adams, 1997; Gersick *et al.*, 1997). It seems that the concept of 'family' has seldom been defined or problematised in these studies as if it were something that naturally and neutrally represents a reality shared and understood by all of us. Seeing the 'family' in family business as a non-cultural, non-historical, apolitical, or even a non-emotional entity has serious consequences for our ability to understand how family and business influence one another in different societal and cultural settings.

Over the past several decades, the Western family has undergone dramatic changes and become increasingly heterogeneous. More and more individuals are living alone in single-parent households or living together in other non-traditional family arrangements. Furthermore, the ethnic diaspora caused by poverty, wars, famine and natural catastrophes has made Western societies more multicultural and family structures and traditions even more diversified than before. Thus, when discussing the meanings of 'family', perhaps the only thing that can be agreed upon is that it refers to a group of people. These disagreements point to the fact that the concept of family is not material but rather a cultural creation, something we construct in our cultural communities. Understanding 'family' as a social construction refers to the idea that the family is also being shaped by ongoing societal discourses and practices.

As individuals are part of families and families are part of larger communities, the larger community and society enter into our understanding of what a family is and what kind of rights and obligations individuals have within a family in the given context. We can, for example, look at two business families that both appear to hold rather traditional family values. Yet, in one of them, the daughter has to marry someone who will bring needed talent or strategic alliances to the business (Hamabata, 1990) and in the other, the daughter working for the business is allowed to marry for love. Seeing business families as representatives of their cultural communities enables us to highlight what kind of rights and obligations are ascribed to different family members within a community and how these rights and obligations influence the ways families do business. The culturally specific ways of doing business can be seen to reflect the specific moral order of the group concerned. Moral order refers to the norms and values of a particular community (Harré, 1983).

Individuals belong to several communities simultaneously and the moral orders of these communities can either support or contradict each other. In order to look at business families from the point of view of the moral order we have, however, to distinguish which moral order has the most significant influence on the business activities of the family, be it ethnicity, locality or something else. This chapter looks at business families within one occupational community, namely, farmers in Finland. Farmers are the most homogeneous group in Finland with respect to social background and economic standing (Alestalo, 1985: 125–34). Farmers are an interesting group, especially with respect to family business studies as farming in Finland (i.e. Suomen maatalous ja maaseutuelinkeinot 1999/2000) and in Europe is mainly organised into familial units (Eurostat, 1995). Farmers are, however, usually excluded from small business analyses regardless of the fact that they are an important element of the small-business-owning population. It is not widely acknowledged that farmers these days are often portfolio founders operating in more than one industrial field (Carter, 1998; Carter and Rosa, 1998; Katila, 2000; Peltola, 2000).

A group-specific familial moral order can influence various aspects of business life. In this chapter, the aim is to focus on the norms and values that regulate labour use in Finnish farm business families. It has been noted that in micro-businesses rendering family labour for the family business is a matter of business survival (e.g. Scase and Goffee, 1982; Wheelock, 1992). The chapter argues, however, that the picture is more complex and contested. Business survival is not sufficient to explain such a phenomenon. Using an ethnographic approach, this chapter explores in detail how the norm of unpaid family labour is acted out at the level of farms in Finland.

The first section discusses families as collectives with specific moral orders rising out of the cultural setting in which they are situated. Here, the role of emotions in moral orders is also addressed. The second section outlines the methodological choices of the study. The third section highlights the role of the norm of unpaid family labour in the system of norms and values comprising the yeoman moral order in Finland using evidence from an ethnographic study of five farm business families. Finally, the fourth section concludes by examining the role of emotions in stabilising the moral order.

Business families as carriers of group-specific moral orders

The image of economic man as a rational, self-interested individual encourages us to accept that people make individual and autonomous decisions about business start-up, growth, etc. In reality, this is seldom the case. People do not make 'individual' decisions but rather decisions within the context set by various collectives (Etzioni, 1988: 4). Therefore, social collectives such as ethnic and racial groups, peer groups at work and neighbourhood groups are the prime decision-making units. To a significant extent, individual decision-making often reflects collective attributes and processes. Thus, as a member of a business family, it is difficult to think of the economic implications of one's business decisions. Instead, one is also forced to consider the social, moral (see Etzioni, 1988; Granovetter, 1985) and emotional implications of decisions. The decisions to support one's community are based not on narrow self-interest but rather on internalised ethics of conduct and norms of reciprocity (Fukuyama, 1995: 9). In a collective, the social context is, to a significant extent, perceived as a legitimate and integral part of one's existence. One has a sense of shared identity and commitment to live up to the moral order of the community (Etzioni, 1988: 5). For example, a member of an Amish community would not open a disco as it would be against her/his collective norms and values.

A moral order refers to the norms and values of a particular community. Each action is publicly marked with respect or contempt. Actions, whatever their practical aim, are treated as displays of character in accordance with local understandings of acceptable and context-appropriate personae. In the moral psychology of personal being, one's actions count not for themselves but for what they reveal about individual character in regard to the communities' moral order. The standing of a person depends in part on the degree to which she/he is capable of fulfilling commitments. It is important to understand that honour can be besmirched not only by one's own actions but also by the actions of a family member that dishonour the whole family (Harré, 1983: 245). A moral order defines what is valuable in a community, worth striving for, and what the basic principles are according to which one is expected to behave (Ylijoki, 1998). A moral order does not, however, causally determine the actions of community members. It could rather be seen as a loose frame within which community members reflect upon their decisions and actions. Moral orders are ambivalent in nature – they can both support and restrict the actions of community members, depending on the context.

Ram's study (1994a) on the Asian-dominated clothing industry in the West Midlands is a good example of the existence of a specific moral order. His study makes a case for the extensive use of family labour and the two sets of moral orders that apply to family members and non-members (ibid.: 63). The emergence of family/non-family moral orders is usually judged as emotional and non-rational, something that endangers the survival of family businesses (Levinson, 1971; Alcorn, 1982; Kets de Vries, 1996). Hence, it is often argued that family moralities and emotions should be kept separate from the business as they are seen to represent contradictory moral orders, for example 'What is right in the corporation is not what's right in a man's home or in his church. What is right in the corporation is what the guy above wants from you. That's what morality is in the corporation' (Jackall, 1988: 109, quoting Fineman, 1997: 552).

In a family business, however, home and corporation are intertwined. The private enters the public in ways that make standard explanations of organisational reality problematic. Emotions play a crucial part in understanding organisations in general and family businesses in particular.

To enhance our understanding of how emotions influence business families and their decision-making, it is important to go beyond individual emotional expressions. Emotions are the personal displays of affected states like joy, love, sadness, shame or guilt. They are, however, only partly individual. They acquire their meaning from the cultural context – national, local and organisational (Ratner, 1989; Lutz and White, 1986, quoting Fineman, 1997: 546; Fineman, 1993). They also transmit the collective subjectivity of groups of individuals, reveal cultural rules and touch upon issues that characterise humans in general (Ruth and Vilkko, 1996).

Emotional displays are also subject to rules and conventions. They are embedded in culturally specific moral orders and normative systems that allow for assessments of the correctness or impropriety of emotions within the group (Averill, 1985; Armon-Jones, 1986; Harré, 1986; Crawford *et al.*, 1992; Oatley, 1993; Harré and Parrot, 1996; Landman, 1996). Different commitments reflect different emotional contracts – with others and with self – and this determines the commitment's potency (Pfeffer, 1982, quoting Fineman, 1997: 551). The emotions of shame and guilt are inherently connected to all moral orders (Harré, 1983; Etzioni, 1988).

Looking at business families from the point of view of a moral order, guilt and shame become relevant emotions in understanding how business families operate. Guilt and shame are not, however, emotions that would be typical to family businesses only; instead they are central to the nature of organisational order in general. They are the sources of self-regulation that social organisations require to function. These emotions are nurtured in the processes of socialisation in a nation's culture and fine-tuned in specific work organisation (Fineman, 1997: 551) and family. When thinking of family it is, however, rather difficult to dismiss the emotion of love altogether. Love refers in the broadest sense to the principle(s) by which people organise their relationships with one another (Averill, 1985: 191). The norms and values of the yeoman moral order in Finland and the emotions supporting it are explored in the following section.

Study design

A study of five farm business families was conducted. All of the five families had received rural investment support from 1987 through 1989 to start new businesses outside the subsidised agricultural sector, although at that time they all were also engaged in farming. All the businesses under study were micro enterprises. The businesses merely created self-employment. An attempt was made to maximise the variability between the cases (see Hammersley, 1992) according to how much the families used the farmer's skills and the farm's resources and how much they needed new skills and new resources. The cases vary from a farm where the entrepreneurs mainly continue farming-like activities by diversifying on land (organic farming, strawberry production) to a farm where the new activities do not have anything to do with the farmer's skills and the farm's resources (veterinarian clinic, carpenter shop).

Diversifying in new sectors or industries is not a new phenomenon in the agricultural sector in Finland (Siiskonen, 1990; Sireni, 1994; Peltola, 2000) nor elsewhere in Europe (Campagne *et al.*, 1990; Fuller, 1990; Reis *et al.*, 1990; Ilbery, 1991; Evans and Ilbery, 1992; Hill, 1993; Carter, 1998). It seems, however, that farmers do not diversify to be able to grow but rather to be able to continue farming (Ilbery, 1991; Haugen and Vartdal, 1994; Katila, 2000; Peltola, 2000). The farm business families under study are therefore seen as representatives of the farming community. It could be argued that the new businesses are founded within the existing web of social and emotional relations and cultural codes.

The study adopts an ethnographic approach (see Spradley, 1980; van Maanen, 1988, 1995) and draws upon two main sources of data: interview material and field notes. The data were collected by living for one full week with each of the five farm business families – observing the activities, participating in them and interviewing different family members. A biographical interview technique was chosen for the study. It was crucial in making visible the moral order and the emotions supporting it that frame the actions of the members of the farm business families. When people tell who they are, what they are striving for, and what is meaningful for them in their lives (Ruth and Kenyon, 1996), they also explain the generally accepted rules of the society in which they are living (Bruner, 1990). Reminiscing about life events triggers emotions that are relived and re-experienced (Cohen, 1993). Self-reflexive judgements are especially sensitive to emotions where narrators' self-esteem and their beliefs about their abilities are concerned (Singer and Salovey, 1993). In biographies episodes of practical activity integrate moral and ethical motives (Polkinghorne, 1991). The interviews highlighted the subjective interpretations, reinterpretations and the individual meaning-giving process of life experiences of growing up on the farm. In biography, a personal story merges with collective memory and makes visible the complicated inter-generational influence of the family (Thompson, 1993: 15).

Using the biographies of different family members and the field notes collected during the participant observation period, narratives were constructed of each of the five families under study. As the narratives are too long to present here, extracts of only one narrative are presented to highlight the arguments made. Parts of the extracts are in italics to indicate a direct quotation from the actor in question. The extracts used in this chapter describe the life and experiences of Kari (42 years old) and his wife Jaana (44 years old) and their two children Tero (their 14-year-old son) and Liisa (their 12-year-old daughter). Kari has continued to work his family farm and has built a new house for his family next to the house where he was born. His older brother and father still live in a nearby house. Three of Kari's brothers and his two sisters left the farm decades ago as young adults.

The norm of unpaid family labour as part of the yeoman moral order in Finland

The basic organisational unit of agriculture in Finland is a family farm that is passed on from generation to generation. The familial basis for the activity sets many at odds with the dominant form of social organisation in which work and family life are sharply segregated. On the farms, husbands, wives, the grandparents and children are often bound together in the most basic tasks of earning a living. Some 88 per cent of active farms are privately owned and 12 per cent by estates and family co-operatives (Suomen maatalous ja maaseutuelinkeinot, 1999/2000). What makes farm businesses special among businesses in general is the fact that the farm is simultaneously a workplace and a home, a production unit and a consumption unit, and a work community and a family. Hence, the farm is a place where public and private cannot be unambiguously defined. In farming families' land, housing, machinery and the skills needed in farming work are transmitted from one generation to the next. Also social values, taken-for-granted ways of behaving (i.e. the local moral order) are transmitted through intergenerational networks with emotion rules to support them.

One of the core norms of the yeoman moral order in Finland is the norm of unpaid family labour. To understand the role of the norm in the system of values and norms comprising the moral order of Finnish family farming, we must see the norm in connection with the other values and norms of the moral order of the group concerned. In familial economic units, like the farm business families in Finland, the business unit and the family unit are closely interrelated (Wheelock, 1992). This entanglement of public and private spheres of life is also manifested in the moral order in the form of values and norms that support the survival and reproduction of the business as well as the family. This chapter, however, focuses on the values that are more closely connected to the survival of the firm than the family. In addition to the norm of unpaid family labour, the other values and norms of the moral order of Finnish farming families are the continuity of the family farm, caring for the older generation and the yeoman economic ethos consisting of hard work, saving and self-sufficiency (Katila, 2000). The following sections will discuss the differential forms of unpaid family labour used in the farm family businesses. It will describe in detail who is doing the work, what kind of work one is expected to do and why.

'Old enough to walk, old enough to work'

In Finnish farm business families, child labour has always been a common practice and to a certain extent still is. When the family owners of the farm business under study were children during the 1950s and 1960s, farming families were usually large and poor. Child labour was crucial for the survival of both the farm and the family. Farming families produced much of the food they needed for their own consumption on the farms. Most families produced at least all the potatoes and bread grain they needed during the year and often the milk as well. Farming families were also self-sufficient in firewood. Thus, during the 1950s and 1960s producing farming products for sale and maintaining the self-sufficiency necessary for the survival of the family required that all able members of the family participated in all work on the farm, as the following extract highlights.

> In Kari's memories, his childhood on the farm evolved around working. He had to work in the sugar beet fields as soon as he was old enough to go on all fours. The next job was driving a tractor at the age of four or five. He was the youngest of the brothers so he drove while his much older and stronger brothers lifted the hay onto the hay poles.
>
> (Katila, 2000)

When the informants were young, child labour was needed on farms. Technological change during that era was, however, extremely fast and there was less and less need for child labour (Alestalo, 1985). The tradition of using familial child labour on the farms has, however, not completely disappeared. It is still a common practice on family farms but not to the extent that it used to be. Nowadays, children are not made to work to ensure family survival but rather to transfer the virtues of industriousness and the core value of the moral order – that of the continuity of the family farm:

> Kari reproduces the work patterns of his childhood in the next generation. His 14-year-old son Tero was driving a tractor as soon as his legs were long enough to reach the gas and brake pedals. At the age of 14, he helps his dad after school with field work and feeding beef cattle. He takes great pride in his work. According to his mom he feels strongly about farming: '*He has wanted to farm since he was a little boy*'. In contrast, Liisa does not care for farm work nor is she expected to. She prefers to help her mother in the kitchen and spend her time reading and playing with the cats and dog. Her father explains her limited role in farming work by her being '*so young and little*'.
>
> Kari wishes that his son would choose another occupation but he has made sure that if he chooses to continue the family farm, he will have all the necessary skills for the task. Kari's older brother once said that they were lucky that it was Kari, and not him, who took over the farm. He could not have produced a successor for the farm as he could not have any children.
>
> (Katila, 2000)

The virtue of industriousness is still highly valued among the rural population in Finland, including rural youth. Young people in rural areas still perceive that every man has an obligation to work (Sireni, 2000). This virtue was part of the yeoman economic ethos throughout the twentieth century (Heinonen, 1998) and it is still actively upheld by farming families. However, both the norm of unpaid family labour and the virtue of industriousness also serve the core value of the moral order, the continuity of the family farm (Katila, 2000). The value of continuity is not an especially Finnish phenomenon, but it is common in countries where family farming is prevalent (Gasson and Errington, 1993; Symes, 1990: 280–91). To secure the continuity of the family farm, children must be taught the tricks of the trade. Formal education still plays a limited role in the reproduction of new farmers in Finland. Farm work is still learned mainly by doing and the main trainers are the parents and grandparents. The norm of unpaid family labour applies to all members of the family but the kind of work one is expected to do varies according to gender.

The Finnish yeoman moral order is strongly gendered, which is also evident from the previous extract. Girls and boys growing up on a farm have differentiated rights and obligations. Boys are expected to learn the occupation and they are entitled to continue the family farm. Men have the right to run the farm and they are socialised and trained accordingly (see also Abrahams, 1991; Kumpulainen, 1999; Sireni, 2000). Girls are mainly expected to do household work and tend the livestock. Both girls and boys growing up on the farm learn important skills but only the skills the boys acquire are sufficient for running the farm. According to Haugen (1994, quoted in Sireni, 2000: 7), boys are actively encouraged to take over the farm, whereas girls are actively encouraged to leave it. Girls are trained to run a farm only when they are the only children in the family, the only ones who could continue.

The assumption of 'free' familial labour

Using unpaid or underpaid child labour is common in many societies around the world but it has been made illegal in Western societies. Western societies have also banned the use of unpaid or underpaid labour of any kind in public spheres of life. This does not, however, mean that unpaid or underpaid labour has disappeared. The legitimate site for unpaid and underpaid work in many societies is the family. The general right of 'free' exchange of factors of production like labour is contested in the business family context or any family context for that matter. What is legally freely exchangeable may not be so socially or emotionally. In the case of new farm business families, labour is mainly informal family labour whose use is based on non-contractual elements. Control of the labour is not based on the employers' authority but rather on a shared moral order articulating the rights and obligations of different family members. Family business in general could thus be seen as sites where the rules of the public spheres of life have merged with family moralities and emotions. This phenomenon is manifested in the extract below describing Kari's life as a young adult.

> In 1982 machine contracting was more profitable than before and Kari bought himself a new machine and worked with two machines until 1988. During the years he harvested peat he had ten months of work for himself and six months for his hired driver. In addition to his welding and machine contracting, he had full responsibility for work in the fields of his family farm. Kari had to fit ploughing, harrowing, sowing and harvesting into his

schedule although he was never paid a penny for the work. He had to get all the money for his private use elsewhere. He spent his days harvesting peat and his nights driving between the family farm and the peat bog. However, when it was time for him to take over the farm he did not resent the idea in any form or fashion. On the contrary, he had farming in his genes. '*I wanted to, I have a rural background and everything. I wanted to get soil under my nails.*'

(Katila, 2000)

In all the families under study, children were never paid for the work they did on the family farm. When they became adults, they kept working on the farm without any financial compensation like the generations before them. All the money they needed for their private use had to be earned elsewhere. The extract shows a typical phenomenon of Finnish agriculture – the irrelevance of monetary incentives on farms where the promise of future succession into an owner-manager position as well as the social obligations to kin are the primary motives for work. Life-long participation in work on the farm family business gives rise to the mutual dependence, expectations, and trust that are important forms of social capital for the family (see Sanders and Nee, 1996). The commitment to your family farm is used seasonally when excess labour is needed. Rendering unpaid labour for the farm is not, however, limited to those adults who expect to take over the farm. For example, Jaana had a job outside the farm but she worked in the strawberry fields in the evenings and on weekends and throughout her summer holidays. Also, Kari's brother who lived in a nearby county came home to work during peak season whenever he was needed and if he could not make it, one of the neighbours would come and help out Kari and Jaana. Communal labour is uncommon in contemporary societies, but it has always been an essential part of the Finnish rural tradition (see Abrahams, 1991).

In this section, I have described the different forms of unpaid familial labour that are used by Finnish farm business families. Using unpaid labour is not, however, a phenomenon limited only to the farming context or to the Finnish context. It is a common phenomenon in micro-businesses in general where familial labour is exploited to secure the survival of the business (for example, Baines and Wheelock, 1998a; Phizacklea and Ram, 1996). In micro-businesses, the business needs and family needs seem to be integrated. Economic reasons are not the only reasons to work (for example, Whatmore, 1991; Baines *et al.*, 1997). Co-operation within the family does not arise out of mere self-interest, but stems from a moral order in which the accumulation of obligations among family members builds a degree of solidarity (Sanders and Nee, 1996). Moral orders do not, however, stand alone. They are supported by an appropriate set of emotions.

Love and guilt as the cement of the moral order

Although moral orders are powerful in themselves, what makes them even more powerful is the appropriate set of supportive emotions. Through the processes of identification and imitation with the parents and the grandparents living in yeoman households, children learn the values and norms of the yeoman moral order and also the appropriate emotions that go with it. The key emotions supporting the Finnish yeoman moral order are love, guilt and shame.

In the extract used in the previous section, Kari explicitly expressed his wish to farm, which was a wish expressed by all those people in the study who lived on their family farms. The relationship they had to farming was different from the relationship they had to wage work, or to their new business activities. The relationship to farm work was deeply emotional. Farming for the farmers in the study seems to represent an occupation where several good things meet. The emotional relationship to farm work was, however, not the only emotional relationship. There was an even stronger relationship to the family farm:

'Hmm ... the feeling, let's say, somewhere around April, when the last patches of snow melt from the woods and the fields are turning grey, and grass starts to grow ... the feeling is something that words can't express. You are full of enthusiasm, like a balloon, and you just run around ... you are all itching to get into the fields again.' To Kari farming is a way of life. He has grown into it and cannot get rid of it. Above all, it's his livelihood. He thinks that farmers are too emotionally involved with their farms. *'People cannot take things rationally when the farm has been passed on from a father to a son, and you have lived in the same place all your life. Some folks take over the farms from their parents and lose everything they have. When I was doing machine contracting it was easy to sell the machines when it was no longer profitable but I cannot give up my farm. It is the anchor of my life. Owning a farm is not like owning any piece of land. It is the land where I was born and raised.'*

(Katila, 2000)

The relationship the farmers in the study had with their family farms could be characterised as one of love. Love does not restrict itself to sex and childcare. Love relationships can extend to members of the larger community and to abstract entities like nature or God (Averill, 1985: 9). When we are talking about loving a farm we are, of course, not talking about romantic love but about companionate love. Companionate love consists of affection, commitment and intimacy (Hatfield and Rapson, 1993: 9). The main element of companionate love – long-term commitment, even a life-long commitment (Sternberg, 1988) – is evident in the extract. The quotation demonstrates Kari's love for land, and not just any land but the land where he was born and raised. The metaphorical expressions the farmers used to describe their relationship to the family farm were strong. They used metaphors such as 'growing into the land', 'having roots in the land' or they described the farm as the 'anchor of their lives' as Kari did. It seem that the love for the family farm is connected to the continuity of the family farm, which is the core value of the yeoman moral order in Finland. Love is, however, not the only emotion supporting the moral order. When we talk of morality, negative emotions also enter the scene.

The core emotions supporting any moral order are the emotions of guilt and shame. A person who feels guilty thinks in terms of duties not performed and obligations not fulfilled (Taylor, 1996). When a farmer takes over the farm from the previous generation he immediately commits himself to the values of the yeoman moral order as well. He is expected to secure the continuity of the family farm. He is responsible not only to himself but also to the previous generations. Breaking the chain of continuation means that one is wasting all the years of labour invested in the farm business, but even more so, it means that one is wasting the hard work and savings of previous generations. Thus, the feelings of guilt come easy. A person who has internalised the value of the continuity of the family farm accepts that loss of the family farm is forbidden. By accepting that it is forbidden, one thereby accepts the authority of whomever or whatever forbids it. What the authority pronounces as wrong must not be done. So the authority becomes the voice of conscience (Taylor, 1996). One is willing to work hard without any financial compensation just to live up to the expectations of the moral order. This means that people are willing to lose everything they have. It could therefore be argued that holding on to the family farm is also a matter of honour. Inability to do so will bring shame on you and your family.

Conclusion

This chapter has taken as its starting point that individuals are part of families and families are part of larger collectives. Membership of a collective, whether based on locality, ethnicity, religion, occupation or any other criteria, is of great importance to the behaviour of business families. The actions of business family members are not seen to rise out of mere self-interest, but they are rather seen to follow the moral order, i.e. the values and norms of a particular community that define what is acceptable and context-appropriate behaviour in a given situation (Harré, 1983). The chapter argues that seeing the business family as a representative of a larger community enables us to understand what kind of rights and obligations family members are expected to have within the community in general and within the business family in particular.

An ethnographic study of five farm business families set out to explore the moral order of the farming community in Finland. This chapter focused on one of the norms of the Finnish yeoman moral order, the norm of unpaid family labour. It is argued that the norm of unpaid family labour is still strong in the community, but it is understandable only in relation to the system of values and norms comprising the Finnish yeoman moral order. The analysis has further revealed that the legitimate site for unpaid labour is the family.

Labour use in the farm business families is not based on contractual elements, but on a shared moral order articulating the rights and obligations of different family members. Working on the family farm could be considered a strong socialising mechanism through which the skills needed in agriculture are passed on from one generation to the other. In addition to the skills, the moral order of the community is also transferred, especially the value of industriousness and the continuity of the family farm.

The study further indicated that the Finnish yeoman moral order is strongly gendered. The norm of unpaid labour is applicable to each and every member of the family but the kind of work one is expected to do varies according to gender. Boys are expected to handle the farm machinery or work in the fields and girls are encouraged to tend the livestock and do household work. Only the skills boys acquire are sufficient for running the farm.

Finally, it is argued that moral orders do not stand alone. They are supported by a set of appropriate emotions. The emotions of companionate love and guilt play a crucial role in the strengthening and reproduction of the Finnish yeoman moral order. The farmers in the study had a love relationship with the land on the family farm. They were committed to it, some even for their whole lives. Loving the land and living up to the expectations of the moral order will entail managing emotions of guilt and shame as well. Guilt and shame are connected to the internalised value of the continuity of the family farm. Losing the farm would mean wasting the hard work and savings of previous generations.

In the light of the study, the attempts of the agricultural policy-makers in Finland to build up a new identity for farmers as farm businessmen, who are driven by profit maximising and economic achievement orientation, (Alasuutari, 1996: 70–3) seem to disregard the fact that the 'rationality' of farming families cannot be understood in purely utilitarian terms. What represents the 'rational', 'success' and 'worthwhile activity' in farm business families does not lie within the activity or the phenomenon itself, but within the social relations and inter- pretive processes that sustain it. Thus, a narrow focus on small, family business in research and policymaking can neglect important aspects of the businesses that are shaped by emotions and moral economy.

Bibliography

Abrahams, R. (1991) *A Place of Their Own: Family Farming in Eastern Finland*, Cambridge: Cambridge University Press.

Adams, G.A., King, L.A. and King, D.W. (1996) 'Relationships of job and family involvement, family social support, and work–family conflict with job and life satisfaction', *Journal of Applied Psychology*, 81, 411–20.

Adler, N. (1983) 'A typology of management studies involving culture', *Journal of International Business Studies*, 3, 29–48.

Alasuutari, P. (1996) *Toinen tasavalta. Suomi 1946–1994*, Jyväskylä: Gummerus.

Alcorn, P.B. (1982) *Success and Survival in the Family-Owned Business*, New York: McGraw-Hill.

Aldrich, H. (1999) *Organisations Evolving*, New York: Sage Publications.

Aldrich, H., Cater, J., Jones, T. and McEvoy, D. (1981) 'Business development and self-segregation: Asian enterprise in three British cities', in C. Peach, V. Robinson and S. Smith (eds) *Ethnic Segregation in Cities*, London: Croom Helm.

Aldrich, H. and Zimmer, C. (1986) 'Entrepreneurship through social networks', in D. Sexton and R. Smilor (eds) *The Art and Science of Entrepreneurship*, New York: Ballinger.

Aldrich, H., Zimmer, C. and McEvoy, D. (1989) 'Continuities in the study of ecological succession: Asian businesses in three British cities', *Social Forces*, 67, 920–44.

Alestalo, M. (1985) 'Yhteiskuntaluokat ja sosiaaliset kerrostumat toisen maailmansodan jälkeen', in M. Valkonen *et al.* (eds) *Suomalaiset. Yhteiskunnan rakenne teollistumisen aikana*, Juva: WSOY.

Alvesson, M. and Sköldberg, K. (2000) *Reflexive Methodology: New Vistas for Qualitative Research*, London: Sage Publications.

Anderson, J.C. and Gerbing, D.W. (1988) 'Structural equation modelling in practice: a review and recommended two-step approach', *Psychological Bulletin*, 103, 411–23.

Ang, J.A., Cole, R.A. and Lin Wuh, J. (2000) 'Agency costs and ownership structure', *Journal of Finance*, 55, 1, 81–106.

Ang, J.S. (1991) 'Small business uniqueness and the theory of financial management', *Journal of Small Business Finance*, 1, 3, 1–13.

Armon-Jones, C. (1986) 'The thesis of constructionism', in R. Harré (ed.) *The Social Construction of Emotions*, Oxford: Basil Blackwell.

Aronoff, C.E. and Ward, J.L. (1992) *Family Business Succession: The Final Test of Greatness* (*Family Business Leadership Series*, 1), Marietta, GA: Business Owner Resources.

Australian Institute of Family Studies (1997) *The Australian Living Standards Study*, Melbourne: Australian Institute of Family Studies.

Averill, J. (1985) 'The social construction of emotion: with special reference to love', in K. Gergen and K. Davis (eds) *The Social Construction of the Person*, New York: Springer-Verlag.

Bacharach, S.B., Bamberger, P. and Conley, S.C. (1990) 'Work processes, role conflict and role overload: the case of nurses and engineers in the public sector', *Work and Occupations*, 17, 199–228.

Baines, S. and Robson, E. (2001) 'Being self-employed and being enterprising: the case of creative work for the media industries', *Journal of Small Business and Enterprise Development*, 8, 4, 349–362.

Baines, S. and Wheelock, J. (1997) *A Business in the Family: An Investigation into the Contribution of Family to Small Business Survival, Maintenance and Growth*, Leeds: Institute for Small Business Affairs.

—— (1998a) 'Working for each other: gender, the household and micro-business survival and growth', *International Small Business Journal*, 17, 1, 16–35.

—— (1998b) 'Reinventing traditional solutions: job creation, gender and the micro-business household', *Work, Employment and Society*, 12, 4, 579–601.

—— (2000) 'Work and employment in small businesses: perpetuating and challenging gender traditions', *Gender, Work and Organization*, 5, 1, 45–55.

Baines, S., Wheelock, J. and Abrams, A. (1997) 'Micro-business owner-managers in social context: household, family and growth or non-growth', in D. Deakins, P. Jennings and C. Mason (eds) *Small Firms: Entrepreneurship in the Nineties*, London: Paul Chapman.

Bandura, A. (1986) *Social Foundations of Thought and Action: A Social Cognitive Theory*, Englewood Cliffs, NJ: Prentice-Hall.

Bank of England (2000) *Finance for Small Firms: A Seventh Report*, London: Bank of England.

Barley, S.R. and Tolbert, P.S. (1997) 'Institutionalization and structuration: studying the links between action and institutions', *Organisation Studies*, 18, 1, 93–117.

Barnes, L.B. (1988) 'Incongruent hierarchies: daughters and sons as company CEOs', *Family Business Review*, 1, 1, 9–21.

Barnett, R.C. and Baruch, G.K. (1985) 'Women's involvement in multiple roles and psychological distress', *Journal of Personality and Social Psychology*, 49, 135–45.

Barrett, G. (1999) 'Overcoming the obstacles: access to bank finance for African-Caribbean enterprise', *Journal of Ethnic and Migration Studies* 25, 303–22.

Barrett, G., Jones, T. and McEvoy, D. (2001) Ethnic Minorities and (de)regulation: retailing and consumer services in the UK, Third Meeting of Thematic Network 'Working on the Fringes': Public Policy and the Institutional Context of Immigrant Businesses, Liverpool, March 22–25.

Barry, B. (1989) 'Development of organisation structure', *Family Business Review*, 2, 3, 293–315.

Barton, S.L. and Matthews, C. (1989) 'Small firm financing: implications for a strategic management', *Journal of Small Business Management*, 27, 1, 1–7.

Bass, B.M. (1981) *Handbook of Leadership* (revised and expanded edn), New York: The Free Press.

Basu, A. (1998) 'An exploration of entrepreneurial activity among Asian small businesses in Britain', *Small Business Economics*, 10, 313–26.

Bechhofer, F., Elliot, M., Rushford, M. and Bland, R. (1974) 'Small shopkeepers: matters of money and meaning', *Sociological Review*, 22, 4, 465–82.

Beck, U. (2000) *The Brave New World of Work*, Cambridge: Polity Press.

Becker, G.S. (1993) 'Nobel Lecture: the economic way of looking at behavior', *Journal of Political Economy*, 101, 3.

Beckhard, R. and Dyer, W.G. (1983) 'Managing change in the family firm – issues and strategies', *Sloan Management Review*, 24, 59–65.

Beehr, T.A., Drexler, J.A. and Faulkner, S. (1997) 'Working in small family businesses: empirical comparisons to non-family businesses', *Journal of Organizational Behavior*, 18, 3, 297–312.

Berg, P.O. (1979) *Emotional Structures in Organizations. A Study of the Process of Change in a Swedish Company*, Lund: Studentlitteratur.

Berger, P. and Luckmann, T. (1967) *The Social Construction of Reality*, New York: Penguin Press.

Binder Hamlyn (1994) *The Quest for Growth: A Survey of UK Private Companies*, London: Binder Hamlyn.

Birley, S. (1997) *The Family and the Business*, London: Grant Thornton.

—— (2000) 'Owner-manager attitudes to family and business issues', in P. Poutziouris (ed.) *Tradition or Entrepreneurship in the New Economy?*, Manchester: Manchester Business School, University of Manchester.

Birley, S., Ng, D.W.N. and Godfrey, A. (1999) 'The family and the business', *Long Range Planning*, 32, 6, 598–608.

Blaschke, J., Boissevain, J., Grotenberg, H. *et al.* (1990) 'European trends in ethnic business', in R. Waldinger, H. Aldrich and R. Ward (eds) *Ethnic Entrepreneurs*, CA: Sage Publications.

Bloodgood, J.M. and Morrow, J.L., Jr (2000) 'Strategic organizational change within an institutional framework', *Journal of Managerial Issues*, 12, 2, 208–26.

Boissevain, J. (1974) *Friends of Friends: Networks, Manipulations and Coalitions*, Oxford: Basil Blackwell.

Bolton Report (1971) *Report of the Committee of Inquiry on Small Firms* (Cmnd 4811), London: HMSO.

Bonacich, E. and Modell, R. (1980) *The Economic Basis of Ethnic Solidarity*, Berkeley, CA: University of California Press.

Bouchiki, H. (1993) 'A constructivist framework for understanding entrepreneurship performance', *Organisation Studies*, 14, 4, 549–70.

Bourdieu, P. (1996) 'On the family as a realised category', *Theory, Culture and Society*, 13, 3, 19–26.

Bouwen, R. and Steyeart, C. (1990) 'Construing organisational texture in young entrepreneurial firms', *Journal of Management Studies*, 29, 6, 637–49.

Brah, A. (1996) *Cartographies of Diaspora: Contesting Identities*, London: Routledge.

Bridge, S., O'Neill, K. and Cromie, S. (1998) *Understanding Enterprise, Entrepreneurship and Small Business*, Basingstoke: Macmillan.

Brief, A.P., Burke, M.J., George, J.M., Dovenson, B.S. and Webster, J. (1988) 'Should negative affectivity remain an unmeasured variable in the study of job stress?', *Journal of Applied Psychology*, 73, 193–8.

Brogger, J. and Gilmore, D.D. (1997) 'The matrifocal family in Iberia: Spain and Portugal compared', *Ethnology*, 36, 1, 13–30.

Brown, F.H. (1993) 'Loss and continuity in the family firm', *Family Business Review*, 6, 2, 111–30.

Bruegel, I., Figart, D. and Mutari, M. (1998) 'Whose full employment? A feminist perspective on work redistribution', in J. Vail, J. Wheelock and M. Hill (eds) *Insecure Times: Living with Insecurity in Contemporary Society*, London: Routledge.

Brunåker, S. (1996) 'Introducing second-generation family members into the family-operated business – a constructionist approach', dissertation, Swedish University of Agricultural Sciences, Uppsala.

—— (1999) 'Understanding the succession process in family businesses', in B. Johannisson and H. Landström (eds) *Images of Entrepreneurship and Small Business*, Lund: Studentlitteratur.

Bruner, J.S. (1990) *Acts of Meaning*, Cambridge, MA: Harvard University Press.

Brunninge, O. and Nordqvist, M. (2001) 'Board composition and strategic change: some findings from family firms and venture capital backed firms', in M. Huse and H. Landström (eds) *Corporate Governance in SMEs*, SIRE Report 2001:1, Halmstad University, Sweden.

Bruns, V. (2001) 'A dual perspective on the credit process between banks and growing privately held firms', JIBS Research Report No. 2001–1, Jönköping International Business School, Sweden.

Brunsson, N. (1985) *The Irrational Organization: Irrationality as a Basis for Organizational Action and Change*, Chichester: John Wiley.

Bryman, A. (1988) *Quantity and Quality in Social Research*, London: Unwin Hyman.

Burke, R.J. and Greenglass, E.R. (1987) 'Work and family', *International Review of Industrial and Organizational Psychology*, 9, 273–320.

Burr, V. (1995) *An Introduction to Social Construction*, London: Routledge.

Butler, J.E. and Hansen, G.S. (1991) 'Network evolution, entrepreneurial success and regional development', *Entrepreneurship and Regional Development*, 3, 1–16.

Bygrave, W.D. (1989) 'The entrepreneurship paradigm (I): a philosophical look at its research methodologies', *Entrepreneurship Theory and Practice*, Fall, 7–26.

Cadbury, Sir A. (chairman) (1992) *Report of the Committee on the Financial Aspects of Corporate Governance*, London: Gee & Co.

Calder, G.H. (1961) 'The peculiar problems of a family business', *Business Horizons*, 4, 3, 93–102.

Campagne, P., Carère, G. and Valceschini, E. (1990) 'Three agricultural regions of France: three types of pluriactivity', *Journal of Rural Studies*, 6, 4, 415–22.

Carter, S. (1998) 'Portfolio entrepreneurship in the farm sector: indigenous growth in rural areas?', *Entrepreneurship and Regional Development*, 10, 17–32.

Carter, S. and Jones-Evans, D. (eds) (2000) *Enterprise and Small Business: Principles, Practice and Policy*, Harlow: Pearson Education Ltd.

Carter, S. and Rosa, P. (1998) 'Indigenous rural firms: farm enterprises in the UK', *International Small Business Journal*, 16, 4, 15–27.

Cashmore, E. (1991) 'Flying business class: Britain's new ethnic elite', *New Community*, 17, 347–58.

Chapman, S. (1996) 'The Fielden fortune. The finances of Lancashire's most successful ante-bellum manufacturing family', *Financial History Review*, 3, 1, 7–28.

Chell, E. (1998) 'A social constructionist perspective of entrepreneurship', paper presented at the Institute for Small Business Affairs, November.

Chell, E. and Baines, S. (2000) 'Networking, entrepreneurship and microbusiness behaviour', *Entrepreneurship and Regional Development*, 12, 2, 195–215.

Chittenden, F., Hall, G. and Hutchinson, P. (1996) 'Small company growth, access to capital markets and financial structure: review of issues and an empirical investigation', *Small Business Economics*, 8, 59–67.

Chrisman, J.J., Chua, J.H. and Sharma, P. (1998) 'Important attributes of successors in family businesses: an exploratory study', *Family Business Review*, 11, 1, 19–30.

Chua, J.H., Chrisman, J.J. and Sharma, P. (1999) 'Defining the family business by behavior', *Entrepreneurship Theory and Practice*, 23, 4, 19–39.

Church, R. (1993) 'The family firm in industrial capitalism: international perspectives on hypotheses and history', *Business History*, 35, 4, 17–43.

Churchill, N.C. and Lewis, V.L. (1983) 'The five stages of small business growth', *Harvard Business Review*, May–June, 30–50.

Cohen, G. (1993) *Memory in the Real World*, Hillsdale, NJ: Lawrence Erlbaum Associates.

Coleman, S. and Carsky, M. (1999) 'Sources of capital for small family-owned businesses: evidence from the National Survey of Small Business Finances', *Family Business Review*, 12, 1, 73–85.

Collins, J., Gibson, K., Alcorso, C., Castles, S. and Tait, D. (1995) *A Shop Full of Dreams: Ethnic Small Business in Australia*, Leichhardt, NSW: Pluto Press.

Cooke, R.A. and Rousseau, D.M. (1984) 'Stress and strain from family roles and work roles and work-role expectations', *Journal of Applied Psychology*, 69, 252–60.

Cookson, G. (1997) 'Family firms and business networks: textile engineering in Yorkshire', *Business History*, 39, 1, 1–20.

Corden, A. and Eardley, T. (1999) 'Sexing the enterprise: gender, work and resource allocation in self-employed households', in L. McKie, S. Bowlby and S. Gregory (eds) *Gender, Power and the Household*, London: Macmillan.

Cosh, A.D. and Hughes, A. (1994) 'Size, financial structure and profitability', in A. Hughes and D. Storey (eds) *Finance and the Small Firm*, London: Routledge.

Cosier, R.A. and Harvey, M. (1998) 'The hidden strengths in family business: functional conflict', *Family Business Review*, 11, 1, 75–9.

Crampton, C.D. (1993) 'Is rugged individualism the whole story? Public and private accounts of a firm's story', *Family Business Review*, 6, 3, 233–62.

—— (1994) 'The entrepreneurial family', unpublished doctoral thesis, Yale University.

Crawford, J., Kippax, S., Onyx, J., Gault, U. and Benton, P. (1992) *Emotion and Gender: Constructing Meaning from Memory*, London: Sage Publications.

Cromie, S. and Adams, S. (1997) 'Management succession in family firms – the challenge of change', in D. Deakins *et al.* (eds) *Small Firms: Entrepreneurship in the Nineties*, London: Paul Chapman.

Cromie, S., Dunn, B., Sproull, A. and Chalmers, D. (1999a) 'Family firms in the Scottish highlands and islands', paper presented to the 22nd ISBA National Small Firms Policy and Research Conference, The Royal Armouries, Leeds, 17–19 November.

Cromie, S. *et al.* (1999b) 'Family firms in Scotland and Northern Ireland: an empirical investigation', *Journal of Small Business and Enterprise Development*, 6, 3, 253–66.

Cromie, S., Stephenson, B. and Monteith, D. (1995) 'The management of family firms: an empirical investigation', *International Small Business Journal*, 13, 11–34.

Crossick, G., Haupt, H.G. and Merriman, J. (1996) 'The petite bourgeoisie in Europe, 1780–1914: enterprise, family and independence', *Economic History Review*, 49, 3, 619–20.

Curran, J. (2000) 'What is small business policy in the UK for? Evaluation and assessing small business policies', *International Small Business Journal*, 18, 3, 36–50.

Curran, J. and Blackburn, R.A. (1991) 'Small firms and networks: methodological strategies – some findings', *International Small Business Journal*, 11, 2, 13–25.

Curran, J. and Burrows, R. (1986) 'The sociology of petit capitalism: a trend report', *Sociology*, 20, 2, 265–79.

Curran, J. and Stanworth, J. (1979a) 'Self selection and the small firm worker – a critique and an alternative view', *Sociology*, 13, 3, 427–44.

—— (1979b) 'Work involvement and social relations in the small firm', *Sociological Review*, 27, 2, 317–42.

—— (1981a) 'Size of workplace and attitudes to industrial relations in the printing and electronics industries', *British Journal of Industrial Relations*, 19, 1, 14–25.

—— (1981b) 'A new look at job satisfaction in the small firms', *Human Relations*, 34, 5, 343–65.

Curran, J. and Storey, D. (2000) 'Small business policy: past experience and future directions', paper presented to Linking Research and Policy: Kingston-SBS Seminar Series, DTI Conference Centre, London, 12 December (available online at http://business. kingston.ac.uk/research/kbssbs/currstor.pdf).

Dahya, B. (1973) 'Pakistanis in Britain: transients or settlers?', *Race* 14, 241–78.

Daily, C.M. and Dollinger, M.J. (1992) 'An empirical examination of ownership structure and family and professionally managed firms', *Family Business Review*, 5, 2, 117–36.

—— (1993) 'Alternative methodologies for identifying family versus nonfamily managed businesses', *Journal of Small Business Management*, April, 79–90.

Danco, L.A. (1980) *Inside the Family Business*, Cleveland, OH: Center for Family Business.

—— (1992) *Beyond Survival: A Guide for the Business Owner and His Family* (15th reprint), Cleveland, OH: Center for Family Business.

D'Aveni, R.A. and Gunther, R.E. (1994) *Hypercompetition: Managing Dynamics of Strategic Maneuvering*, New York: The Free Press.

Davis, J.A. (1982) 'The influence of life stage on father–son work relationships in family companies', unpublished thesis, Harvard Business School.

Davis, P. (1983) 'Realising the potential of the family business', *Organizational Dynamics*, Summer, 47–56.

Davis, P.S. and Harveston, P.D. (1998) 'The influence of family business succession process: a multi-generational perspective', *Entrepreneurship Theory and Practice*, Spring, 31–53.

Davis, P. and Stern, D. (1980) 'Adaptation, survival, and growth of the family business: an integrated systems perspective', *Human Relations*, 34, 4, 207–24.

—— (1988) 'Adaptation, survival, and growth of the family business: an integrated systems perspective', *Family Business Review*, 1, 1, 69–85.

Deakins, D., Majmudar, M. and Paddison, A. (1997) 'Developing success strategies for ethnic minorities in business: evidence from Scotland', *New Community*, 23, 325–42.

Deetz, S. (1992) *Democracy in an Age of Corporate Colonization: Developments in Communication and the Politics of Everyday Life*, New York: State University.

Deveaux, M. (2000) 'Conflicting equalities? Cultural group rights versus sex equality', *Journal of Political Studies*, 48, 522–39.

De Visscher, F.M., Aronoff, C.F. and Ward, J.L. (1995) *Financing Transitions: Managing Capital and Liquidity in the Family Business* (*Family Business Leadership Series*), Marietta, GA: Business Owner Resources.

Dex, S., Willis, J., Paterson, R. and Sheppard, E. (2000) 'Freelance workers and contract uncertainty: the effects of contractual changes in the television industry', *Work, Employment and Society*, 14, 2, 283–305.

DiMaggio, P.J. and Powell, W.W. (1983). 'The iron cage revisited: institutional isomorphism and collective rationality in organizational fields', *American Sociological Review*, 48, 147–60.

Donckels, R. (1997) *Family Businesses on their Way to the New Millennium*, Brussels: Small Business Research Institute.

Donckels, R. and Fröhlich, E. (1991) 'Are family businesses really different? European experiences from STRATOS', *Family Business Review*, 7, 149–60.

Donnelley, R.G. (1964) 'The family business', *Harvard Business Review*, 42, 93–105.

Drucker, P.F. (1995) *Managing in a Time of Great Change*, Oxford: Butterworth-Heinemann.

DTI (2000) 'Consultation on the Small Business Service: summary of replies and Government's response' (available online at http://www.dti.gov.uk/sbs/execsum.htm).

Dun and Bradstreet (1999) Unpublished raw data, 479 St Kilda Road, Melbourne, Victoria 3004, Australia.

Dunkley, J. (1997) 'Strategic HRM and the family-controlled SME', paper presented at the Small Business and Enterprise Development Conference, University of Sheffield.

Dunn, B. (1995a) 'Success themes in Scottish family enterprises: philosophies and practices through generations', *Family Business Review*, 8, 1, 17–28.

—— (1995b) *The Challenges Facing Scotland's Family Enterprises: Perspectives for Family Firms, Advisers and Education*, Glasgow: Centre for Family Enterprise, Glasgow Caledonian University.

—— (1996) 'Family enterprises in UK – a special sector?', *Family Business Review*, 9, 2, 139–56.

—— (1999a) 'The family factor: the impact of family relationship dynamics on business-owning families during transitions', *Family Business Review*, 12, 1, 41–60.

—— (1999b) 'Who's ready, willing and able? A longitudinal study of the succession transition process in family enterprises', paper presented at Family Business Network Conference, Stockholm, 16 September.

—— (1999c) 'Emotional and developmental influences on the management of generational transitions by business-owning families', unpublished doctoral thesis.

Dunn, B. and Hughes, M. (1995) 'Themes and issues in the recognition of family businesses in the UK', paper presented to the 18th Institute for Small Business Affairs National Small Firms Conference, University of Paisley, 15–17 November.

Dyer, W.G. (1986) *Cultural Change in Family Firms: Anticipating and Managing Business and Family Transitions*, San Francisco: Jossey-Bass.

—— (1989) 'Integrating professional management into a family-owned business', *Family Business Review*, 2, 3, 221–35.

—— (1994a) 'Potential contribution of organisational behaviour to the study of family-owned business', *Family Business Review*, 7, 2, 109–32.

—— (1994b) 'Toward a theory of entrepreneurial careers', *Entrepreneurship Theory and Practice*, Winter, 7–21.

Dyer, W.G. and Handler, W. (1994) 'Entrepreneurship and family business: exploring the connections', *Family Business Review*, 19, 1, 71–83.

Dyer, W.G. and Sánchez, M. (1998) 'Current state of family business theory and practice as reflected in *Family Business Review*', *Family Business Review*, 11, 4, 287–95.

Edwards, J.R. and Rothbard, N.P. (2000) 'Mechanism linking work and family: clarifying the relationship between work and family constructs', *Academy of Management Review*, 25, 1, 178–99.

Eisenhardt, K.M. (1989) 'Building theories from case study research', *Academy of Management Review*, 14, 4, 532–50.

Ericson, T., Melander, A. and Melin, L. (2001) 'The role of the strategist', in H.W. Volberda and T. Elfring (eds) *Rethinking Strategy*, London: Sage Publications.

Erikson, E.H. (1950) *Childhood and Society*, New York: Norton.

Eriksson, M. (2000) *Strategi, kalkyl, känsla*, Stockholm: EFI, Stockholm School of Economics.

Etzioni, A. (1988) *The Moral Dimension: Toward a New Economics*, London: The Free Press.

European Commission (1996) 'SMEs: recommendation of the Commission', *Official Journal of the European Communities*, L107/6, 1–2.

Eurostat (1995) *Europe in Figures*, Luxembourg: Office for the Official Publications of the European Union.

Evans, N. and Ilbery, B. (1992) 'Farm-based accommodation and the restructuring of agriculture: evidence from three English counties', *Journal of Rural Studies*, 8, 1, 85–96.

Fernandez-Kelly, P. and Garcia, A. (1990) 'Power surrendered, power restored: the politics of work and family among Hispanic garment workers in California and Florida', in L. Tilly and P. Guerin (eds) *Women and Politics in America*, New York: Russell Sage Foundation.

Fiegener, M.K., Brown, B.M., Prince, R.A. and File, K.M. (1994) 'A comparison of successor development in family and non-family business', *Family Business Review*, 7, 4, 313–29.

Finch, J. and Mason, J. (1993) *Negotiating Family Responsibilities*, London: Routledge.

Fineman, S. (1993) *Emotion in Organizations*, London: Sage Publications.

—— (1997) 'Emotion and organizing', in S. Glegg, C. Hardy and W. Nord (eds) *Handbook of Organization Studies*, London: Sage Publications.

Flap, H., Kumcu, A. and Bulder, B. (1999) 'The social capital of ethnic entrepreneurs and their business success', in J. Rath (ed.) *Immigrant Businesses: The Economic, Political and Social Environment*, London: Macmillan.

Fletcher, D. (1997) 'Organisational networking, strategic change and the family business', unpublished doctoral thesis, Nottingham Trent University.

—— (2000) 'Family and enterprise', in S. Carter and D. Jones-Evans (eds) *Enterprise and Small Business: Principles, Practice and Policy*, Harlow: Pearson Education Ltd.

—— (2001) 'Experiencing professional management in the small, family firm', paper presented at 17th EGOS Colloquium, Lyons, 5–7 July.

—— (2002) '"In the company of men": a reflexive tale of cultural organizing in a small organization', *Gender, Work and Organization*, August, 9, 4, 397–418.

Florin Samuelsson, E. (1999) 'Redovisning och små, växande familjeföretag' (in Swedish), *JIBS Research Reports No. 1999–1*, Jönköping International Business School, Sweden.

Flyvbjerg, B. (1991) *Rationalitet og magt, Band II Et case-baseret studie av planlaegning, politik og modernitet*, Copenhagen: Akademisk Forlag.

Folbre, N. (1994) *Who Pays for the Kids? Gender and the Structures of Constraint*, London: Routledge.

Foster, A.T. (1995) 'Developing leadership in the successor generation', *Family Business Review*, 8, 3, 201–9.

Fox, M., Nilikant, V. and Hamilton, R.T. (1996) 'Managing succession in family-owned businesses', *International Small Business Journal*, 15, 1, 15–25.

Frone, M.R., Barnes, G.M. and Farrell, M.P. (1994) 'Relationship of work–family conflict to substance use among employed mothers: the role of negative affect', *Journal of Marriage and the Family*, 56, 1019–30.

Frone, M.R., Russell, M. and Cooper, M.L. (1992) 'Antecedents and outcomes of work–family conflict: testing a model of the work–family interface', *Journal of Applied Psychology*, 77, 1, 65–78.

Frone, M.R., Yardley, J.K. and Markel, K.S. (1997) 'Developing and testing an integrative model of the work–family interface', *Journal of Vocational Behavior*, 50, 145–67.

Fukuyama, F. (1995) *Trust: The Social Virtues and the Creation of Prosperity*, London: Hamish Hamilton.

Fuller, A. (1990) 'From part-time farming to pluriactivity: a decade of change in rural Europe', *Journal of Rural Studies*, 6, 4, 361–73.

Gallo, M.A. and Vilaseca, A. (1996) 'Finance in family business', *Family Business Review*, 9, 4, 387–401.

—— (1998) 'A financial perspective on structure, conduct and performance in the family firm: an empirical study', *Family Business Review*, 11, 1, 35–47.

Gambetta, D. (1993) *The Sicilian Mafia. The Business of Private Protection*, London: Harvard University Press.

Gartner, W.B. (1990) 'What are we talking about when we talk about entrepreneurship?', *Journal of Business Venturing*, 5, 1, 15–28.

Gartner, W.B., Bird, B.J. and Starr, J.A. (1992) 'Acting "as if": differentiating entrepreneurial from organizational behavior', *Entrepreneurship Theory and Practice*, 16, Spring, 13–31.

Gasson, R., Crow, G., Errington, A., Hutson, J., Marsden, T. and Winter, D.M. (1988) 'The farm as a family business: a review', *Journal of Agricultural Economics*, 39, 1–41.

Gasson, R. and Errington, A. (1993) *The Farm Family Business*, Wallingford: CAB International.

GEEF (2001) 'A comparison of taxes, relevant to the transfer of businesses – identifying best practices', prepared by European Group of Owner Managed and Family Enterprises, 28 May.

George, J.M. and Brief, A.P. (1990) 'The economic instrumentality of work: an examination of the moderating effects of financial requirements and sex on the pay–life satisfaction relationship', *Journal of Vocational Behavior*, 37, 357–68.

Gergen, K.K. (1999) *An Invitation to Social Construction*, London: Sage Publications.

Gergen, K.K. and Gergen, M.M. (1991) 'Toward reflexive methodologies', in F. Steier (ed.) (1992) *Research and Reflexivity*, London: Sage Publications.

Gersick, C.J.G. (1991) 'Revolutionary change theories: a multilevel exploration of the punctuated equilibrium paradigm', *Academy of Management Review*, 16, 1.

Gersick, K.E., Davis, J.A., McCollom, M.E., Hampton and Lansberg, I. (1997) *Generation to Generation: Lifecycles of Family Business*, Boston: Harvard Business School Press.

Gersick, K.E., Lansberg, I., Desjardins, M. and Dunn, B. (1999) 'Stages and transitions: managing change in the family business', *Family Business Review*, 12, 4, 287–97.

Giddens, A. (1984) *The Constitution of Society*, Berkeley, CA: University of California Press.

Gittins, D. (1985) *The Family in Question: Changing Households and Familiar Ideologies*, London: Macmillan.

Goss, D. (1991) *Small Business and Society*, London: Routledge.

Grabher, G. (ed.) (1993) *The Embedded Firm and the Socio-Economics of Industrial Networks*, London: Routledge.

Granger, B., Stanworth, J. and Stanworth, C. (1995) 'Self-employment career dynamics: the case of unemployment "push" in UK book publishing', *Work, Employment and Society*, 9, 499–516.

Granovetter, M. (1985) 'Economic action and social structure: the problem of embeddedness', *American Journal of Sociology*, 91, 3, 481–510.

—— (1992) 'Economic action and social structure: the problem of embeddedness', in R. Swedberg and M. Granovetter (eds) *The Sociology of Economic Life*, San Francisco: Westview Press.

Gray, C. (1998) *Enterprise and Culture*, London: Routledge.

Greenhaus, J.H. and Beutell, N.J. (1985) 'Sources of conflict between work and family roles', *Academy of Management Review*, 10, 76–88.

Greenwood, R. and Hinings, C.R. (1996) 'Understanding radical organizational change:

bringing together the old and new institutionalists', *Academy of Management Review*, 21, 4, 1022–54.

Grell, O.P. and Woolf, S. (eds) (1996) 'Domestic strategies: work and the family in France and Italy, 1600–1800', *Historical Journal*, 39, 1, 257–63.

Gubrium, J.F. and Holstein, J.A. (1990) *What is Family?*, Mountain View, CA: Mayfield Publishing.

Guzzo, R.A. and Abbott, S. (1990) 'Family firms as utopian organizations', *Family Business Review*, 3, 23–33.

Hall, A., Melin, L. and Nordqvist, M. (2000) 'Entrepreneurial strategies in family businesses: the impact of culture on the strategy process', paper presented at the Family Business Network conference, Academic Research Forum, 11th Annual World Conference, London, October.

Hamabata, M.M. (1990) *Crested Kimono: Power and Love in the Japanese Business Family*, London: Cornell University Press.

Hammersley, M. (1992) *What's Wrong with Ethnography?*, London: Routledge.

Handler, W.C. (1989a) *Managing the Family Firm Succession Process: The Next Generation Family Member's Experience*, unpublished doctoral thesis, Boston: Boston University Graduate School of Management.

—— (1989b) 'Methodological issues and considerations in studying family businesses', *Family Business Review*, 2, 257–76.

—— (1992) 'The succession experience of the next generation', *Family Business Review*, 5, 3, 283–307.

—— (1994) 'Succession in family business: a review of the research', *Family Business Review*, 7, 2, 133–58.

Hardill, I. (1998) 'Trading places: case studies of the labour market experiences of women in rural in-migrant households', *Local Economy*, 13, 2, 102–13.

Hareven, T. (1975) 'Family time and industrial time: family and work 1912–22: the role of family and ethnicity in the adjustment to urban life', *Labor History*, 16, 249–65.

Hargreaves Heap, S. (1989) *Rationality in Economics*, Oxford: Basil Blackwell.

Harré, R. (1983) *Personal Being*, Oxford: Basil Blackwell.

—— (1986) 'An outline of the social constructionist viewpoint', in R. Harré (ed.) *The Social Construction of Emotions*, Oxford: Basil Blackwell.

Harré, R. and Parrot, G.W. (1996) 'Overview', in R. Harré and G.W. Parrot (eds) *The Emotions: Social, Cultural and Biological Dimensions*, London: Sage Publications.

Harris, D., Martinez, J.I. and Ward, J.L. (1994) 'Is strategy different for the family-owned business?', *Family Business Review*, 8, 2, 159–73.

Harvey, M. and Evans, R. (1994) 'Family business and multiple levels of conflict', *Family Business Review*, 7, 4, 331–48.

—— (1995) 'Life after succession in the family business: is it really the end of problems?', *Family Business Review*, 8, 1, 3–16.

Hatfield, E. and Rapson, R. (1993) 'Love and attachment processes', in M. Lewis and J. Haviland (eds) *Handbook of Emotions*, New York: The Guilford Press.

Haugen, M. (1994) 'Rural women's status in family and property law: lessons from Norway', in S. Whatmore, T. Marsden and P. Lowe (eds) *Gender and Rurality* (*Critical Perspectives on Rural Change Series*, 6), London: David Fulton Publishers.

Haugen, M. and Vartdal, B. (1994) *Small Business among Farmers: A New Strategy for Diversification*, Paper no. 1/94, Center for Rural Research, Trondheim: University of Trondheim.

Heinonen, V. (1998) *Talonpoikainen etiikka ja kulutuksen henki. Kotitalousneuvonnasta kuluttajapolitiikkaan 1900-luvun Suomessa*, Helsinki: Bibliotheka Historica 33.

Helweg, A. (1986) *Sikhs in Britain*, London: Oxford University Press.

Hershon, S.A. (1975) 'The problem of management succession', unpublished doctoral thesis.

Herz Brown, F. (1991) *Reweaving the Family Tapestry: a Multigenerational Approach to Families*, New York: Norton.

Heuberger, G. (ed.) and Gutwein, D. (1997) 'The Rothschilds: essays on the history of a European family' (review), *Journal of Economic History*, 57, 1, 214–16.

Hill, B. (1993) 'The "myth" of the family farm: defining the family farm and assessing its importance in the European community', *Journal of Rural Studies*, 9, 4, 359–70.

Hoel, B. (1984) 'Contemporary clothing sweatshops: Asian female labour and collective organisation', in J. West (ed.) *Work, Women and the Labour Market*, London: Routledge & Kegan Paul.

Hofstede, G. (1991) *Cultures and Organizations: Software of the Mind*, London: McGraw-Hill.

Holland, P.G. and Boulton, W.B. (1984) 'Balancing the "family" and the "business" in family business', *Business Horizons*, March–April, 16–21.

Hollander, B. (1983) *Family-Owned Businesses as a System: A Case Study of the Interaction of Family, Task and Market Place Components*, unpublished doctoral thesis, Pittsburgh: Graduate Faculty of Education, University of Pittsburgh.

—— (1984) 'Towards a model for family-owned business', paper presented at meeting of the Academy of Management, Boston.

Hollander, B. and Bukowitz, W.R. (1990) 'Women, family culture, and family business', *Family Business Review*, 3, 2 139–51.

Hollander, B. and Elman, N.S. (1988) 'Family-owned businesses: an emerging field of inquiry', *Family Business Review*, 1, 2, 145–64.

Holliday, R. (1992) 'Cutting new patterns for small firms' research', in K. Caley, E. Chell, F. Chittendden and C. Mason (eds) *Small Enterprise Development Policy and Practice in Action*, Lancashire: Lancashire Enterprises.

—— (1995) *Investigating Small Firms: Nice Work*, London: Routledge.

Holliday, R. and Letherby, G. (1993) 'Happy families or poor relations – an exploration of familial analogies in the small firm', *International Small Business Journal*, 11, 2, 54–63.

Hollis, M. (1983) 'Rational preferences', *The Philosophical Forum*, 14, 3–4.

—— (1994) *The Philosophy of Science: An Introduction*, Cambridge: Cambridge University Press.

Holme, C. (1992) 'Self development and the small organisation', *Training and Development UK*, August, 16–19.

House, J.S., Strecher, V., Metzner, H.L. and Robbins, C.A. (1986) 'Occupational stress and health among men and women in Tecumseh Community Health Study', *Journal of Health and Social Behavior*, 27, 62–77.

House, J.S., Wells, J.A., Landerman, L.R., McMichael, A.J. and Kaplan, B.H. (1979) 'Occupational stress and health among factory workers', *Journal of Health and Social Behaviour*, 20, 139–60.

Hoy, F. and Verser, T.G. (1994) 'Emerging business, emerging field: entrepreneurship and the family firm', *Entrepreneurship Theory and Practice*, 18, Fall, 9–23.

Hudson, J. (2001) 'Capital succession', in A. Jolly (ed.) *The Growing Business Handbook*, London: Kogan Page.

Hughes, R.L., Ginnett, R.C. and Curphy, G.J. (1996) *Leadership: Enhancing the Lessons of Experience* (2nd edn), Boston: Irwin McGraw-Hill.

Hung, H. (1998) 'A typology of the theories of the roles of governing boards', *Corporate Governance: An International Review*, 6, 2, 101–11.

Huse, M. (1995) *Tante, barbar eller klan: om styrets rolle* (in Norwegian), Bergen: Fagbokforlaget.

—— (1998) 'Researching the dynamics of board-stakeholder relations', *Long Range Planning*, 31, 218–26.

Ibarra, H. (1993) 'Personal networks and minorities in management: a conceptual framework', *Academy of Management Review*, 18, 1, 56–87.

Ilbery, B. (1991) 'Farm diversification as an adjustment strategy on the urban fringe of the West Midlands', *Journal of Rural Studies*, 7, 3, 207–18.

Ingram, P. and Simons, T. (1995) 'Institutional and resource dependence determinants of responsiveness to work–family issues', *Academy of Management Journal*, 38, 5, 1460–82.

Jackall, R. (1988) *Moral Mazes: The World of Corporate Managers*, New York: Oxford University Press.

James, H.S. (1999a) 'What can the family contribute to business? Examining contractual relationships', *Family Business Review*, 12, 1, 61–71.

—— (1999b) 'Owners as manager, extended horizons and the family firm', *International Journal of the Economics of Business*, 6, 1, 41–55.

Janesick, V. (1998) 'The dance of qualitative research design: metaphor, methodolatry and meaning', in N.K. Denzin and Y.S. Lincoln (eds) *Strategies of Qualitative Enquiry*, Thousand Oaks, CA: Sage Publications.

Jensen, M.C. and Meckling, W.H. (1976) 'Theory of the firm: managerial behaviour, agency costs and ownership structure', *Journal of Financial Economics*, 3, 305–60.

Johannisson, B. (1987a) 'Beyond process and structure: social exchange networks', *International Studies of Management and Organisation*, 17, 1, 3–23.

—— (1987b) 'Anarchists and organisers: entrepreneurs in a network perspective', *International Studies of Management and Organisation*, 17, 1, 49–63.

—— (ed.) (1992) *Entreprenörskap på svenska*, Malmö: Almqvist & Wiksell.

—— (2000) 'Modernising the industrial district – rejuvenation or managerial colonisation', in M. Taylor and E. Vatne (eds) *The Networked Firm in a Global World: Small Firms in New Environments*, Aldershot: Ashgate.

Johannisson, B. and Forslund, M. (1998) *Det medelstora familjeföretaget – en ideologisk kraftsamling* (FSF-rapport 1998:7), Örebro: FSF.

Johannisson, B. and Huse, M. (2000) 'Recruiting outside board members in the small family business: an ideological challenge', *Entrepreneurship and Regional Development*, 12, 4, 353–78.

Johnson, G. (1986) *Strategic Change and the Management Process*, Oxford: Basil Blackwell.

—— (1988) 'Rethinking incrementalism', *Strategic Management Journal*, 9, 75–91.

Jones, T., McEvoy, D. and Barrett, G. (1994a) 'Labour-intensive practices in the ethnic minority firm', in J. Atkinson and D. Storey (eds) *Employment, the Small Firm and the Labour Market*, London: Routledge.

—— (1994b) 'Raising capital for the ethnic minority firm', in A. Hughes and D. Storey (eds) *Finance and the Small Firm*, London: Routledge.

—— (1997) 'Universalism versus particularism in ethnic minority business studies', Conference on South Asian Entrepreneurship, University of Reading, 29 September.

—— (1999) 'Market potential as a decisive influence on ethnic business development', in J. Rath (ed.) *Immigrant Businesses: The Economic, Political and Social Environment*, London: Macmillan.

Jordan, B., James, S., Kay, H. and Redley, M. (1992) *Trapped in Poverty: Labour Market Decisions in Low Income Households*, London: Routledge.

Jöreskog, K.G. and Sörbom, D. (1989) *LISREL 7: A Guide to the Program and Application*, Chicago: SPSS Inc.

Joseph, M. (1999) 'Trends in private equity', in C. Gasson and A. Jolly (eds) *Corporate Finance Handbook*, London: Kogan Page.

Judge, W.Q. and Zeithaml, C.P. (1992) 'Institutional and strategic choice perspectives on board involvement in strategic decision process', *Academy of Management Journal*, 35, 4, 766–94.

Kahn, R.L., Wolfe, D.M., Quinn, R.P., Snoek, J.D. and Rosenthal, R.A. (1964) *Organizational Stress: Studies in Role Conflict and Ambiguity*, New York: John Wiley.

Kanter, R.M. (1977) *Work and Family in the United States: A Critical Review and Agenda for Research and Policy*, New York: Russell Sage.

—— (1989) 'Work and family in the United States: a critical review and agenda for research and policy', *Family Business Review*, 2, 1, 77–114.

Karlsson-Stider, A. (2000) 'Familjen och Firman' (in Swedish), doctoral dissertation, EKI Stockholm School of Economics, Stockholm.

Katila, S. (2000) *Moraalijärjestyksen rajaama tila: maanviljelijä-yrittäjäperheiden selviytymisstrategiat* ('Framed by Moral Order: The Survival Strategies of Farm-based Businesses') (*Acta Universitatis Oeconomicae Helsingiensis* A-174), Helsinki: School of Economics and Business Administration.

Kaye, K. (1996) 'When the family business is a sickness', *Family Business Review*, 9, 4, 347–68.

Kepner, E. (1983) 'The family and the firm: a coevolutionary perspective', *Organisational Dynamics*, 12, 1, 57–70.

Kerr, M. and Bowen, M. (1988) *Family Evaluation*, New York: Norton.

Kets de Vries, M. (1985) 'The dark side of entrepreneurship', *Harvard Business Review*, January–February, 160–7.

—— (1993) 'The dynamics of family controlled firms: the good and the bad news', *Organisational Dynamics*, 21, 3, 59–71.

—— (1996) *Family Business: Human Dilemmas in the Family Firm*, London: International Thomson Business Press.

Kibria, N. (1994) 'Household structure and family ideologies: the dynamics of immigrant economic adaptation among Vietnamese refugees', *Social Problems*, 41, 81–96.

Kim, K. and Huhr, W. (1985) 'Ethnic resources utilisation of Korean immigrant entrepreneurs in the Chicago minority area', *International Migration Review*, 18, 82–111.

Kimhi, A. (1997) 'Intergenerational succession in small family businesses: borrowing constraints and optimal timing of succession', *Small Business Economics*, 9, 4, 309–18.

Klein, K.J., Dansereau, F. and Hall, R.J. (1994) 'Levels issues in theory development, data collection and analysis', *Academy of Management Review*, 19, 2, 195–229.

Kumpulainen, M. (1999) *Maan ja talouden välissä. Vilsi kertomusta suomalaisen maatilan luontosuhteen muutoksesta*, Joensuun yliopisto, Maantieteenlaitos, julkaisuja No. 5.

Kundnani, A. (2000) 'Stumbling on: race and class in England', *Race and Class*, 41, 1–18.

Lambert, S.J. (1990) 'Processes linking work and family: a critical review and research agenda', *Human Relations*, 43, 249–57.

Landman, J. (1996) 'Social control of "negative emotions": the case of regret', in R. Harré and G.W. Parrot (eds) *The Emotions: Social, Cultural and Biological Dimensions*, London: Sage Publications.

Landström, H. and Johannisson, B. (2001) 'Theoretical foundations of Swedish entrepreneurship and small-business research', *Scandinavian Journal of Management*, 17, 2, 225–48.

Lansberg, I. (1983) 'Managing human resources in family firms: the problem of institutional overlap', *Organisational Dynamics*, 12, 1, 39–46.

—— (1988) 'The succession conspiracy', *Family Business Review*, 1, 2, 119–43.

—— (1996) 'The succession conspiracy', in R. Bechard (ed.) *The Best of Family Business Review*, Brookline, MA: The Family Firm Institute.

—— (1999) *Succeeding Generations: Realizing the Dream of Families in Business*, Boston: Harvard Business School Press.

—— (2001) 'The reflective practitioner: a tribute to Dick Beckhard', *Family Business Review*, 14, 1, 3–11.

Lansberg, I. and Astrachan, J. (1994) 'Influence of family relationships on succession planning and training: the importance of mediating factors', *Family Business Review*, 7, 1, 39–60.

Larson, A. (1992) 'Network dyads in entrepreneurial settings: a study of the governance of exchange relationships', *Administrative Science Quarterly*, 37, 76–104.

Leach, P. (1994) *The Stoy Hayward Guide to the Family Business*, London: Kogan Page.

Leiter, M.P. and Durup, M.J. (1996) 'Work, home, and in-between: a longitudinal study of spillover', *Journal of Applied Behavioral Science*, 32, 1, 29–47.

Levin, I. (1993) 'Family as mapped realities', *Journal of Family Issues*, 14, 1, 82–91.

Levinson, D.J. (1978) *The Seasons of a Man's Life*, New York: Basic Books.

—— (1996) *The Seasons of a Woman's Life*, New York: Knopf.

Levinson, H. (1971) 'Conflicts that plague the family business', *Harvard Business Review*, March–April, 49, 71–80.

Light, I. (1984) 'Immigrant and ethnic enterprise in North America', *Ethnic and Racial Studies*, 7, 195–216.

Light, I. and Bonacich, E. (1988) *Immigrant Entrepreneurs: Koreans in Los Angeles 1965–82*, Berkeley, CA: University of California Press.

Litz, R.A. (1995) 'The family business: toward definitional clarity', *Family Business Review*, 8, 2, 71–81.

Lombardini, S. (1996) 'Family, kin and the quest for community: a study of three social networks in early modern Italy', *History of the Family*, 1, 3, 227–58.

Longenecker, J.G. and Schoen, J.E. (1978) 'Management succession in the family business', *Journal of Small Business Management*, July, 1–6.

Lopez-Gracia, J. and Aybar-Arias, C. (2000) 'An empirical approach to the financial behaviour of small and medium-sized companies', *Small Business Economics*, 14, 55–63.

Loscocco, K.A. and Spitze, G. (1990) 'Working conditions, social support and the well-being of female and male factory workers', *Journal of Health and Social Behavior*, 31, 313–27.

Lowe, P. and Talbot, H. (2000) 'Policy for small business support in rural areas: a critical assessment of the proposals for the small business service', *Regional Studies*, 54, 5, 479–85.

Lutz, C.A. and White, G. (1986) 'The anthropology of emotions', *Annual Review of Anthropology*, 15, 405–36.

Lyon, M. (1973) 'Ethnicity in Britain: the Gujerati tradition', *New Community* 2, 399–419.

McCloskey, D. (1998) 'Bourgeois virtue and the history of P and S', *Journal of Economic History*, 58, 2.

McCollom, M.E. (1988) 'Integration in the family firm: when the family system replaces controls and culture', *Family Business Review*, 1, 4, 399–417.

—— (1990) 'Problems and prospects in clinical research on family firms', *Family Business Review*, Fall, 245–62.

—— (1992) 'Organizational stories in a family-owned business', *Family Business Review*, 5, 1, 3–23.

McCounaughy, D.L. and Phillips, G.M. (1999) 'Founders versus descendants: the profitability, efficiency, growth characteristics and financing in large, public, founding-family-controlled firms', *Family Business Review*, 12, 2, 123–31.

MacDonald, R. (1996) 'Welfare dependency, the enterprise culture and self-employed survival', *Work Employment and Society*, 10, 3, 431–47.

McMahon, R.G.P. and Stanger, A.M.J. (1995) 'Understanding the small enterprise financial objective function', *Entrepreneurship Theory and Practice*, Summer, 21–39.

Mäki, U., Gustavsson, B. and Knudsen, C. (1993) *Rationality, Institutions and Economic Methodology*, London: Routledge.

Malone, S.C. (1989) 'Selected correlates of business continuity in family business', *Family Business Review*, 2, 4, 341–53.

Mariussen, A., Wheelock, J. and Baines, S. (1997) 'The family business tradition in Britain and Norway: modernisation and reinvention?', *International Studies of Management and Organisation*, 27, 3, 64–85.

Matlay, H. (1996) 'Vocational education and training in the small business sector of the British economy', unpublished PhD thesis, Department of Continuing Education, University of Warwick.

—— (1997) 'Training and human resource management in small businesses: a mixed methodology approach', paper presented at the VET Conference, University of Huddersfield.

—— (1998) 'The paradox of training in the small business sector of the British economy', *Journal of Vocational Education and Training*, 49, 4, 573–89.

—— (1999) 'Vocational education and training in Britain: a small business perspective', *Education and Training*, 41, 1, 6–13.

—— (2000a) 'Vocational education and training in small businesses: setting a research agenda for the twenty-first century' (editorial article), *Education and Training*, 42, 4–5, 200–1.

—— (2000b) 'S/NVQs in Britain: employer-led or ignored?', *Journal of Vocational Education and Training*, 52, 1, 135–47.

—— (2001) *Training and HRD Needs in Small, Medium-sized and Large Businesses: An Empirical Evaluation*, Birmingham: Enterprise Research and Development Centre, University of Central England.

Matthews, C.H., Vasudevan, D.P., Barton, S.L. and Apana, R. (1994) 'Capital structure decision making in privately held companies: beyond the finance paradigm', *Family Business Review*, 7, 4, 349–67.

Medalie, J.H. and Goldbourt, U. (1976) 'Angina pectoris among 10,000 men, II: psychosocial and other risk factors as evidenced by a multivariate analysis of a five-year incidence study', *American Journal of Medicine*, 60, 910–21.

Melin, L. and Nordqvist, M. (2000) 'Corporate governance processes in family firms: the role of influential actors and the strategic arena', proceedings from the 45th ICSB World Conference, Brisbane.

Metcalf, H., Modood, T. and Virdee, S. (1996) *Asian Self-Employment: The Interaction of Culture and Economics*, London: Policy Studies Institute.

Meyer, J. and Rowan, B. (1977) 'Institutionalized organisations: formal structure as myth and ceremony', *American Journal of Sociology*, 83, 310–63.

Michaelas, N. (1998) 'Financial policy and capital structure choice in UK privately held companies', PhD thesis, Manchester Business School, University of Manchester.

Michaelas, N., Chittenden, F. and Poutziouris, P. (1998) *The Application of the Theory of Capital Structure to the Private Company Sector* (Working Paper No. 383), Manchester: Manchester Business School.

Miles, R. (1982) *Racism and Migrant Labour*, London: Routledge, Kegan & Paul.

Miles, M.B. and Huberman, A.M. (1994) *Qualitative Data Analysis* (2nd edn), Thousand Oaks, CA: Sage Publications.

Miller, D. (1990) *The Icarus Paradox: How Excellent Companies Can Bring About Their Own Downfall*, New York: Harper & Row.

Mintzberg, H., Ahlstrand, B. and Lampel, J. (1998) *Strategy Safari*, New York: The Free Press.

Mishra, C.S. and McConaughy, D.L. (1999) 'Founding family control and capital structure: the risk of loss of control and the aversion of debt', *Entrepreneurship Theory and Practice*, Summer, 53–64.

Mitchell, J.C. (1969) 'The concept and use of social networks', in J. Mitchell (ed.) (1973) *Social Networks in Urban Situations*, Manchester: University of Manchester Press.

—— (ed.) (1973) *Social Networks in Urban Situations*, Manchester: University of Manchester Press.

Mitter, S. (1986) 'Industrial restructuring and manufacturing homework', *Capital and Class*, 27, 37–80.

Morph, M. (1989) *The Work/Life Dichotomy: Prospects for Reintegrating People and Jobs*, New York: Quorum Books.

Morris, B. (1997) 'Is your family wrecking your career? (and vice versa)', *Fortune*, 135, 70–90.

Morris, M.H., Williams, R.O., Allen, J.A. and Avila, R.A. (1997) 'Correlates of success in family business transitions', *Journal of Business Venturing*, 12, 385–401.

Muller, M. (1996) 'Good luck or good management? Multigenerational family control in two Swiss enterprises since the nineteenth century', *Entreprises et histoire*, 12, 19–48.

Muncie, J. and Sapsford, R. (1997) 'Issues in the study of "the family"', in J. Muncie, M. Wetherell, M. Langan, R. Dallos and A. Cochrane (eds) *Understanding the Family*, London: Sage.

Myers, S.C. (1984) 'The capital structure puzzle', *Journal of Finance*, 34, 3, 575–92.

Myers, S.C. and Majluf, N.S. (1984) 'Corporate financing and investment decisions when firms have information the investors do not have', *Journal of Financial Economics*, 13, 187–221.

Nager, R.W., Aronoff, C.E. and Ward, J.L. (1995) *American Family Business Survey: 1995*, Houston: Arthur Andersen Center for Family Business.

Naman, J.L. and Slevin, D.P. (1993) 'Entrepreneurship and the concept of fit: a model and empirical tests', *Strategic Management Journal*, 14, 137–53.

Nee, V. and Wong, H. (1985) 'Asian-American socioeconomic achievement: the strength of family bonds', *Sociological Perspectives*, 28, 281–306.

Nelson, D. (1975) *Managers and Workers: Origins of the New Factory System in the United States, 1880–1920*, Madison: University of Wisconsin Press.

Nelson, M.K. and Smith, J. (1999) *Working Hard and Making Do: Surviving in Small Town America*, Berkeley, CA: University of California Press.

Neubauer, F. and Lank, A.G. (1998) *The Family Business – Its Governance for Sustainability*, London: Macmillan Business.

Newby, H. (1977) *The Deferential Worker*, Harmondsworth: Penguin.

North, D. (1990) *Institutions, Institutional Change and Economic Performance*, Cambridge: Cambridge University Press.

NUD_IST (Non-numerical Unstructured Data Indexing, Searching and Theorising) (1997) *User Guide*, Victoria: La Trobe University, Qualitative Solutions and Research Pty Ltd.

Oatley, K. (1993) 'Social construction of emotions', in M. Lewis and J. Haviland (eds) *Handbook of Emotions*, New York: The Guilford Press.

Ocasio, W. (1999) 'Institutionalized action and corporate governance: the reliance on rules of CEO succession', *Administrative Science Quarterly*, 44, 384–416.

Ödman, P.-J. (1991) *Tolkning, förståelse, vetande: Hermeneutik i teori och praktik*, Stockholm: Almqvist & Wiksell Förlag AB.

O'Hara, P. (1995) 'Household labour, the family and macro-economic stability in the US, 1940s–1990s', *Review of Social Economy*, 8, 1, 89–120.

Oliver, C.E. (1997) 'Sustainable competitive advantage: combining institutional and resource-based views', *Strategic Management Journal*, 18, 9, 697–713.

ONS–Office of National Statistics (1996) *Social Focus on Ethnic Minorities*, London: HMSO.

Ouchi, W.G. (1980) 'Markets, bureaucracies and clans', *Administrative Science Quarterly*, 25, 129–41.

Papero, D. (1995) 'Anxiety and organizations', in *The Emotional Side of Organisations, Applications of Bowen Theory*, Georgetown Family Center Conference on Organisations, 22–23 April, p. 56.

Parasuraman, S., Purohit, Y.S., Godshalk, V.M. and Beutell, N.J. (1996) 'Work and family variables, entrepreneurial career success, and psychological well-being', *Journal of Vocational Behavior*, 48, 275–300.

Parker, D. (1994) 'Encounters across the counter: young Chinese people in Britain', *New Community*, 20, 621–34.

Parsons, T. (1959) 'The social structure of the family', in R. Anshen (ed.) *The Family: Its Function and Destiny*, New York: Harper & Row.

Patton, M.Q. (1990) *Qualitative Evaluation and Research Methods* (2nd edn), Newbury Park, CA: Sage Publications.

Peltola, A. (2000) *Viljelijäperheiden monitoimisuus suomalaisilla maatiloilla*, Maatalouden taloudellinen tutkimuslaitos, julkaisuja 96.

Penrose, E. (1959/1995) *The Theory of the Growth of the Firm*, Oxford: Oxford University Press.

Pettigrew, A. (1992) 'On studying managerial elites', *Strategic Management Journal*, 13, 163–82.

Pettigrew, A. and Whipp, R. (1991) *Managing Change for Competitive Success*, Oxford: Blackwell.

Pettit, R.R. and Singer, R.F. (1985) 'Small business finance: a research agenda', *Financial Management*, Autumn, 47–61.

Pfeffer, J. (1982) *Organizations and Organization Theory*, Marshfield, MA: Pitman.

Phizacklea, A. (1990) *Unpacking the Fashion Industry*, London: Routledge.

Phizacklea, A. and Ram, M. (1996) 'Being your own boss: ethnic minority entrepreneurs in comparative perspective', *Work, Employment and Society*, 10, 2, 319–39.

Polkinghorne, D. (1991) 'Narrative and self-concept', *Journal of Narrative and Life History*, 1, 2/3, 135–53.

Poutziouris, P. (2000) 'Venture capital and small medium-size family companies: an analysis from the demand perspective', in P. Poutziouris (ed.) *Family Business – Tradition or Entrepreneurship in the New Economy*, book proceedings, 11th Annual Family Business Network World Conference, FBN-London, 255–82.

—— (2001a) 'The views of family companies on venture capital evidence from the UK SME economy', *Family Business Review*, 14, 3.

—— (2001b) 'Models of entrepreneurial development', in A. Jolly (ed.) *The Growing Business Handbook*, London: Kogan Page.

—— (2001c) 'Understanding family firms', in A. Jolly (ed.) *The Growing Business Handbook*, London: Kogan Page.

Poutziouris, P. and Chittenden, F. (1996) *Family Businesses or Business Families?*, Leeds: Institute for Small Business Affairs, in association with National Westminster Bank.

Poutziouris, P., Chittenden, F. and Michaelas, N. (1999) *The Financial Development of Smaller Private and Public Ltd Companies*, Liverpool: Tilney Fund Management Publication.

—— (2001) 'Modelling the impact of taxation (direct and compliance cost) on the UK small business economy', in C. Evans, J. Hasseldine and J. Pope (eds) *Taxation Compliance Costs: A Festschrift for Cedric Sandford*, Sydney: Prospect Media Pty Ltd.

Poutziouris, P., Michaelas, N. and Chittenden, F. (1998) *The Financial Affairs of UK SMEs: Family and Private Companies* (Working Paper No. 738), Manchester: Manchester Business School.

Poutziouris, P., Michaelas, N., Chittenden, F. and Sitorous (2000) *The Financial Structure, Behaviour and Performance of SMEs: Family and Private Companies*, Manchester: Small Business and Enterprise Development Conference, April.

Prahalad, C.K. and Bettis, R.A. (1986) 'The dominant logic: a new linkage between diversity and performance', *Strategic Management Journal*, 7, 485–501.

Rainnie, A. (1989) *Industrial Relations in Small Firms: Small Isn't Beautiful*, London: Routledge.

Rajagopolan, N. and Spreitzer, G.M. (1996) 'Towards a theory of strategic change: a multi-lens perspective and integrative framework', *Academy of Management Review*, 22, 1, 48–79.

Raley, M. and Moxey, A. (2000) *Rural Microbusinesses in the North-East of England: Final Survey Results*, Newcastle upon Tyne: Centre for Rural Economy, Department of Agricultural Economics and Food Marketing, University of Newcastle.

Ram, M. (1991) 'The dynamics of workplace relations in small firms', *International Small Business Journal*, 10, 1.

—— (1994a) *Managing to Survive – Working Lives in Small Firms*, Oxford: Blackwell.

—— (1994b) 'Unravelling social networks in ethnic minority firms', *International Small Business Journal*, 12, 3, 42–53.

Ram, M., Abbas, T., Sanghera, B., Barlow, G. and Jones, T. (forthcoming) 'Making the link: households and small business activity in a multi-ethnic context', *Community, Work and Family*.

Ram, M., Arrowsmith, J., Gilman, M. and Edwards, P. (2001) 'Once more into the sunset? Asian clothing firms after the National Minimum Wage', paper prepared for the 3rd Conference of the International Thematic Network on Public Policy and the Institutional Context of Immigrant Businesses, 'Working on the Fringes: Immigrant Businesses, Economic Integration, and Informal Practices', Liverpool, 22–5 March.

Ram, M. and Hillin, G. (1994) 'Achieving breakout: developing mainstream ethnic minority business', *Small Business Enterprise and Development* 1, 15–21.

Ram, M. and Holliday, R. (1993a) 'Keeping it in the family: family culture in small firms', in F. Chittenden, M. Robertson and D. Watkins (eds) *Small Firms: Recession and Recovery*, London: Paul Chapman.

—— (1993b) 'Relative merits: family culture and kinship in small firms', *Sociology*, 27, 4, 629–48.

Ram, M. and Jones, T. (1998) *Ethnic Minority Enterprise in Britain*, London: Small Business Research Trust.

Ram, M., Jones, T., Abbas, T. and Sanghera, B. (2002) 'Ethnic minority enterprise in its urban context: South Asian restaurants in Birmingham', *International Journal of Urban and Regional Research*, 26, 1, 26–40.

Ram, M., Sanghera, B., Abbas, T., Barlow, G. and Jones, T. (2000) 'Ethnic minority business in comparative perspective: the case of the independent restaurant sector', *Journal of Ethnic and Migration Studies*, 26, 495–510.

Rath, J. (2002) 'Needle games: mixed embeddedness of immigrant entrepreneurs', in J. Rath (ed.) *Unravelling the Rag Trade: Immigrant Entrepreneurship in Seven World Cities*, Oxford: Berg Publishers.

Ratner, C. (1989) 'A social constructionist critique of the naturalistic theory of emotion', *Journal of Mind and Behaviour*, 10, 3, 211–30.

Razin, E. and Langlois, A. (1996) 'Metropolitan characteristics and entrepreneurship among immigrants and ethnic groups in Canada', *International Migration Review*, 30, 703–27.

Regnér, P. (2001) 'Complexity and multiple rationalities in strategy processes', in H.W. Volberda and T. Elfring (eds) *Rethinking Strategy*, London: Sage Publications.

Reid, R., Dunn, B., Cromie, S. and Adams, J. (1999) 'Family orientation in family companies: a model and some empirical evidence', *Journal of Small Business and Enterprise Development*, 6, 1, 55–67.

Reis, J., Hespanha, P., Pires, A. and Jacinto, R. (1990) 'How "rural" is agricultural pluriactivity?', *Journal of Rural Studies*, 6, 4, 395–9.

Reynolds, P.D. (1995) 'Family firms in the start-up process: preliminary explorations', paper presented to the 1995 Annual Meeting of the International Family Business Program Association, 20–22 July, Nashville, TN.

Riordan, D. and Riordan, M. (1993) 'Field theory: an alternative to systems theories in understanding the small family business', *Journal of Small Business Management*, 31, 2, 66–78.

Robinson, V. (1986) *Transients, Settlers and Refugees*, Oxford: Clarendon.

Romano, C.A., Tanewski, G.A. and Smyrnios, K. (1997) 'Capital structure decision making: a model for family business', 9th Family Business Network Conference, Paris.

Rosa, P. (1993) 'Gender and small business co-ownership: implications for enterprise training', paper presented at INTENT, Stirling University.

Rosa, P., Hamilton, D., Carter, S. and Burns, H. (1994) 'The impact of gender on small business management: preliminary findings of a British study', *International Small Business Journal*, 12, 3, 25–32.

Rosenblatt, P.C. (1991) 'The interplay of family system and business system in family farms during economic recession', *Family Business Review*, 4, 45–57.

Roure, J. (1998) *A Formula for Successful Growth*, Barcelona: IESE, University of Navarra (with J. Prats and J. Pistrui).

Ruth, J.-E. and Kenyon, G. (1996) 'Biography in adult development and ageing', in J. Birren *et al.* (eds) *Ageing and Biography*, New York: Springer Publishing Company.

Ruth, J.-E. and Vilkko, A. (1996) 'Emotion in the construction of autobiography', in C. Malatesta, C. Magai and S. McFadden (eds) *Handbook of Emotion, Adult Development and Ageing*, San Diego: Academic Press.

Salaff, J. and Hu, S.M. (1996) 'Working daughters of Hong Kong: filial piety or power in the family', *Asian Thought and Society*, 21, 61, 187–9.

Sanders, J. and Nee, V. (1996) 'Immigrant self-employment: the family as social capital and the value of human capital', *American Sociological Review*, 61, 2, 231–49.

Scase, R. and Goffee, R. (1982) *The Entrepreneurial Middle Class*, London: Croom Helm.

Schein, E.H. (1995) 'The role of the founder in creating organisational culture', *Family Business Review*, 8, 3, 221–38.

Schön, D. (1983) *The Reflective Practitioner: How Professionals Think in Action*, New York: Basic Books.

Schumpeter, J.A. (1934) *The Theory of Economic Development*, Oxford: Oxford University Press.

Scott, M., Roberts, I., Holroyd, G. and Sawbridge, D. (1989) *Management and Industrial Relations in Small Firms*, London: Department of Employment, Research Paper No. 70.

Seymour, K.C. (1993) 'Intergenerational relationships in the family firm: the effect on leadership succession', *Family Business Review*, 6, 3, 263–81.

Shanker, M.C. and Astrachan, J.H. (1996) 'Myths and realities: family businesses' contribution to the US economy – a framework for assessing family business statistics', *Family Business Review*, 9, 2, 107–19.

Sharma, P., Chrisman, J.J. and Chua, J.H. (1997) 'Strategic management of the family business: past research and future challenges', *Family Business Review*, 10, 1, 1–35.

Shucksmith, M. (2000) *Exclusive Countryside? Social Inclusion and Regeneration in Rural Britain*, York: Joseph Rowntree Foundation.

Siiskonen, P. (1990) *Emännän ja isännän roolin muutos maatalouden uudenaikaistuessa: Tutkimus maatilan emännän ja isännän muuttuvista rooleista työnjaon avulla tarkasteltuna*, Mikkeli: Helsingin yliopiston maaseudun tutkimus- ja koulutuskeskus.

Simon, H. (1947) *Administrative Behavior: A Study of Decision-making Processes in Administrative Organizations*, Collier Macmillan, Canada, Ltd.

—— (1976) 'From substantive to procedural rationality', in S. Latsis (ed.) *Method and Appraisal in Economics*, Cambridge: Cambridge University Press.

Singer, J.A. and Salovey, P. (1993) *The Remembered Self: Emotion and Memory in Personality*, New York: The Free Press.

Sireni, M. (1994) 'Monitoimisuus: syrjäseudun maatalouden selviytymiskeino?', in J. Oksa (ed.) *Syrjäisen maaseudun uudet kerrostumat*, Joensuun yliopisto, Karjalan tutkimuslaitoksen julkaisuja Nro 110, 53–64.

—— (2000) 'Kunnon työtä ja oikeaa elämää kotiseudulla: Työn ja kotipaikkakunnan merkitys syrjäseudun nuorelle aikaiselle', *Alue ja Ympäristö*, 29:00, 1–16.

Sjöstrand, S.-E. (1997) *The Two Faces of Management – The Janus Factor*, London: International Thomson Business Press.

Small, S.A. and Riley, D. (1990) 'Toward a multidimensional assessment of work spillover', *Journal of Marriage and the Family*, 52, 51–61.

Smircich, L. and Stubbart, C. (1985) 'Strategic management in the enacted world', *Academy of Management Review*, 10, 4, 724–736.

Smyrnios, K. and Romano, C. (1994) *The Price Waterhouse/Commonwealth Bank Family Business Survey*, Melbourne: Syme Department of Accounting, Monash University.

—— (1999) *The 1999 Australian Family Business Lifestyle Audit*, Melbourne: AXA Australia Family Business Research Unit, Monash University.

Smyrnios, K., Romano, C. and Tanewski, G. (1997) *The Australian Family and Private Business Survey*, Melbourne: National Mutual Family Business Research Unit, Monash University.

Spector, P.E. (1987) 'Interactive effects of perceived control and job stressors on affective reactions and health outcomes for clerical workers', *Work and Stress*, 1, 2, 155–62.

Spradley, J.P. (1980) *Participant Observation*, New York: Holt, Rinehart & Winston.

Srinavasan, S. (1995) *The South Asian Petty Bourgeoisie in Britain*, Aldershot: Avebury.

Stafford, K., Duncan, K.A., Dane, S. and Winter, M. (1999) 'A research model of sustainable family businesses', *Family Business Review*, 12, 3, 197–208.

Stafford, W. (1995) 'Ferdinand Tönnies on gender, women and the family', *History of Political Thought*, 16, 3, 391–415.

Stake, R.E. (1995) *The Art of Case Study Research*, Thousand Oaks, CA: Sage Publications.

Stanworth, J. and Stanworth, C. (1995) 'The self-employed without employees – autonomous or atypical?', *Industrial Relations Journal*, 26, 3, 221–9.

Steindl, J. (1945) *Small and Big Business: Economic Problems of the Size of Firm*, Oxford: Basil Blackwell.

Stempler, G.L. (1988) *A Study of Succession in Family-owned Businesses*, Ann Arbor, MI: UMI Dissertation Services.

Sternberg, R. (1988) 'Triangulating love', in R. Sternberg and M. Barnes (eds) *The Psychology of Love*, London: Yale University Press.

Stevenson, H.H. and Gumpert, D.E. (1985) 'The heart of entrepreneurship', *Harvard Business Review*, March–April: 85–94.

Steyeart, C. and Bouwen, R. (1992) 'Opening the domain of entrepreneursip: a social constructionist perspective', paper presented at the Research in Entrepreneurship (RENT)VI workshop, Barcelona, November.

Stinnett, N. and DeFrain, J. (1985) *Secrets of Strong Families*, New York: Little, Brown & Co.

Stopford, R.D. and Baden-Fuller, C.W.F. (1994) 'Creating corporate entrepreneurship', *Strategic Management Journal*, 15, 521–36.

Storey, D. (1994) *Understanding the Small Business Sector*, London: Routledge.

Storey, D. and Strange, A. (1992) *Entrepreneurship in Cleveland, 1979–1989: A Study of the Effects of the Enterprise Culture*, Warwick: Centre for Small and Medium-sized Enterprises, Warwick Business School, University of Warwick.

Storey, D. and Sykes, N. (1996) 'Uncertainty, innovation and management', in P. Burns and J. Dewhurst (eds) *Small Business and Entrepreneurship* (2nd edn), London: Macmillan.

Stoy Hayward (1989) *Staying the Course: Survival Characteristics of the Family-owned Business*, London: Stoy Hayward.

—— (1992) *Managing the Family Business in the United Kingdom: A Stoy Hayward Survey in Conjunction with London Business School*, London: Stoy Hayward.

Stoy Hayward and the London Business School (1990) *Managing the Family Business in the UK*, London: Stoy Hayward and the London Business School.

Strauss, A. and Corbin, J. (1998) *Basics of Qualitative Research: Techniques and Procedures for Developing Grounded Theory* (2nd edn), Thousand Oaks, CA: Sage Publications.

Suomen maatalous ja maaseutuelinkeinot (1999/2000) *Maatalouden taloudellinen tutkimuslaitos*, Finland, Publications 95

Symes, D. (1990) 'Bridging the generations: succession and inheritance in a changing world', *Sociologica Ruralis*, 3/4, 280–91.

Tagiuri, R. and Davis, J.A. (1982) 'Bivalent attributes of the family firm', *Family Business Review*, 9, 2, 199–208.

Taylor, G. (1996) 'Guilt and remorse', in R. Harré and G.W. Parrot (eds) *The Emotions: Social, Cultural and Biological Dimensions*, London: Sage Publications.

Thomas, J. (2000) 'The exercise of leadership in family business: perceptions of owners and managers, family and non-family, in the Australian small to medium enterprise sector', unpublished PhD dissertation, University of South Australia.

Thomas, L.T. and Ganster, D.C. (1995) 'Impact of family-supportive work variables on work–family conflict and strain: a control perspective', *Journal of Applied Psychology*, 80, 6–15.

Thompson, P. (1993) 'Family, myth, models, and denials in the shaping of individual life paths', in D. Bertaux and P. Thompson (eds) *Between Generations: Family Models, Myths and Memories* (*International Yearbook of Oral History and Life Stories*, 2, 13–38).

Tichy, N.M., Tushman, M.L. and Fomburn, C. (1979) 'Social network analysis for organisations', *Academy of Management Review*, 4, 4, 507–19.

Tobin, D.R. (1996) *Transformational Learning: Renewing Your Company through Knowledge and Skills*, New York: John Wiley.

Tricker, B. (1996) 'Corporate governance: the ideological imperative', in H.T. Thomas and D. O'Neal (eds) *Strategic Integration*, Chichester: John Wiley.

Turnbull, S. (1997) 'Corporate governance: its scope, concerns and theories', *Corporate Governance: An International Review*, 5, 4.

van Dijk, T.A. (1998) *Ideology – A Multidisciplinary Approach*, London: Sage Publications.

van Dijkhuizen, N. and Reiche, H. (1980) 'Psychosocial stress in industry: a heartache for middle management?', *Psychotherapy and Psychosomatics*, 34, 124–34.

Van Maanen, J. (1988) *Tales of the Field*, Chicago: University of Chicago Press.

—— (1995) *Representation in Ethnography*, London: Sage Publications.

Volberda, H.W. and Elfring, T. (eds) (2001) *Rethinking Strategy*, London: Sage Publications.

Waldinger, R., Aldrich, H., Ward, R. and Associates (1990) *Ethnic Entrepreneurs: Immigrant Business in Industrial Society*, Newbury Park, CA: Sage Publications.

Ward, J.L. (1987) *Keeping the Family Business Healthy: How to Plan for Continuing Growth, Profitability, and Family Leadership*, San Francisco: Jossey-Bass.

—— (1991) *Creating Effective Board for Private Enterprises*, San Francisco: Jossey-Bass.

Ward, R. (1987) 'Ethnic entrepreneurs in Britain and Europe', in R. Goffee and R. Scase (eds) *Entrepreneurs in Europe*, Beckenham: Croom Helm.

—— (1991) 'Economic development and ethnic business', in J. Curran and R. Blackburn (eds) *Paths of Enterprise*, London: Routledge.

Watson, T.J. (1994a) *In Search of Management: Culture, Chaos and Control in Managerial Work*, London: Routledge.

—— (1994b) 'Entrepreneurship and professional management: a fatal distinction', *International Small Business Journal*, 13, 2, 34–46.

—— (2002) *Organising and Managing Work: Organisational, Managerial and Strategic Behaviour in Theory and Practice*, Harlow: FT Prentice-Hall.

Weidenbaum, M. (1996) 'The Chinese family business enterprise', *California Management Review*, 96, 141–57.

Welsch, J. (1993) 'The impact of family ownership and involvement on the process of management succession', *Family Business Review*, 6, 1, 31–54.

Werbner, P. (1984) 'Business on trust: Pakistani entrepreneurs in the garment trade', in R. Ward and R. Jenkins (eds) *Ethnic Communities in Business: Strategies for Economic Survival*, Cambridge: Cambridge University Press.

—— (1990) 'Renewing an industrial past: British Pakistani entrepreneurship in Manchester', *Migration*, 8, 17–41.

Westhead, P. (1997) 'Ambitions, "external" environment and strategic factor differences between family and non-family companies', *Entrepreneurship and Regional Development*, 9, 127–57.

Westhead, P. and Cowling, M. (1997) 'Performance contrasts between family and non-family unquoted companies in the UK', *International Journal of Entrepreneurial Behaviour and Research*, 3, 1, 30–52.

—— (1998) 'Family firm research: the need for a methodological rethink', *Entrepreneurship Theory and Practice*, 23, 1, 31–56.

Westhead, P., Cowling, M. and Storey, D. (1996) *The Management and Performance of Unquoted Family Companies in the United Kingdom* (Working Paper 42), Coventry: Centre for Small and Medium-sized Enterprises, University of Warwick.

Westhead, P. and Wright, M. (eds) (2000) *Advances in Entrepreneurship*, Cheltenham: Edward Elgar Publishing.

Whatmore, S. (1991) *Farming Women: Gender, Work and Family Enterprise*, London: Macmillan.

Wheelock, J. (1991) 'The flexibility of small business family work strategies', 14th National Small Firms Policy and Research Conference, 'Small Enterprises Development: Policy and Practices in Action', Blackpool.

—— (1992) 'The flexibility of small business family work strategies', in K. Caley, E. Chell, F. Chittenden and C. Mason (eds) *Small Enterprise Development: Policy and Practice in Action*, London: Paul Chapman.

—— (1996) 'People and households as economic agents', in M. Mackintosh *et al.* (eds) *Economics and Changing Economies*, London: International Thomson Business Press.

—— (1999a) 'Who dreams of failure? Insecurity in modern capitalism', in J. Vail, J. Wheelock and M. Hill (eds) *Insecure Times: Living with Insecurity in Contemporary Society*, London: Routledge.

—— (1999b) 'Fear or opportunity? Insecurity in employment', in J. Vail, J. Wheelock and M. Hill (eds) *Insecure Times: Living with Insecurity in Contemporary Society*, London: Routledge.

Wheelock, J. and Baines, S. (1998) 'Dependency or self-reliance? The contradictory case of work in UK small business families', *Journal of Family and Economic Issues*, 19, 1, 53–74.

Wheelock, J. and Oughton, E. (1996) 'The household as a focus for research', *Journal of Economic Issues*, 30, 1, 143–59.

Whittington, R. (1993) *What Is Strategy and Does It Matter?*, London: Routledge.

Wilson, P. and Pahl, R. (1988) 'The changing social construct of the family', *Sociological Review* 36, 232–66.

Wilson, P. and Stanworth, J. (1988) 'Growth strategies in small Asian and Afro-Caribbean businesses', *Employment Gazette*, Jan 8–14.

Wortman, M.S. (1994) 'Theoretical foundations for family-owned business: a conceptual and research-based paradigm', *Family Business Review*, 7, 1, 3–27.

Yin, R.K. (1984) *Case Study Research: Design and Methods* (*Applied Social Research Methods Series*, 5), Beverly Hills, CA: Sage Publications.

—— (1989) *Case Study Research: Design and Methods* (revised edn) (*Applied Social Research Methods Series*, 5), Newbury Park, CA: Sage Publications.

Ylijoki, O.-H. (1998) *Akateemiset heimokulttuurit ja noviisien sosialisaatio*, Tampere: Vastapaino.

Zaretsky, E. (1976) *Capitalism, the Family and Personal Life*, London: Pluto Press.

Zedeck, S. (ed.) (1992) *Work, Families, and Organizations*, San Francisco: Jossey-Bass.

Zhou, M. (1992) *Chinatown: The Socioeconomic Potential of an Urban Enclave*, Philadelphia: Temple University Press.

Zingales, L. (1997) 'Corporate governance', in P. Newman (ed.) *The New Palgrave Dictionary of Economics and the Law*, Basingstoke: Macmillan.

Index